"Respite, ritual, and celebration around the table, ideas intrinsic to all cultures but often overlooked, are at the heart of every dish in Adeena Sussman's *Shabbat*. Her mouthwatering recipes present an intoxicating reminder of how restorative cooking can be, how it can speak to our modern cravings while honoring ancient tradition, and the powerful role it plays in human connection. Adeena's ability to combine very personal experience with masterful technique in the kitchen elevates even the simplest bite, resulting in food that is at once satisfying, sacred, and abundantly soulful."

—GAIL SIMMONS, food expert, TV host, and author of
Bringing It Home: Favorite Recipes from a Life of Adventurous Eating

"Adeena does it again. *Shabbat* has the perfect selection of what you need/ should be making every weekend. Hearty, colorful, full of flavor, and approachable, you'll be reaching for this book over and over again, and it will quickly become a classic in your home kitchen."

—EDEN GRINSHPAN, chef, TV host, and author of *Eating Out Loud*

"I have been following Adeena for years (total fangirl here!) [and] I could not be more excited to add another one of her books to my collection. *Shabbat* is celebrated on the seventh day of the week and is about rest, reflection, and, of course, enjoying good food with loved ones. I can't think of a better way to celebrate this day (or any day, for that matter) than with this beautiful book. I look forward to cooking my way through these delightful, easy-to-follow recipes that highlight the culture and cuisine of Israel."

—TIFFANI THIESSEN, actress and author of *Pull Up a Chair*

SHABBAT

Adeena Sussman

Photography by Dan Perez | Styling by Nurit Kariv

SHABBAT
שבת

Recipes and Rituals from My Table to Yours

AVERY | an imprint of Penguin Random House | New York

AVERY

an imprint of Penguin Random House LLC
penguinrandomhouse.com

Most Avery books are available at special quantity
discounts for bulk purchase for sales promotions,
premiums, fund-raising, and educational needs.
Special books or book excerpts also can be
created to fit specific needs. For details, write
SpecialMarkets@penguinrandomhouse.com.

Library of Congress Cataloging-in-Publication
Data has been applied for.

ISBN 9780593327777
eBook ISBN 9780593327784

Printed in China
10 9 8 7 6 5 4 3 2 1

Book design by Ashley Tucker

In loving memory of my mother, Steffi Sussman, z"l
My first and forever Shabbat Queen

CONTENTS

INTRODUCTION

It's Friday morning in Tel Aviv, and my Shabbat kitchen is beginning to hum.

I've already rubbed a whole chicken with garlic confit and lemon zest, giving the flavors time to permeate the bird before it goes in for a roast in the late afternoon. It's almost time to punch down a batch of golden challah dough before braiding it into loaves, brushing them with beaten egg, anointing them with sesame seeds, and baking them until burnished and glossy. Whole carrots are simmering, ready to be sliced into a Moroccan-style salad bathed in a spicy, cumin-y, lemony dressing and studded with the sweet surprise of Medjool dates.

I'll be at the ready in case people stop by unannounced at any point today—and they usually do—with a zippy dip of artichoke hearts, feta, chili, and herbs that's just begging to meet a slice of that challah (I knew there was a reason I made an extra loaf). It'll be chilly tomorrow, so I'm planning on making a hamin (also known as cholent)—a hearty stew of meat, white beans, grains, and seasonings that I will put together later today, stash in a low-temperature oven, and forget about until Saturday morning, when it will be uncovered and demolished by me, my husband, our family, and any last-minute guests.

This is how I get ready for Shabbat (the Hebrew word for Sabbath) in Israel, where I've lived for the better part of a decade. Here, weekend cooking is celebrated, taking on a multitude of cultural and immigrant inflections and offering something for everyone who wants to get in the kitchen and cook, bake, or merely assemble something delicious.

Weekend food in Israel is special yet unbuttoned, lavish yet relaxed, and perfect for entertaining a crowd, no matter the size.

Most of all, it's food with meaning, centered around a tradition with ancient roots and conceptualized around the ideas of rest, relaxation, and reflection, a focus that feels decidedly modern right now. It isn't lost on me that Shabbat is the north star of my kitchen identity; after all, it's been a central part of my whole life. But it took almost leaving Shabbat cooking behind to realize how much I actually needed this respite. Shabbat is a weekly opportunity to slow down, chill out, and feast along the way.

I was actually born on Shabbat, the Jewish day of rest that begins just before sundown every Friday and ends nearly twenty-five hours later, when the first three precocious stars push their way into the inky-blue sky on Saturday night.

A "Shabbat baby," my grandma Mildred would tell me once I was old enough to understand the significance of having been introduced to the world on the Jewish calendar's most spectacular day of the week, one where anything considered "work" was cast aside. Instead of the mundane labor that inundated the week, on Shabbat we wrapped ourselves in a voluntary cocoon of peaceful and spiritual tranquility.

I grew up enveloped in Shabbat's magic, aware of how my family's life revolved around this sacred bubble, one that Rabbi Abraham Joshua Heschel called "a palace in time." I also became aware, on an almost cellular level, of how amazing cooking for Shabbat could be—in both the making and the eating—and what a joy it was to have these special cornerstones marked into our calendar like clockwork.

In my childhood home in Palo Alto, California, our weekdays were a mere prelude to Shabbat, which traces itself all the way to the biblical story of creation. As it is told, God created the world in six days, and on the seventh day, He (or maybe She?) rested. And so we rested, too—and we ate. Shabbat wasn't only about food, but it was a *lot* about food. In addition to time for sleep and for prayer, it was about gathering people around the table and holding them close without interruption, distraction, television, and the stress of the workweek.

My mother, Steffi, would begin preparations in earnest on Wednesday, writing out her menus on recycled scraps of paper in her elegant cursive, then sending my father, Stan, to bring frozen kosher meat from a dedicated freezer in our garage (kosher meat wasn't easily available, so we picked it up monthly after a giant truck had unloaded it into an empty room connected to a local synagogue).

As the chicken and stew meat defrosted, she put our chipped white KitchenAid mixer through its paces, kneading challah dough and whipping egg whites for chocolate chip meringues. I can still remember the first baking tip I ever learned from my mom, who showed me and my older sister, Sharon, how to cut large sheets of brown paper from grocery bags into a perfect replacement for parchment (she had so many kitchen "hacks" before that was even a thing).

Both my parents were early risers, and my mother used the time to cook. After she got a master's degree in linguistics when I was seven, she worked at local colleges teaching English to adults, so planning for Shabbat in advance was key. My bedroom was closest to the kitchen, and on Thursdays and Fridays I would wake up to intoxicating aromas, accompanied by the sound of pots clanging and cabinet doors slamming. Who could sleep through that? It's no wonder I became a morning riser, too, subjecting all future roommates to the same blissful symphony. (Good thing my permanent roommate, my husband, Jay, sleeps out of earshot.)

As a result of a 107-degree fever that caused nerve damage, my mother was hard of hearing, and those early mornings were the only time she allowed herself the luxury of being outside of her bedroom without her tiny hearing aids installed. The noise she made and the aromas she coaxed from the stove colluded to create a joyous cacophony of purpose. It was like an olfactory alarm clock tipping us off to the crispy potato kugels, steaming pots of chicken soup, tomatoey roasts, and fudgy brownies cooling on the counter for that weekend's meals.

Shabbat officially began when my father went off to shul (synagogue) and my mother, sister, and I—freshly scrubbed, combed, and dressed in our best—gathered around a tray holding silver candlesticks. (Women also sometimes attended shul, but it was more customary, at least in Orthodox homes, for women to stay home. We all went to shul together on Shabbat morning.) My mother would strike a match, light four candles—one for each member of our immediate family—and we would all move our palms in a circular motion three times, beckoning special Shabbat energy before covering our eyes and blessing the candles.

> Our father would give each of us girls a special blessing, and I can still feel his warm hands on the top of my head, something that centered me no matter what weekday drama might have rocked my childhood/adolescent world.

Once my father came home, we would sit and talk for a few minutes, then head to the table and begin singing. First we would harmonize "Shalom Aleichem," an incantation meant to welcome in the angels who were said to have ushered my father—and Shabbat—home safely. Then we'd sing "Eshet Chayil" ("Woman of Valor"), an acrostic poem set to music that described the perfect woman according to the parameters of an ancient, traditional view—essentially, a domestic goddess (and knowing full well that we women are *wayyy* more than that).

Our father would give each of us girls a special blessing, and I can still feel his warm hands on the top of my head, something that centered me no matter what weekday drama might have rocked my childhood/adolescent world.

Next he recited the kiddush, the ritual blessing over wine, holding a silver cup and passing it around for a sip of treacly Concord grape Manischewitz poured from a heavy crystal decanter (the good stuff was served later, with the meal). After we washed our hands, my father would bless the two loaves of challah with yet one more prayer, slice the bread, and dinner would begin. In their season, we started with artichokes accompanied by a lemony mayo dip. Next, we slurped crystal-clear chicken soup that had been cooked over a low flame for the course of a whole night, with the vegetables and deliciously overcooked chicken served on the side, followed by tender, juicy roast chicken, a crispy potato or lusciously sweet noodle kugel (casserole), fresh vegetables, and a simple salad.

More often than not, we also had company. In addition to our friends and family, we often welcomed many strangers. Every week the phone would ring, with visitors saying they had heard we offered Shabbat hospitality and were there possibly, perhaps, by any chance, a few seats at our table?

Some weeks it was a scholar speaking at nearby Stanford University. Other times it was my high school friends (of all religions . . . or no religion at all). Other times it was a young family seeking treatment at the medical center, or a Nobel Prize–winning mathematician. Sometimes it was a recently divorced mom who bunked with her kids on the pullout sofa in the living room. One summer, after I came home from camp, my dad schlepped my duffel bag into my bedroom, pointed at my bed, and said, "The chief rabbi of France slept there for a few days."

So much about Shabbat was about the food and the table that the two are inseparable in my mind. During the week we ate meals, but on Shabbat we had celebrations. Between bites of chopped liver, we sang songs. We learned from our guests about happenings in far corners of the world. We listened to stories from our grandparents and had their ears to hear ours. My sister and I felt heard and seen, cherished, loved, and celebrated, and we had Shabbat to thank for all of this. If I ever have to wonder why I'm so comfortable surrounded with people, it's because of Shabbat, having witnessed firsthand groups of people linked together by a ritualistic table laden with delicious food and, more importantly, infused with graciousness.

After college, I spent a few years in Jerusalem with two close friends in a run-down apartment we furnished with the cheapest used refrigerator and dining table we could find. It was there that I took everything I had absorbed at home and cooked Shabbat meals with my friends, hosting many other young expats who were thousands of miles away from their families and craving a bit of the special sauce only a Shabbat meal could provide.

> My sister and I felt heard and seen, cherished, loved, and celebrated, and we had Shabbat to thank for all of this.

A few years later I moved to New York to pursue a career in food, at the same time drifting from my religious observance, mostly abandoning the tradition of preparing Shabbat dinner as well. Just like on any other night of the week, I would dine out at noisy restaurants and drink at even noisier bars. But what I thought would feel like freedom instead often left me unmoored, empty, and exhausted.

Without the anchor of that meal and the opportunity to unwind my week, I felt a bit lost. That's when I realized that staying home, hosting loved ones, and cooking food had imbued the beginning of the weekend, and in fact my life, with a deeper sense of meaning. Although I left many of the stricter religious traditions behind me for good, I started making Shabbat meals again, knowing that it was just what I needed—and continue to need to this day.

That remains even more true for me here in Israel, where Shabbat is practically a national holiday. Religious or not (only half the Jewish population identifies as ritually observant), Israelis revere Shabbat for the edible opportunities it offers, in the form of open-ended meals where time stops and relaxation is the order of the day.

In a hectic place where still moments are few and far between, Shabbat is a quieter, meditative time, when meals serve as magnets for togetherness and the day leaves time for actual naps (not weekday catnaps), going somewhere to pray, reading on beaches, taking hikes, walking over to the museum, or doing absolutely nothing at all.

I cook for Shabbat most of all because it feeds my soul. It's a weekly spiritual check-in with a delicious payoff. In this book, most of the dishes are my personal interpretation of this divine time. The bulk were created by me or inspired by the Shabbat meals of my youth, mixed in with a fair number learned from local cooks I admire who shared their traditions and stories with me. The recipes paint a picture of oneg shabbat (Shabbat delight), one plate at a time, and they await your attention, interpretation, and embrace.

It is my hope that Shabbat can be your palace in time, your personal haven for friends, family, and yourself, one where cooking can be a gateway to making Shabbat and its tantalizing food sacred to you in your own way.

Shabbat Shalom.

A FEW STAPLES

These are some kitchen staples you'll want to buy or make to create the recipes in this book. Many of them appeared in *Sababa*, and I am repeating some here, often in abbreviated or adapted form.

AMBA Makes 2 cups

Peel 1 large or 2 medium completely unripe green-skinned mangoes (1 to 1¼ pounds total), such as Tommy Atkins variety; discard the peels. Grate the peeled mangoes on the large holes of a box grater straight into a medium saucepan. Add 2 cups water, 1 finely diced medium onion, 1½ tablespoons chopped jalapeño (with seeds), 2 tablespoons kosher salt, 3 chopped garlic cloves, 1 tablespoon ground turmeric, 1½ teaspoons yellow mustard seeds, 1 teaspoon ground fenugreek, ½ teaspoon ground cumin, and ½ teaspoon sweet paprika. Bring to a boil, reduce the heat to medium-low, and cook, stirring, until the mango and onion have softened and the liquid has reduced slightly, 20 to 25 minutes. Remove from the heat, cool slightly, then stir in 3 tablespoons fresh lemon juice and 1 teaspoon fish sauce (optional, but this gives a great funky tang). Transfer to a blender or food processor and puree until smooth and glossy, 20 seconds. Store in an airtight container in the refrigerator for 1 month.

BAHARAT SPICE BLEND Makes ¾ cup

In a bowl, combine 6 tablespoons ground cinnamon, 3 tablespoons finely ground black pepper, 2 tablespoons ground allspice, 2 teaspoons ground cardamom, 2 teaspoons freshly grated or ground nutmeg, 1 teaspoon ground ginger, and 1 teaspoon ground cloves. Store in an airtight container for up to 6 months.

HARISSA Makes 1 cup

Arrange 7 dried chilies de arbol and 1 dried guajillo chile (or 3 more chilies de arbol) in a bowl and cover with 1 cup boiling water; soak 1 hour. Drain, discard the water, then open the peppers and remove and discard as many seeds as you can; coarsely chop the flesh. Toast 1 teaspoon each caraway, cumin, and coriander seeds in a small skillet over low heat until fragrant, 2 minutes. Cool, then grind them in a spice grinder to a fine powder. Add the spices to the bowl of a food processor with 2 garlic cloves, the chopped chilies, ¼ cup olive oil, 1 tablespoon fresh lemon juice, 1 tablespoon sweet paprika, and 2 teaspoons kosher salt. Process the mixture and press it through a fine-mesh sieve into a bowl, discarding any solids. Pack the harissa into a jar with a tight-fitting lid, cover with another tablespoon of olive oil, and store in the fridge for up to 1 month.

TAHINI SAUCE Makes 2½ cups

In a large bowl, combine 1 cup pure tahini paste, 2 minced garlic cloves, and 2 teaspoons kosher salt. Whisk in ⅓ cup freshly squeezed lemon juice until incorporated, then whisk in ½ cup water until the tahini is thick, creamy, and just pourable, 25 to 30 seconds. Thin with more water or lemon juice as needed, and season with salt to brighten it up. Refrigerate in an airtight container for up to 4 days; let come to room temperature and loosen with water and lemon juice to taste.

LABANEH Makes 2 cups

Arrange a large, clean linen towel, flour sack, or triple layer of cheesecloth inside a medium bowl. In another bowl, whisk together 4 cups whole-milk yogurt, 1 tablespoon freshly squeezed lemon juice, and 2 teaspoons kosher salt. Transfer the mixture to the towel-lined bowl. Gather up two opposite sides of the towel and tie them into a knot, then loop the two remaining opposite sides through and tie them into a knot, leaving the ends for hanging. Find a space over a kitchen or bathroom sink or shower or tub and hang the labaneh, letting the liquid drip into a bowl if you're not working over a sink or shower. Drain a minimum of 4 hours (for a consistency similar to Greek yogurt) and a maximum of 24 (for something more like cream cheese), depending on how thick you like your labaneh. Transfer to an airtight container and refrigerate for up to 1 month.

POMEGRANATE MOLASSES Makes 1 cup

In a small saucepan, whisk 5 cups pure pomegranate juice and 2 tablespoons honey. Bring to a low boil over medium-high heat; boil until reduced to 2 cups (use a measuring cup to gauge the volume), 25 minutes. Reduce the heat to medium-low. Simmer, stirring occasionally, until small bubbles form all over the top. Reduce the heat to low; simmer until the liquid is visibly thickened but not as thick as honey (it will thicken as it cools); the bubbles will be foamy and small. Remove the pan from the heat and dip a spoon into the molasses; if you run your finger over the back of the spoon, a distinct stripe will form. Refrigerate in an airtight container for up to 6 months.

PRESERVED LEMONS Makes 2 cups

Wash a 24-ounce jar and its lid (preferably plastic) in soapy water; dry. Working with 8 lemons and 1 cup kosher salt, use a sharp knife to cut an *X* shape through each lemon so it is quartered but not cut all the way through. Working over a bowl, hold a lemon open in your hand. Pack a heaping tablespoon of the salt inside, close the lemon, and fit it into the jar. Repeat with the remaining lemons and salt, fitting the lemons in the jar as tightly as possible. Sprinkle more salt on the lemons as you go along. Juice will gush out of the lemons and fill the jar. If needed, add more freshly squeezed lemon juice to cover the salted lemons and fill the jar. Seal tightly, place the jar on a plate to catch any leaks, and leave it in a sunny place for at least 2 weeks and up to 3 months, flipping the jar occasionally and adding lemon juice during the first few days to keep the jar filled with liquid. Refrigerate for up to 1 year.

PRESERVED LEMON PASTE Makes 1½ cups

Remove as many seeds as you can from 1 cup (2 large) preserved lemons. Roughly chop the lemons and add them to a bullet-style blender or the small bowl of a food processor with 1 teaspoon sweet paprika and ½ cup extra-virgin olive oil. Blend until creamy and smooth, 1 minute. Refrigerate in an airtight container for up to 1 month.

RECIPES CONTINUE

SCHUG Makes 2 cups

In a food processor, process 2 cups each packed fresh parsley and cilantro (including tender stems), 20 garlic cloves, 10 medium jalapeños (trimmed, but seeds and veins left intact), 2 teaspoons kosher salt, 2 teaspoons ground cumin, 2 teaspoons freshly ground black pepper, and 2 teaspoons freshly squeezed lemon juice until smooth, adding 1 to 2 tablespoons water and scraping down the sides of the processor if the mixture sticks to the sides, about 1 minute. Transfer to an airtight container, cover with 2 tablespoons olive oil, seal, and refrigerate for up to 1 month.

ZA'ATAR SPICE BLEND Makes ¾ cup

Arrange 1 cup picked fresh hyssop (za'atar) leaves (or oregano leaves) on a paper towel–lined microwave-safe plate and microwave, stopping and stirring every 30 seconds, until dry and crumbly, 2 to 2½ minutes. Crumble the dried leaves by hand or in a spice grinder until almost fine and combine them in a medium bowl with 3 tablespoons dried marjoram, 3 tablespoons toasted sesame seeds, 4 teaspoons dried thyme, 1 tablespoon ground sumac, and 1 teaspoon fine sea salt. Store in an airtight container for up to 3 months.

A FEW OTHER NOTES

SALT

I always use Diamond Crystal kosher salt where kosher salt is called for. If you are using Morton, or a heavier, denser kosher salt, please halve the amount.

METRIC MEASUREMENTS

I have added metric measurements (in grams) to the baking recipes. More and more American cookbooks are continuing to do so, catching up with bakers around the globe. The recipes will all work with their conventional measurements, but if you like, by all means use the metrics.

CHALLAHS, BREADS & CRACKERS

GOLDEN CHALLAH

If there is one recipe that defines Shabbat, it's challah, and my table isn't complete until a pair of loaves sit on the table. The wonderful challah recipe from *Sababa* contains olive oil and honey, and while it has made regular bakers out of many of you, I wanted this one to be even simpler, using vegetable oil and plain white sugar instead of olive oil and honey. I also add a tiny pinch of turmeric, which gives the challah the most gorgeous golden hue without imparting any flavor. The key to the challah's perfect crumb is allowing plenty of rising time, both before and after braiding. I am a devotee of a simple three-strand plait; Instagram was practically created for incredible eight-strand artworks, but the simple, meditative back-and-forth of a three-strand braid means you'll be able to do this one with your eyes closed. My recipe recommends kneading by hand after pulling the initial dough together in a stand mixer, but if you want to machine-knead, by all means use the mixer to do so.

Makes 2 large or 3 medium challahs

Active Time:
35 minutes

Total Time (including rising and cooling time):
4 hours 30 minutes

---

1 cup (236 grams/ml) warm water (110° to 115°F, a little hotter than you think), plus up to ¼ cup (60 grams/ml) more

½ cup (100 grams) plus 2 tablespoons (24 grams) sugar

Two ¼-ounce (7-gram) packets active dry yeast (4½ teaspoons/14 grams total)

½ cup (110 grams/ml) vegetable oil, plus ½ tablespoon (7 grams/ml) for greasing the bowl

⅛ teaspoon ground turmeric

4 large eggs

6 cups (780 grams) all-purpose flour, plus more as needed

2½ teaspoons (14 grams) fine sea salt

½ cup (70 grams) sesame seeds

Flaky sea salt, such as Maldon, or kosher salt

1. In the bowl of a stand mixer, whisk the warm water and the 2 tablespoons (24 grams) sugar (I use a fork—no need to dirty the whisk). Whisk in the yeast and let it get foamy and fluffy for 5 to 6 minutes (if this doesn't happen, your yeast is dead! Start over!). Whisk in the remaining ½ cup (100 grams) sugar, ½ cup (110 grams/ml) of the oil, the turmeric, and 3 of the eggs until incorporated.

2. Add the flour and fine sea salt, then fit the mixer with the paddle attachment to incorporate the ingredients well and mix on medium speed, stopping the mixer and using a silicone spatula to coax any loose flour into the dough, until the dough is shaggy but unified, 3 minutes. If the dough does not hold its shape at all and looks more like a wet blob, add more flour, ¼ cup at a time, to achieve the desired texture; if the dough

RECIPE CONTINUES

feels dry and crumbly, add up to ¼ cup more water. If you wish to knead in the mixer, continue to knead on medium speed until the dough is smooth and plush without being sticky and pulls away from the mixer without leaving any dough on the sides or bottom of the bowl, 5 to 6 minutes (the dough may seem ready earlier, but kneading this long helps develop the gluten, which will make for a stronger, better dough with better crumb and structure).

Transfer to a very lightly floured work surface (if you have a marble countertop, I recommend starting without flour and only adding it if the dough feels impossibly sticky in an all-over-your-hands way).

3. Using the heel of one hand to lean into the dough and the other to rotate it, knead until a very smooth dough forms, another 9 to 10 minutes. If you get tired, rest for a second, throw some dishes in the sink, then keep kneading for another minute or two. You should be able to hold the ball of dough and not have it stick to your hands, but it also shouldn't feel too dry or tear across the top; you're looking for smooth!

4. Add the remaining ½ tablespoon oil to a large metal bowl and use a pastry brush or your hands to coat the bowl with the oil. Add the dough, flip it to coat lightly in oil, seal with plastic wrap, then cover with a clean kitchen towel and let the dough sit in a warm place until at least doubled but ideally tripled in size, 1 hour 30 minutes to 2 hours for double and 3 hours for triple (tripling makes the dough lighter, so if you have time, I recommend it). Uncover the dough and punch it down with your fist, then transfer the dough from the bowl to the work surface.

5. Cut the dough into 2 equal-sized pieces (or 3 for smaller challahs), then cut each larger piece into 3 smaller pieces.

6. Line a large baking sheet with parchment paper. Press down on each piece of dough to release any air bubbles, roll each into a 12-inch log (or a 10-inch log if you are making 3 challahs), then roll out and taper the ends of each log to form 16-inch logs (or 12-inch logs for 3 challahs). Let the logs rest for 5 minutes to allow the gluten to relax. Pinch the top ends together, pressing down the pinched top with a chef's knife to secure the dough. Braid the logs, forming a challah that is slightly tapered on both ends and plump and generous as it reaches the center. Tuck the ends

Two Challahs on the Table

According to the biblical story, while the Jewish people were in the desert, attempting to travel from Egypt to Israel, they were hungry. To feed them, God sent down manna from heaven (aha—now we know where that phrase comes from!), and it took on the taste of whatever it was the Jews wanted to eat. During the week, they each received one piece of manna, but before Shabbat they received two, so they wouldn't have to work by gathering their meal. Today, we place two loaves of challah on the table for Shabbat meals to symbolize those two pre-Shabbat portions of manna.

under and arrange the loaves on the parchment-lined sheet, leaving at least 4 inches between loaves. Let rise, covered, in a warm, draft-free place, until the challahs puff and nearly double in volume, 1 hour.

7. During the last 15 minutes of rising, set a rack in the center of the oven and preheat the oven to 350°F.

8. Beat the remaining egg in a small bowl, then brush the challahs thoroughly all over with the egg, making sure not to neglect the sides of the challah all the way down to the parchment (so that the sesame seeds will coat the whole challah). Coat each challah with ¼ cup of the sesame seeds (or about 2½ tablespoons if you're making 3 challahs). Sprinkle with the flaky sea salt and bake until the challahs are golden and fluffy and the undersides are a lovely golden brown color and sound hollow when tapped, 34 to 36 minutes for 2 large loaves, 28 to 30 minutes for 3 medium loaves.* Cool and slice.

*Another way to determine if challah is done? Insert a meat thermometer into the center. If it reads 190–195°F, you're there.

CHALLAH ROLLS

For making sandwiches or when you're a smaller crowd, perfect little challah rolls are the way to go. Though I make a suggestion for shaping, you can always just form the challah into balls and bake them that way. I like to wrap them individually and freeze, then defrost and use as needed.

Makes 15 rolls

Active Time:
25 minutes

**Total Time
(including rising and cooling time):**
4 hours 15 minutes

All-purpose flour,
for dusting

1 recipe Golden Challah
dough (page 20),
fully risen

1 large egg, beaten,
for brushing

Sesame, nigella, or other
seeds of your choice

Line a baking sheet with parchment paper. On a clean, lightly floured work surface, divide the dough into 15 equal-sized pieces. Roll each one into a 10-inch log. Working with one piece at a time, bend the log into a horseshoe shape, then cross one end over the other so the top third resembles the letter *O* and the bottom two-thirds resembles the lower side of an *X*. Pull the lower right corner up and through the *O*, then tuck the lower left corner behind the *O* and pinch the 2 pieces together. Place on the parchment-lined sheet, leaving at least 4 inches between rolls, brush with the egg wash (save the rest for the second brushing), and let rise, uncovered, until almost doubled in size, 1 hour to 1 hour 15 minutes. During the last 15 minutes of rising time, set a rack in the center of the oven and preheat the oven to 350°F. Brush the rolls again with the egg wash, then sprinkle with seeds and bake until golden and puffed, 19 to 20 minutes.

Kneading by Hand

Though most of the bread recipes in this book have a machine-kneading option, there's no substitute for hand kneading—it's the best way to get a feel for the texture, elasticity, and moisture level of dough. I sometimes find that dough that feels sticky in the mixer may not need more flour, just a hand-knead; it seems to respond to the human touch, coaxing the dough into its desired state once it's received a little TLC. Even if you choose to knead in a stand mixer, do yourself a favor and consider pulling the dough from the mixer a minute early and finishing the process by hand on a smooth, clean, dry surface, incorporating as little flour at a time as possible on the countertop.

PULL-APART CHALLAH STICKS

Making these sweet little braids has become a favorite way to prepare challah in our home. The toppings can be adjusted to suit your taste or audience; choose a variety of whole seeds, salts, and seasonings, or, if you like, keep it simple and top the entire pan with one thing. As they rise and bake, the challahs become kissing cousins, meeting one another at the sides. Each braid is perfect for one or two people, and after baking, they freeze beautifully as individuals, ready to be defrosted and served with dips and breads, or alongside a bowl of soup.

Makes eight 12 × 2-inch challah sticks

Active Time:
1 hour

Total Time (including rising and cooling time):
4 hours 40 minutes

1 recipe Golden Challah dough (page 20), fully risen

1 large egg, beaten, for brushing

Sesame seeds, sunflower seeds, nigella or black sesame seeds, za'atar, ground sumac, flaky sea salt, and/or other toppings of your choice

1. Line a baking sheet with parchment paper. Divide the dough into 8 equal-sized pieces. Cut each into 3 smaller pieces and roll each piece into a 12-inch log, keeping the logs you're not braiding covered with a towel to prevent drying out. Pinch the top ends together and braid into long, narrow challahs about 1 inch wide × 12 inches long, pinching the ends once braided and arranging them on the parchment-lined sheet, leaving ½ to 1 inch between each challah. Cover and let rise in a warm, draft-free place until puffed and nearly doubled in size, 45 minutes to 1 hour.

2. During the last 15 minutes of the challah rising, set a rack in the center of the oven and preheat the oven to 350°F. Uncover and brush each challah with egg and sprinkle generously with the toppings of your choice. Bake until the challahs are golden, have risen, and touch one another, 25 to 26 minutes. Cool until easy to handle and serve warm or at room temperature.

WATER CHALLAH

In the shtetls of Eastern Europe in the eighteenth and nineteenth centuries, eggs were expensive and hard to come by, so festive and indulgent recipes that did not require eggs were prized for their simplicity and affordability. At the Vishnitz challah factory in Bnei Brak (see page 42), run by members of the Hasidic Jewish sect of the same name, the challahs are made using an eggless recipe often known as "water challah." This type of loaf typically produces a darker, crunchier exterior, and I'm not complaining. I brush the challah with a combination of nondairy milk and maple syrup to keep it vegan, and the recipe can easily be doubled.

Makes 2 medium challahs

Active Time:
25 minutes

**Total Time
(including rising and cooling):**
5 hours 15 minutes

1½ cups (350 grams/ml) warm water (110°F to 115°F, a little warmer than you think), plus more as needed

3 tablespoons (38 grams) sugar

One ¼-ounce (7-gram) packet active dry yeast (2¼ teaspoons)

3 tablespoons (42 grams/ml) plus 2 teaspoons (10 grams/ml) neutral oil

4¾ cups (618 grams) all-purpose flour, plus more as needed

2½ teaspoons (14 grams) fine sea salt

2 tablespoons (30 grams/ml) almond milk (or other vegan milk of your choice)

2 teaspoons (10 grams) maple syrup or light brown sugar

3 tablespoons (27 grams) nigella seeds, black sesame seeds, poppy seeds, or seeds of your choice

1. In the bowl of a stand mixer, whisk the warm water and sugar (I use a fork—no need to dirty a whisk). Whisk in the yeast and let it get foamy and fluffy for about 10 minutes (if this doesn't happen, your yeast is dead. Start over!). Mix in the 3 tablespoons (42 grams/ml) oil, then add the flour and mix until a shaggy dough forms, adding an additional 1 to 2 tablespoons warm water, if needed, to help the dough come together.

2. Scrape any dough from the paddle attachment back into the bowl, then fit the mixer with the dough hook and knead for 2 minutes. Add the salt and continue to knead until the dough is smooth and elastic and pulls away from the sides of the bowl, adding flour by the tablespoon as needed, 5 to 6 minutes; the dough should be moist and plush but not sticky. To knead the dough by hand, dump it onto a lightly floured work surface and knead until the dough is plush but not sticky, 9 to 10 minutes.

3. Lightly coat a large bowl (it could be the mixer bowl itself) with the remaining 2 teaspoons oil (10 grams/ml), place the ball of dough in the bowl, flip it gently to coat, cover with plastic wrap, and cover with a kitchen towel. Let the dough rise at room temperature until the dough has at least doubled in size (I like mine almost tripled in size), 2 hours to 2 hours 30 minutes in a colder room or 1 hour 30 minutes to 2 hours in a warmer room.

4. Line a baking sheet with parchment paper. Uncover the dough, turn it out onto the counter, and cut it into 2 equal-sized pieces. Divide each half into 3 pieces and roll each one out into a rope about 11 to 12 inches long. Let the logs rest for 5 minutes to allow the gluten to relax. Pinch the top ends of the ropes together and braid them, then tuck the ends under, weighing down the pinched end with a chef's knife to secure the dough. Repeat with the second half of dough. Place the loaves on the parchment-lined baking sheet and let rise, uncovered, until fluffy and high, about 1 hour 30 minutes.

5. During the last 15 minutes of the second rise, arrange a rack in the center of the oven, and preheat the oven to 365°F.

6. In a small bowl, whisk together the almond milk and maple syrup. Gently brush the tops and sides of the challahs with the liquid, sprinkle with the seeds, and bake until the crust is deeply golden brown and the bottoms sound hollow when tapped, 25 to 30 minutes. Cool before slicing or tearing.

SESAME PAVLOVA CHALLAH

Challah can feel downright dessert-like all on its own, but somehow additions of streusel, cinnamon sugar, chocolate chips, and even frosting have become popular in recent years. Here's my contribution to the genre, which I've nicknamed the Pavlova Challah. By letting the challah dough bake for 10 minutes first, removing it from the oven, slathering on a layer of sweet meringue and a sprinkling of sesame seeds, and returning it to the oven to bake again, the top develops a gorgeous, swirly, crunchy topping with a soft, chewy center. Many recipes call for leaving the oven door propped open to cool and crisp the meringue post-baking, and I do the same; bake these at the end of the day or when you know you don't need your oven afterward for a few hours. Do it properly and you will be rewarded with a challah variation that may seem like a novelty but may just become a permanent part of your repertoire.

Makes 3 medium or 2 large challahs

Active Time:
1 hour

Total Time (including rising and cooling time):
4 hours 45 minutes

---

1 recipe Golden Challah dough (page 20)

1 large egg, for brushing the challah

Pinch of salt

3 large egg whites

1 teaspoon (6 grams/ml) white vinegar, plus more for cleaning the mixer

½ cup (100 grams) sugar

3 tablespoons (27 grams) sesame seeds

1½ teaspoons flaky sea salt, such as Maldon, for sprinkling

1. Prepare the challah up to shaping and rising the braided loaves. Whisk the egg with the pinch of salt. During the last 10 minutes of rising time, brush the sides of the challah with the egg wash, leaving the tops unbrushed (this will help the meringue adhere and bake without additional moisture).

2. Preheat the oven to 350°F.

3. Wipe the bowl of a stand mixer and its whisk attachment (or the whisk beaters from a handheld electric mixer) with vinegar to clean them. Fit the mixer with the whisk attachment and beat the egg whites at medium-high speed until white and frothy, about 1½ minutes. Add the vinegar, and with the mixer running, beat in the sugar in

RECIPE CONTINUES

a slow, steady stream. Beat at high speed until the meringue is glossy and holds stiff peaks, 5 to 6 minutes (beating for this long creates a stronger meringue). You should have about 3 cups meringue.

4. Bake the challahs without the meringue until they begin to rise but are still pale in color and are not baked through, 10 minutes.

5. Remove the challahs from the oven and cool on a rack for 5 minutes. Working quickly, dollop a third of the meringue over the top of each medium challah (or about half if you're making 2 large challahs), spread it evenly over the loaves into a ¼-inch layer, forming some decorative peaks, and if making three medium challahs, sprinkle each challah with 1 tablespoon sesame seeds and ½ teaspoon flaky sea salt; if making 2 large challahs, sprinkle each with 1½ tablespoons sesame seeds and ¾ teaspoon flaky salt. Return to the oven and bake until the meringue is lightly browned and dry to the touch and the sesame seeds are toasted, an additional 20 to 25 minutes for smaller challahs and 30 to 35 minutes for larger challahs (if the meringue is still soft, lower the temperature to 200°F and bake until the meringue is drier, another 5 minutes). Turn off the oven, prop the door open with the handle of a wooden spoon, and let the challahs cool in the oven for at least 1 hour and up to 4 hours (this allows the meringue to crisp further as it cools). Slice the challah with a serrated knife and eat immediately. This challah is best enjoyed the day it's made, but can be stored, loosely wrapped in foil, for up to 3 days. Toast leftovers before serving.

JACHNUN
(Rolled Yemenite Sabbath Bread)

If ever there was a weekend Shabbat cult food, jachnun—deep golden coils of buttery dough baked low and slow—fits the bill. As is the case with yeasty, brioche-like kubaneh bread, jachnun, which contains only baking powder, is traditionally placed in the oven or on a hot plate before Shabbat on Friday, then devoured the following morning after synagogue prayers. It's sold in almost every makolet (mini-market) and from food trucks and carts all over the country, and in the neighborhood where I live (Tel Aviv's Yemenite Quarter), tiny jachnun joints (usually open only on Friday and Saturday) sell it by the piece with its traditional accompaniments: resek (grated tomato), schug (hot sauce), and hard-cooked eggs.

As a teenager, my friend Merav Tzanani Perez—known as Tamati at the coffee shop her husband, Miki, named after her—would have a traditional Shabbat dinner with her family at home, then go out clubbing until the wee hours. Upon coming home, she'd become intoxicated anew with the buttery aroma of jachnun slowly baking in the oven. "I wanted to sneak into the pot and demolish all of it," said Merav. "But I'd go to bed, then wake up to those jachnun rolls, sweet and slightly golden and crusty on the outside." Merav arranged for me to visit her mother, Ramia, at home to learn how to make jachnun. As a newlywed, Ramia, a retired nursery school teacher, learned to prepare a variety of Yemenite breads, which she would sell on Fridays. Watching Ramia, I found a similarity between jachnun and strudel (see page 350) in that pieces of dough are stretched gossamer-thin before use. Though it's a much more rustic process, jachnun is roughly croissant-like, with flaky layers that can be pulled apart once cooked. These days, Ramia makes the dough less often but still in huge batches, which she freezes and distributes to her children and grandchildren to take and bake at home. Merav, for one, is grateful. "I never learned how to make jachnun," she told me. "Maybe now I'll try."

Makes 12 jachnun

Active Time:
1 hour 30 minutes

**Total Time
(including cooking time):**
12 hours 30 minutes

RECIPE AND INGREDIENTS CONTINUE

7 cups (910 grams) all-purpose flour

⅓ cup (67 grams) sugar, plus more as needed

1 tablespoon (18 grams) fine sea salt, plus more as needed

½ teaspoon (2 grams) baking powder

1 tablespoon (21 grams) honey

2¼ cups (532 grams/ml) lukewarm (115°F) water, plus more as needed

1 tablespoon (14 grams/ml) vegetable oil, for greasing, plus more as needed

¾ cup (1½ sticks/ 6 ounces/170 grams) very soft (but not melted) unsalted butter, plus more as needed

8 large eggs, shells gently washed with soap and dried

8 vine-ripened tomatoes (about 1½ pounds)

Schug (page 16)

1. In a large bowl, combine the flour, sugar, salt, baking powder, and honey. Add the water and use your hands to mix a loose, sticky dough, 2 to 3 minutes. Let the dough rest for 10 minutes, then grab a corner of the dough from underneath, pull the dough, and fold it over the top and across the dough, rotating the bowl a bit each time and repeating three or four times total. Seal the bowl with plastic wrap, cover with a clean kitchen towel, and let it rest in a warm place for 1 hour. Lightly oil a baking sheet with the oil, then use oiled hands to divide the dough into 12 equal-sized pieces and transfer them to the baking sheet. Cover loosely with a large plastic bag and let the dough rest again for 10 minutes.

2. Preheat the oven to 200°F. Cut two parchment circles the same size as the bottom of a 9- or 10-inch kubaneh pan (an aluminum pot with a tight-fitting lid) or another pot with a heavy lid. Butter one side of one of the parchment rounds and set it into the pan, buttered side up. Use oiled hands to lightly grease the counter, then place one of the dough pieces on the counter. Scoop up 1½ tablespoons of the butter with your hands and use it to help spread the dough as thinly as you can into an almost-translucent rectangle (it may tear a bit; that's OK), about 12 inches wide × 18 inches long.

3. Using both hands, take both ends from one long side of the dough and fold them toward the center, then take the other long ends and fold them over to create a long, narrow three-layered rectangle (this is called an envelope fold). Starting at one narrow end, roll into a log, trying to lift slightly as you fold to aerate the log, pulling the sides out so you end up with a uniform log. Arrange the jachnun in the prepared pan or pot, then repeat with more butter and dough, arranging 3 or 4 logs, then layering the next 3 or 4 in the opposite direction. Butter one side of the remaining parchment round and place it, buttered side down, on top of the jachnun. Nestle the eggs in their shells on top of the parchment and cover tightly, sealing with foil if the lid is not tight.

4. Bake in the oven (or on the lowest setting of a hotplate) until the jachnun is deeply golden and the layers can easily be pulled apart, 11 to 12 hours.

5. Right before serving, grate the tomatoes on a box grater into a bowl; discard the skins. Season with pinches of sugar and salt to create the ultimate vine-ripened tomato taste. Separate the jachnun rolls and serve them alongside the eggs with the grated tomato and schug.

DABO
(Ethiopian Shabbat Bread)

I first met my incandescent friend Fanta Prada while passing by her Ethiopian restaurant, Balinjera ("Ba li" is Hebrew for "I want," and injera is Ethiopia's signature fermented, crenellated bread), in my neighborhood near the shuk. A force of nature who worked as a model around the world for years and also picked up a law degree along the way, Fanta has made it her life's mission to share the beauty of Ethiopian-Jewish life with the world—something she does at the restaurant and her cultural center, Battae, which hosts groups from Israel and abroad. Fanta came to Israel in 1991 with thousands of other Ethiopian Jews— believed by many to be one of the twelve lost tribes of Israel—as part of Operation Solomon, a covert airlift mission to rescue Ethiopia's Jewish community from famine and civil war. "The excitement and anticipation of getting to our homeland after waiting for generations is something I can still feel like it was yesterday," she told me. A talented, energetic cook, Fanta is also the primary host of her large extended family. For Shabbat she makes sweet, fluffy dabo bread, an unbraided and usually round loaf that, unlike the better-known injera, isn't made with teff but rather with regular all-purpose flour. One day last year I was lucky enough to learn how to make it with Fanta at her home. After kneading the dough with spices, she allowed it to rise quickly before baking it on the stovetop to develop a golden crust on both sides. The dough released from the pot, tall and majestic, like Fanta herself, and I could barely wait for it to cool before tearing in. Fragrant and yeasty, it's the perfect foil for Shabbat soups and stews.

Serves 8 to 10

Active Time:
15 minutes

**Total Time
(including rising time):**
1 hour 30 minutes

RECIPE AND INGREDIENTS CONTINUE

6 cups (780 grams) all-purpose flour

2½ tablespoons (23 grams) instant (rapid-rise) yeast

⅛ teaspoon ground cloves

⅛ teaspoon ground cardamom

⅛ teaspoon ground ginger

⅛ teaspoon ground cinnamon

¾ teaspoon ground turmeric

2 teaspoons (12 grams) fine sea salt

3 cups (705 grams/ml) very warm water (about 130°F)

3 tablespoons (42 grams/ml) olive oil, plus more for greasing

2 tablespoons (42 grams) honey

In the bowl of a stand mixer fitted with the paddle attachment, combine the flour, yeast, cloves, cardamom, ginger, cinnamon, turmeric, and salt. Add the water, oil, and honey and mix until a sticky dough forms, 2 to 3 minutes. Lightly oil the bottom and sides of a round 6- to 8-quart soup pot. Line the bottom and sides with parchment, pour in batter in (it will be thick and sticky), and use oiled hands to smooth the top of the dough. Let it rise, uncovered, for 30 minutes. Place the pot on a large burner; cook over low heat for 30 to 35 minutes, rotating occasionally to prevent burning. Remove from the heat, use oven mitts to invert onto a parchment-lined plate, then return to the pot, cooked side up. Peel off top layer of parchment. Cook until underside is golden, rotating occasionally to prevent burning, 35 to 40 minutes. Loosen sides of bread with a knife; invert into a cooling rack for 20 minutes before serving.

PLETZLACH
(Poppy Onion Crackers)

Onion board, or pletzlach, was a fixture of my childhood visits to New York and of restaurants like the legendary Ratner's on the Lower East Side. You can find relatives of pletzlach at bakeries in ultra-Orthodox neighborhoods in Israel, where they're a sort of catchall weekday bread. My grandmother Mildred used to make a sweet, almost cookie-like version, and after she died, my uncle Dan; sister, Sharon; and I gathered our family to try to re-create her recipe. What emerged was something similar to this cracker, and over the years I've refined it into a crisp, oversized sheet that I like to break into jagged shards and serve with soups—a natural pairing that would have made my bubbe proud.

Serves 6 to 8

Active Time:
15 minutes

**Total Time
(including resting time):**
1 hour

2 large eggs

½ cup (110 grams/ml) vegetable oil, plus more for your hands

1 tablespoon (12 grams) sugar

2 cups (260 grams) all-purpose flour

4 tablespoons (32 grams) poppy seeds

½ cup (32 grams) dried onion flakes

1 teaspoon (4 grams) baking powder

½ teaspoon (3 grams) fine sea salt

¼ teaspoon finely ground black pepper

Flaky sea salt, for sprinkling

1. Arrange two racks in the bottom and top thirds of the oven. Preheat the oven to 375°F. In a large mixing bowl, whisk the eggs, oil, and sugar. In a medium mixing bowl, whisk together the flour, 3 tablespoons (24 grams) of the poppy seeds, ¼ cup (16 grams) of the onion flakes, the baking powder, sea salt, and pepper and add to the egg mixture. Mix with a wooden spoon, then using lightly oiled hands, knead the dough into a cohesive ball, about 30 seconds. Divide the dough into 2 equal-sized pieces, wrap in plastic, and chill for 30 minutes.

2. Roll one piece of dough out between two pieces of parchment paper to ⅛-inch thickness.

3. Peel away the top piece of parchment. Transfer the dough (still on the bottom piece of parchment) to a baking sheet, prick with a fork, brush lightly with water, and sprinkle with ½ tablespoon (4 grams) of the poppy seeds, 2 tablespoons (16 grams) of the onion flakes, and flaky sea salt, pressing them in lightly with your hands. Repeat with the remaining dough on another baking sheet. Bake, switching and rotating the baking sheets halfway through, until golden brown and crisp, 13 to 14 minutes. Let cool, then break into pieces and serve. The crackers can be frozen in an airtight container for up to 3 months or stored in an airtight container on the counter for 1 week.

BNEI BRAK:
A WORLD APART, CLOSE BY

I set out from Tel Aviv for the ultra-Orthodox city of Bnei Brak late on a Thursday night and arrived a mere twenty minutes later, a reminder of just how physically close a place can be even if it feels a universe away. Bnei Brak is one of the most population-dense cities in the world, home to 180,000 mostly ultra-Orthodox Israelis shoehorned into a space originally designed to house half as many. Hasidic and Haredi (both rigorously Orthodox streams of Judaism) Jews are often thought to be insular, but perhaps due to its proximity to Tel Aviv, Bnei Brak feels more open and welcoming than other ultra-Orthodox neighborhoods in Israel where I've spent time.

I was here with culinary guide Netanel Zelikovitch to witness firsthand the nocturnal pre-Shabbat food scene that attracts Bnei Brak residents and visitors alike to its stores, delicatessens, and heimishe (which translates to "homestyle" in Yiddish) restaurants.

"I hope you're hungry," he said as we approached our first stop, Shtisel (no relation to the television show of the same name). Inside, customers were loading up on rich, almost custardy potato kugels, teriyaki salmon, schnitzel, gefilte fish, and mayonnaise-laden baba ghanouj. Netanel ladled cholent, a traditional stew, into a Styrofoam bowl from a giant cauldron whose level never seemed to recede; people stood on the street eating their steaming portions standing up or packed them to take home for Shabbat itself. Netanel grabbed a handful of arbes (peppery chickpeas), meant to be a symbol of fertility, for us to nosh on before we moved on to the Vishnitz challah factory.

Open since 1950, Vishnitz is probably the most famous bakery in Israel, making and selling thousands upon thousands of challahs every week.

CONTINUES

BNEI BRAK *(continued)*

Deep in the back of the massive space, the smell of fermented yeast permeates the air as workers feed dough into machines that automatically form it into balls, then logs. The challahs are then braided by hand, brushed with melted shortening, and sprinkled with sesame seeds. Next, they are transferred to metal trays boasting patina only achieved by decades of use. After a bake in massive, rotating industrial ovens, challahs by the hundreds are rolled out on massive carts, where customers hand-select their loaves, slip them into brown paper bags, and queue at the glass-windowed booth near the entrance to pay.

On Fridays, the lines snake around the block; the factory shuts down as close to Shabbat's entrance as possible, reopening again on Saturday night as soon as the first loaves come out of the oven.

Next, Netanel received a mysterious call. After a short walk, he motioned me up five flights of stairs to the home of Mrs. Bress (like many devoutly re-

At Mrs. Bress's home, light switches are taped shut or covered with special guards to help her family avoid turning on lights, which is forbidden on Shabbat.

ligious women, she preferred to leave out her first name and did not want to be pictured), a local mother of thirteen who raised her family in the three-bedroom apartment. She was preparing traditional gefilte fish for Shabbat and invited us in for a taste. "There is never a Shabbat when one of my children and their family are not staying with me," she said as she opened a freezer stocked with desserts and produced cookies and cakes for us to take with us on our way out. We ended the night at Moti's, a thirteen-year-old restaurant that serves a full buffet of Ashkenazi Shabbat food: cholent, kishke (stuffed derma, a casing filled with animal fat and starch), helzeleh (stuffed turkey neck), kugel, and more. At midnight the place was packed with long tables full of Yeshiva bochers (students), families, and Tel Aviv refugees eager to fill up on rib-sticking food that would most likely keep them full until Shabbat actually started the following afternoon. I said my farewells to Netanel, and we promised to meet again—if only so I could attempt to document Mrs. Bress's gefilte fish recipe for myself.

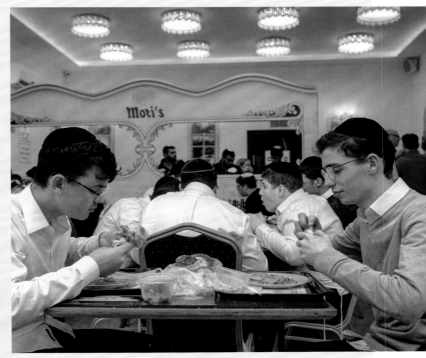

BREAKFAST & BRUNCH

CRISPY EGGPLANT & GOAT CHEESE TART

Nurit Kariv made this tart as the centerpiece of the lovely family Shabbat brunch she hosted at her home (see page 54), and it's become an instant classic at my place. It starts with one of the best pastry dough bases I've ever encountered; simultaneously flaky and sturdy, it comes together in a snap with the aid of a food processor and slices like a dream. The crispy eggplant that tops a layer of creamy goat cheese is easier than you think, and any extra eggplant pieces make a perfect little stack of "fries." At the end, it gets drizzled with a tangy dressing and topped with fresh basil. Serve with Nurit's Spinach Salad with Oranges & Pine Nuts (page 138) for an ideal Shabbat repast.

Serves 8

Active Time:
45 minutes

Total Time:
3 hours

FOR THE DOUGH:

1½ cups (195 grams)
all-purpose flour

1 teaspoon (6 grams)
kosher salt

½ cup (1 stick/4 ounces/
114 grams) cold unsalted
butter, cut into ½-inch
cubes, plus more for
greasing the pan

1 large egg, lightly
beaten with 1 tablespoon
(15 grams/ml) ice water

SPECIAL EQUIPMENT:

2 pounds dried beans
(or pie weights),
for blind-baking

FOR THE EGGPLANT:

1 medium eggplant
(about 1 pound)

½ teaspoon kosher salt,
plus more as needed

Vegetable oil, for frying

⅓ cup potato starch

One 6-ounce tube-style
goat cheese, cut into
¼-inch rounds

2 tablespoons chopped
fresh basil, for garnish

FOR THE DRESSING:

2 tablespoons olive oil

1½ tablespoons freshly
squeezed lemon juice

½ teaspoon Dijon
mustard

¼ teaspoon kosher salt

¼ teaspoon freshly
ground black pepper

RECIPE CONTINUES

1. Make the dough: Pulse the flour and salt in a food processor until combined. Add the butter and pulse until the mixture resembles coarse meal, 10 to 15 pulses. Drizzle in the egg mixture evenly and pulse until the dough just comes together, another 10 pulses. Transfer the dough to a large piece of plastic wrap and gather the dough together, forming a 5-inch disk and wrapping it. Chill until firm, 1 hour. Preheat the oven to 350°F. Grease the bottom and sides of a 9- or 10-inch pie plate or tart pan with a removable bottom with butter. Roll out the dough into a 12-inch round between two sheets of parchment. Peel off one of the layers, then fit the dough into the pan. Trim the edges to fit the pan. Prick the dough all over with a fork, then cover the dough with parchment and fill with beans or pie weights. Bake until the crust is fragrant and lightly golden around the edges, 20 to 25 minutes. Remove the pan from the oven, carefully remove the parchment and pie weights, return the pan to the oven, and bake until the tart shell is golden and crisp, another 15 to 20 minutes. Remove to a rack and cool completely in the pan.

2. Cook the eggplant: Peel the eggplant, then cut it lengthwise into ½-inch planks. Cut the planks into long ½-inch-thick pieces, then cut them into 4-inch batons. Transfer the batons to a large bowl and sprinkle with the salt; toss so the salt adheres, 5 seconds. Line a large rimmed baking sheet with paper towels, arrange the eggplant on top, cover with another layer of paper towels, and let the eggplant sit for 30 to 45 minutes to release its moisture. During the last 5 minutes, heat ¼ inch of oil in a wide, high-sided skillet over medium heat. Gently press down on the paper towels one last time to absorb any additional moisture and discard the towels. Transfer the eggplant back to the large bowl, add the potato starch, and toss to coat completely, shaking off any excess. Working in two batches, fry in a single layer until the eggplant is golden and crisp, 3 to 4 minutes per side. Transfer with tongs to drain on paper towels, sprinkle lightly with salt, and repeat with the remaining eggplant.

3. Make the dressing: Whisk the oil, lemon juice, mustard, salt, and pepper in a medium bowl (or shake in a jar with a tight-fitting lid) until smooth and emulsified, 10 to 15 seconds.

4. To assemble the tart, arrange the goat cheese in the bottom of the tart shell and use an offset spatula to spread the cheese evenly over the pastry. Working from the center of the tart in a single tight, concentric layer, arrange the fried eggplant over the cheese. Remove the rim of the tart pan (if using) and transfer the tart to a serving plate. Drizzle with the dressing and garnish with the basil. Serve immediately. The tart shell and dressing can be made 1 day in advance; fry the eggplant, spread the goat cheese, and finish the dish just before serving.

SHARING PITA
with Creamy Scrambled Eggs & Labaneh

Think of this as the Dutch baby of breads—an oversized pita that miraculously puffs like the original and serves as a welcoming landing spot for a pile of tangy yogurt and soft scrambled eggs. I love this breakfast because there is a high probability you can make it without leaving your house to source any of the ingredients, and what's more the essence of weekend cooking than that? Stirring cumin and red pepper flakes into the eggs makes them extra savory and a little bit special. Yes, you can use a knife and fork for this, but this one is really meant to be torn by hand and eaten with abandon, dipping and swiping the toppings as the bread comes apart. Feel free to take a shortcut by starting with four or six store-bought pitas, then divide the yogurt and eggs among them for a single-serve experience.

Serves 6

Active Time:
1 hour

**Total Time
(including rising time):**
3 hours

FOR THE PITA:

1½ cups (190 grams) all-purpose flour, plus more as needed

½ cup (60 grams) whole wheat flour

¾ cup (177 grams/ml) warm water (about 115°F)

1 tablespoon (13 grams) sugar

2 teaspoons (6 grams) instant (rapid-rise) yeast

1 tablespoon (14 grams/ml) olive oil

1½ teaspoons (9 grams) fine sea salt

FOR THE EGGS AND LABANEH:

10 large eggs, lightly beaten

½ teaspoon ground cumin

¼ teaspoon dried red pepper flakes

1 teaspoon kosher salt

3 tablespoons unsalted butter

1 teaspoon finely grated lime zest

½ cup Labaneh (page 15 or store-bought) or Greek yogurt

2 tablespoons chopped fresh chives

FOR THE CUCUMBER-RADISH SALAD:

6 Persian cucumbers, quartered lengthwise and cut across into 2-inch lengths

4 small radishes, quartered

1 scallion (green and white parts), very thinly sliced

2 tablespoons olive oil

2 tablespoons fresh lime juice

½ teaspoon kosher salt

RECIPE CONTINUES

1. Make the pita: In the bowl of a stand mixer, use a wooden spoon to mix ½ cup (65 grams) of the all-purpose flour, ¼ cup (30 grams) of the whole wheat flour, ½ cup (118 grams/ml) of the warm water, 1 teaspoon of the sugar, and the yeast. Rest, uncovered, until puffed and foamy, 20 to 25 minutes.

2. Add the remaining 1 cup (130 grams) all-purpose flour, ¼ cup (30 grams) whole-wheat flour, ¼ cup (30 grams/ml) water, and 2 teaspoons sugar, the olive oil, and salt. Attach the dough hook and bring the dough together over low speed, then raise the speed to medium and knead the dough until slightly springy but still soft and sticky, and pulling away from the sides of the bowl, 5 to 6 minutes (after 6 minutes, add more flour by the tablespoonful if needed, but try not to add too much). Remove the dough hook, cover the dough with a clean kitchen towel, and let it rest in a warm place until doubled in size, 45 minutes to 1 hour. Refrigerate another 45 minutes to 1 hour (this helps develop the flavor and texture of the dough). Alternatively, if you're baking the following morning, the dough can be refrigerated overnight immediately after mixing, then continued the next morning.

3. Flour a work surface, uncover the dough, gently transfer it to the work surface, and shape it into a large ball, tucking the ends under. Cover with a clean kitchen towel and let rise for 15 minutes (or 45 minutes to 1 hour if it was refrigerated overnight).

4. While the dough is rising, arrange a rack about 8 inches from the broiler and place two clean, inverted, and stacked heavy baking sheets or a pizza stone in the oven. Preheat the oven to the highest temperature that it will go (500°, 525°, or even 550°F).

5. Uncover the dough, gently flour the ball, and use a rolling pin to roll it up and down to form a 10-inch oval, dusting the top and bottom with flour as necessary. Rotate the dough 90 degrees, then roll the dough again; it should roll into a beautiful 10-inch round. Slide the round onto a sheet of parchment, cover the round with another clean towel, and let it sit for 10 to 15 minutes, until the pita has puffed up to about twice its original height.

6. Make the eggs: At this point, whisk the eggs, cumin, red pepper flakes, and salt in a bowl and set aside.

7. Make the cucumber-radish salad: Toss the cucumbers, radishes, scallion, olive oil, lime juice, and salt in a bowl, transfer to a serving platter, and chill until ready to use.

8. Uncover the dough, open the oven, and using the parchment as a sling, place the round on the top baking sheet, working quickly and closing the oven so it holds its high temperature. Bake the pita until it's puffed and golden, 4 to 5 minutes. Using two large spatulas, remove the pita from the baking sheet. Let the pita cool for 5 minutes.

9. While the pita cools, melt the butter in a 10- or 12-inch skillet over medium-low heat. Add the eggs and cook, stirring often, until the eggs are creamy, custardy, glossy, and still wet, 6 to 8 minutes. Transfer the pita to a serving platter, pile the eggs on top, then stir the lime zest into the labaneh and dollop it on top. Garnish the eggs with the chives and serve with the cucumber-radish salad.

BRUNCH AT NURIT'S

I have known Nurit Kariv for six years now, first as a colleague and now as a friend. As Israel's most respected food stylist, she has helped me express my craft with simplicity, beauty, elegance, and honesty. Every picture in *Sababa* and this book has benefited from her talents, and one of the reasons she is so masterful at her craft is because, at the heart of it, she is a wonderful home cook. She knows what a dish needs, what it doesn't, and how to make food that disappears as quickly as it gets put out. At home in North Tel Aviv, where she lives with her husband, Yoti, Nurit often hosts her three adult children and a gaggle of spouses, partners, children, and friends for Shabbat-morning brunch. Shabbat meals take on many differ-

ent iterations in Israel, and not all of them are connected to religious ritual. On a late-winter Saturday I arrived to the most intoxicating aroma of pastry baking and eggplant frying as Nurit arranged flowers in vases of her own design. In their spacious, lived-in kitchen, Yoti was cracking open a bottle of wine, and I helped Nurit assemble her delicious eggplant tart (see page 48), an egg salad loaded with caramelized onions (see page 80), a roasted kohlrabi and cherry tomato salad (see page 112), and more. Everything was simple and sensational, each dish's elements as delicious alone as they were when combined as only Nurit can do. At work, Nurit is a whirlwind of activity. At home, it was a joy to watch her relaxed, improvising behind the stove and beaming at the sight of her grandchildren, who call her Saftul, a take on *savta*, the Hebrew word for "grandma." Most of all, after we sat down to eat, I was happy to see her off her feet, reveling in her own beautiful world as opposed to working to beautify ours.

FRIDAY FRITTATA

There are few things more Shabbat-friendly than a frittata, a crustless quiche found all over the world. There's kuku sabzi, the Persian rendition front-loaded with herbs, and Spanish torta, studded with potatoes and onions; Italian frittatas tend to contain cheese and vegetables. Here, I add chickpeas for protein (please use canned to save time) and a generous amount of cheese (feel free to omit for a dairy-free dish). If you make the frittata fresh and serve it hot, good for you. But if you're serving later or the next day (as I do, eating it straight out of the fridge, piece by piece), I recommend simply enjoying this one cold or letting it come to room temperature. You can also take it with you for a Shabbat picnic lunch or, later in the week, pack it for a brown-bag meal.

Serves 8

Active Time:
20 minutes

Total Time:
35 minutes

---

10 large eggs

2 cups shredded sharp white Cheddar or kashkaval cheese (8 ounces)

¼ cup chopped fresh herbs of your choice, such as dill, parsley, cilantro, or a mix

1½ teaspoons kosher salt

¼ teaspoon freshly ground black pepper

½ teaspoon paprika

6 tablespoons olive oil

1 large onion, diced

1 large jalapeño, seeded and finely minced

4 garlic cloves, finely minced

5 ounces greens of your choice (chard, spinach, kale, etc.), thinly sliced (about 4 cups)

One 14-ounce can chickpeas, drained and rinsed

Set a rack in the top third of the oven; preheat to 300°F. In a medium bowl, whisk the eggs, then stir in the cheese, herbs, 1 teaspoon of the salt, the pepper, and paprika. Heat 3 tablespoons of the oil over medium-low heat in an ovenproof 10-inch, heavy cast-iron or nonstick skillet. Add the onions and cook, stirring until lightly golden, 8 to 9 minutes. Add the jalapeño and garlic and cook, stirring, 1 more minute. Raise the heat to medium, add the greens in three batches and cook, stirring occasionally, until slightly wilted, 1 to 2 minutes per batch. Continue to cook until all the greens are wilted, 3 to 4 minutes. Add the chickpeas and remaining ½ teaspoon salt and cook, stirring, 1 minute. Add the remaining 3 tablespoons oil to the skillet, pour in the egg mixture, and gently stir to make sure the eggs get between and beneath the cooked greens. Cook until the outside is set, 5 to 6 minutes. Transfer to the oven and cook until the frittata is just beginning to set (the surface may be a little bit runny), 10 minutes. Keeping a close eye on the frittata, turn on the broiler, and broil until gently puffed and golden, 1 to 2 minutes. Serve out of the skillet, or invert the frittata onto a plate, cut into 8 wedges, and serve.

POTATO BLINTZES
with Mushroom Sauce

There was only one type of blintz in my childhood home: Golden kosher brand, which we would unearth from the freezer, dusting off the frost from the package as though we were discovering a long-lost treasure. My mother would bring the sweet cheese-filled version to room temperature, then turn the blintzes into the famous sweet soufflé listed on the package, serving it for family gatherings or a dairy Shabbat lunch. But I was always partial to the savory potato blintzes, which we would top with sour cream and sautéed mushrooms for a special weekend dinner or treat. Making homemade blintzes is a revelation; I've been doing it ever since I discovered chef Thomas Keller's no-fail version (adapted slightly here) for a photo shoot many years ago. Once you get the hang of it, it's the ultimate meditative activity. And, yes, this recipe is hands-on and time-consuming, but totally worth the payoff. The crepes freeze well—just layer them between sheets of wax paper or plastic wrap, then peel off and use when needed.

Serves 4 to 6

Active Time:
1 hour 45 minutes

Total Time:
1 hour 45 minutes

FOR THE CREPES:

Pinch of ground white pepper (optional)

Scant 1 cup (125 grams) all-purpose flour

Pinch of kosher salt

3 large eggs, lightly beaten

1¼ cups (352 ml/grams) whole milk

4 tablespoons (½ stick/2 ounces) unsalted butter, melted but not piping hot

1 tablespoon minced fresh chives

FOR THE POTATO:

1¼ pounds russet potatoes (about 2 large), peeled and cut into ½-inch pieces

6 tablespoons (¾ stick/3 ounces) unsalted butter, softened

1 medium onion, finely diced (1½ cups)

6 ounces sharp white Cheddar cheese, shredded (1½ cups)

2 tablespoons finely chopped fresh chives, plus more for garnish

Kosher salt to taste

Pinch of ground white pepper (optional)

FOR THE MUSHROOM SAUCE AND FINISHING THE BLINTZES:

6 tablespoons (¾ stick/3 ounces) unsalted butter

4 ounces white button mushrooms, trimmed and thinly sliced (2 cups)

4 ounces fresh shiitake mushrooms, trimmed and thinly sliced (1½ cups)

4 ounces oyster or shimeji mushrooms, trimmed and thinly sliced (1½ cups)

1 teaspoon fresh thyme leaves, plus more for garnish

Kosher salt to taste

2 garlic cloves, minced

1 cup heavy cream

RECIPE CONTINUES

1. Make the crepes: In a medium bowl, whisk together the flour and salt. Gently whisk in the eggs and milk, then the butter. Strain the batter through a fine-mesh strainer into a separate bowl, pressing any solids with a silicone spatula, and stir in the chives.

2. Heat an 8-inch nonstick crepe pan over medium heat until hot. Spray with nonstick spray, then use a small ladle to pour about 2½ tablespoons of the batter into the center of the skillet. Rotate the skillet in a circular motion to cover the bottom of the pan evenly with the batter (if you hear it sizzle in the pan, your heat is too high). Cook for 30 to 45 seconds to set the batter, then use a small, narrow spatula to gently flip the crepe. Cook for 5 seconds more to set, remove the crepe, and place it with the nicer side down on a paper towel. Repeat for the remaining crepes, spraying the pan as needed and layering the paper towels and crepes. (Crepes can be stored between layers of plastic wrap, sealed, and frozen for up to 3 months, then defrosted and used as needed.)

3. Make the filling: Place the potatoes in a medium saucepan, add enough water to cover the potatoes, plus an additional 2 inches of cold water, and bring to a boil over high heat. Reduce the heat to medium-low and simmer until very soft, about 15 minutes.

4. While the potatoes are cooking, melt 2 tablespoons of the butter in a large skillet over medium heat. Add the onions, reduce the heat to medium-low, and cook, stirring, until lightly golden, 9 to 10 minutes.

5. When the potatoes are soft, drain them in a colander and return them to the pot. Add the remaining 4 tablespoons butter. Mash with a potato masher or fork until soft and creamy,

1 to 2 minutes. Stir in the onions, cheese, and chives until combined and season to taste with salt and white pepper (if using). Cover and let the mixture rest until cool enough to handle (you should have about 3 cups filling).

6. Make the sauce: Melt 2 tablespoons of the butter in a large skillet over medium-high heat. Add half of the mushrooms and ½ teaspoon of the thyme and cook, turning the mushrooms once, until browned, 5 to 6 minutes. Season lightly with salt and transfer them to a paper towel–lined plate. Repeat with another 2 tablespoons of the butter and the remaining mushrooms and thyme and transfer to the plate with the rest of the mushrooms.

7. Lower the heat to medium and add the garlic to the skillet. Cook until fragrant, stirring constantly, about 10 seconds. Add the cream, white pepper (if using), and the reserved mushrooms. Cook, stirring frequently, until the cream has thickened, 3 to 4 minutes. Season to taste and keep warm.

8. To assemble the blintzes, place ¼ cup of the filling on each crepe about 2 inches from one end, shaping it into a 3 × 1-inch log. Fold the lower edge of the crepe over the filling, then fold the sides inward and continue to roll the blintz burrito-style. Repeat with the remaining crepes and filling.

9. Melt 1 tablespoon of the butter in a large nonstick skillet over medium heat. Add half the blintzes, seam side down, and cook until deep golden brown on each side, flipping once, 2 to 3 minutes per side. Transfer to a platter and repeat with the remaining 1 tablespoon butter and blintzes; cover loosely with foil to keep warm. Spoon the mushroom sauce over the warm blintzes to serve. Garnish with additional thyme and chives.

CHEESY SPINACH & PHYLLO PIE

Lale Abouaf and I had been planning to cook in person for almost two years, but the pandemic had other ideas. I first learned about Lale, who lives in Izmir, Turkey, from her daughter Leslie, a fellow Tel Avivian who told me that her mother was known at home for being a wonderful Shabbat cook. As a member of Izmir's dwindling Jewish community—where there once were 40,000 Jews, there now remain about 2,500—Lale grew up observing Shabbat quietly, Jewish in a majority Muslim country. The community in Izmir (known as Smyrna in pagan times) traces its history back to antiquity but disappeared during the Byzantine era, not to be reestablished until the 1500s. In recent decades, many have decamped to Israel, where all three of Lale's daughters now live. Via Zoom we made delicious, individually shaped phyllo-encased bourekas (savory filled pastries), which she often serves for Shabbat lunch, especially during the summer, when she and her family spend time in the coastal town of Çeşme. Spinach is integral to Turkish cooking, and it was in high season when we "met" virtually, so she used it for her flaky triangles. I took inspiration from her delicious filling and turned it into a cheesier, Greek-ish Turkish pie, which is a bit faster to assemble and still yields admirably crispy results. A few months later, when Lale was in Tel Aviv, we had a joyful in-person reunion at a local cafe, where she gifted me gorgeous bright-red Marash chili flakes, a tea set, and Turkish coffee from home. We hugged like old friends, promising to meet again soon—hopefully not on Zoom.

Serves 6 to 8

Active Time:
45 minutes

Total Time:
1 hour 40 minutes

RECIPE AND INGREDIENTS CONTINUE

FOR THE PIE:

6 tablespoons olive oil

1 pound fresh spinach leaves, washed and drained

1 medium onion, finely diced (1½ cups)

3 garlic cloves, minced

6 ounces feta cheese, drained and crumbled

6 ounces kashkaval or sharp white Cheddar cheese, grated (about 1½ cups)

½ cup chopped fresh dill

1 large egg, lightly beaten

½ cup chopped scallion greens

3 tablespoons chopped fresh za'atar or oregano leaves, or 1 tablespoon dried

½ teaspoon freshly ground black pepper

5 standard (9 × 14-inch) sheets phyllo dough, thawed in the refrigerator overnight

6 tablespoons (¾ stick/3 ounces) unsalted butter, melted

1 tablespoon sesame seeds

FOR THE CUCUMBER YOGURT:

2 medium Persian cucumbers

1 cup Greek yogurt (fat level of your choice)

2 tablespoons freshly squeezed lemon juice

2 tablespoons chopped fresh dill

¼ teaspoon kosher salt

1. Make the pie: Arrange a rack in the center of the oven and preheat the oven to 350°F.

2. In a large pot, heat 3 tablespoons of the olive oil over medium heat. Add the spinach and cook, stirring occasionally, for 3 minutes. Turn off and let sit, covered, for 5 minutes. Spread the spinach out evenly on a sheet pan to cool, then, using your hands, squeeze all the water from the spinach. Repeat a second time to ensure all the water is removed. Finely chop the spinach.

3. Dry out the pot that was used for the spinach and heat the remaining 3 tablespoons olive oil over medium heat. Add the onion and cook, stirring occasionally, until lightly golden, 8 to 9 minutes. Add the garlic and continue to cook until softened, 1 minute.

4. Transfer the onions to a large bowl, then add the spinach, feta, kashkaval, dill, egg, scallion greens, za'atar, and pepper; gently stir until incorporated.

5. Arrange the phyllo on the counter and cover it with a clean kitchen towel to prevent it from drying out. Brush the bottom of a 10-inch round baking dish with the melted butter and fit two piece of phyllo into the bottom and sides of the dish, overlapping them at the bottom and letting the ends extend past the edges of the dish by a good 5 to 6 inches. Brush everywhere generously with butter, then fit the bottom with another two phyllo sheets, arranging them so the sides extend around the part not covered by the first two pieces; brush again with butter. Gently spread the filling over the phyllo, smoothing it out and spreading it to the edges. Lay the fifth sheet of phyllo over the center of the filling, then brush it with butter. Fold all the phyllo inward so the phyllo covers the filling. Brush the top with more butter, sprinkle with the sesame seeds, and bake until the phyllo is golden and crisp, 50 to 55 minutes.

6. While the pie is baking, make the cucumber yogurt: Grate the cucumbers into a medium bowl. Add the yogurt, lemon juice, dill, and salt and stir to combine. Cover and chill until ready to use.

7. Remove the pie from the oven, cool slightly, cut into pieces, and serve with the cucumber yogurt.

BAHARAT CHOCOLATE CHIP BANANA BREAD

If banana bread isn't easy to make, is it even worth it? I first tried this recipe using the more traditional method of creaming butter and sugar with an electric mixer, but eventually I settled on hand mixing, for a cake that comes together in minutes. I actually prefer using vegetable oil to butter here; it encourages a lovely, plush texture that lasts to the final slice (and keeps the cake non-dairy). Baharat spice plays warm, cozy, and complex, dovetailing harmoniously with the generous amount of chocolate chips. The drizzle of tahini is optional, but highly recommended.

Serves 8

Active Time:
10 minutes

Total Time:
1 hour 10 minutes

½ cup (110 grams/ml) vegetable oil, plus more for greasing the pan

½ cup (65 grams) pecans

2 cups (260 grams) plus 1 teaspoon (3 grams) all-purpose flour

1½ tablespoons (12 grams) Baharat Spice Blend (page 14 or store-bought)

1½ teaspoons (9 grams) baking soda

1½ teaspoons (9 grams) fine sea salt

⅔ cup (132 grams) granulated sugar

½ cup (115 grams) packed dark brown sugar

2 large eggs

4 large or 6 medium very ripe bananas (2 pounds/907 grams unpeeled), mashed (2 cups mashed)

2¼ teaspoons (11 grams/ml) pure vanilla extract

⅔ cup (120 grams) chocolate chips

Pure tahini paste, for drizzling

1. Preheat the oven to 350°F. Lightly grease an 8½ × 4½-inch loaf pan with oil. Arrange the pecans on a sheet tray and toast, tossing once midway through, until slightly darkened and aromatic, 5 minutes. Cool, then roughly chop.

2. In a medium bowl, whisk together the 2 cups of flour, the baharat, baking soda, and salt.

3. In a large bowl, vigorously whisk the granulated sugar, brown sugar, oil, and eggs by hand until creamy, 1 to 2 minutes.

4. Add the flour mixture to the wet ingredients and use a wooden spoon or spatula to mix until just combined. Add the bananas and 2 teaspoons of the vanilla and mix just until combined. In a small bowl, toss the chocolate chips with the remaining ¼ teaspoon vanilla until coated, then toss with the remaining 1 teaspoon flour until coated. Gently fold the chocolate chips into the batter along with the pecans. Scrape the batter into the prepared pan and smooth the top.

5. Bake until a tester inserted into the center comes out clean and the top is golden and hard to the touch, 55 minutes to 1 hour. Transfer to a wire rack and cool for 15 minutes, then turn out onto a rack and let cool completely (if you can resist) before slicing. Top with tahini, if desired, and serve.

HALVAH BERRY BREAD PUDDING
with Tahini Drizzle

When I have leftover challah, I make an indulgent bread pudding that benefits from sweet hawaiij, a spice blend that Yemenite Jews stir into boiling water and drink as a post-meal digestif. Unlike its savory counterpart, which is used in soups and stews, this one is laced with ginger and cardamom and packs some surprisingly sweet heat. I started out buying the mixture at spice stores in the shuk, but lately I've taken to making my own, either grinding whole spices or using store-bought for a lickety-split execution. Adding hawaiij to this bread pudding, along with halvah and a rich, three-ingredient tahini drizzle, is my favorite kind of dessert: one that fuses childhood flavors with ones that speak to my life right now.

Serves 8 to 10

Active Time:
15 minutes

**Total Time
(including minimum resting time):**
1 hour 30 minutes

---

3 tablespoons unsalted butter, melted and cooled slightly, plus more for greasing the pan

1 day-old loaf challah (about 1 pound), cut into 2-inch cubes (about 9 cups)

8 ounces halvah (flavor of your choice), crumbled (about 1 cup)

1 cup fresh or frozen raspberries

4 cups whole milk

1 cup heavy cream or half-and-half

6 large eggs

⅔ cup granulated sugar

⅓ cup light brown sugar

1 tablespoon pure vanilla extract

2 teaspoons Sweet Hawaiij (page 68)

1 teaspoon ground cinnamon

½ teaspoon fine sea salt

Tahini Drizzle (recipe follows)

1. Grease a 9 × 13-inch baking dish with butter, then arrange the bread evenly in the dish. Sprinkle ⅔ cup of the halvah and the berries evenly all over the dish, moving some bread to let the halvah nestle between pieces.

2. In a bowl, whisk the milk, heavy cream, eggs, granulated sugar, brown sugar, vanilla, hawaiij, cinnamon, and salt, then drizzle in the melted butter. Pour the mixture over the bread, tilting the dish and moving the bread in places to let the liquid soak in. Let the custard sit at room temperature for at least 30 minutes, or cover and refrigerate overnight to absorb the liquid.

3. Preheat the oven to 350°F. Crumble the remaining ⅓ cup halvah over the top and bake until the top is golden but the bottom half is still very moist, 40 to 45 minutes (or up to 1 hour if you're baking directly from the refrigerator). Remove from the oven, let cool slightly, and drizzle with Tahini Drizzle.

TAHINI DRIZZLE

Makes ¾ cup
Active Time: 3 minutes
Total Time: 3 minutes

½ cup half-and-half

¼ cup pure tahini paste

2 tablespoons sugar

½ teaspoon fine sea salt

In a small bowl, mix the half-and-half, tahini, sugar, and salt until combined. Drizzle can be refrigerated in an airtight container for 1 week.

SWEET HAWAIIJ

I first encountered this versatile spice blend back in 2005, when I spent time with sisters-in-law Ilana Saad and Dafna Tzanani, who took me under their wings when I was writing an article about Yemenite cooking for *Gourmet* magazine. After one of the many meals we cooked and ate together, they brought delicate tea glasses to the table, filled them with boiling water, then spooned pale, fragrant hawaiij le' cafe (sweet hawaiij "coffee," recipe follows) into the water. Mace, or *mashya* in both Hebrew and Arabic, which is one of the star ingredients here, starts out its life as the bright-red webbing that encases a whole nutmeg pod. And indeed, when dried and ground, it tastes like a mellower version of nutmeg, with notes of cinnamon. If you can't find mace, just use more nutmeg.

Makes a scant ⅓ cup

Active Time:
5 minutes

Total Time:
5 minutes

IF USING WHOLE SPICES:

3 tablespoons whole cardamom pods

One 2-inch cinnamon stick

One 2-inch piece whole dried ginger

4 whole cloves

1 dried mace web (optional), or ½ teaspoon additional freshly grated nutmeg

1 teaspoon freshly grated nutmeg

1. Place the cardamom pods on a kitchen towel and fold it over to cover them. Use a mortar and pestle or heavy mug to gently break the skins. Peel and discard the papery outer layer from the pods to reveal the black seeds inside.

2. Combine the cardamom seeds with the cinnamon stick, ginger, cloves, mace (if using), and nutmeg in an electric spice grinder and process until finely ground, 45 to 60 seconds. Pass the mixture through a fine-mesh strainer into a bowl, then return the larger pieces to the grinder and process until finely ground, another 30 seconds. Store in an airtight container for up to 6 months.

IF USING DRIED SPICES:

1½ tablespoons ground ginger

1½ tablespoons ground cardamom

1½ teaspoons ground cinnamon

½ teaspoon ground or freshly grated nutmeg

¼ teaspoon ground cloves

¼ teaspoon ground mace (optional)

Pass the spices through a fine-mesh strainer into a bowl. Store in an airtight container for up to 6 months.

SWEET HAWAIIJ "COFFEE"

Serves 1

1 cup boiling water

1 teaspoon Sweet Hawaiij

1 teaspoon honey, or more to taste

Combine the boiling water, hawaiij, and honey in a mug, stir, and let the spices settle to the bottom for a minute before drinking.

SLOW-ROASTED TOMATO & FETA TART

Puff pastry may have experienced a period of . . . ahem . . . overuse, marked by the Shabbat-table ubiquity of individual-appetizer pastry rounds served hot and topped with a savory mushroom sauce. This recipe goes in the opposite direction, showcasing to excellent effect the versatility of things I often have in the house and allowing me to serve them at room temperature. My Shabbat strategy for this one is to bake the pastry, leave it whole for ease, then have the tomatoes and cheese ready. Then I assemble the tart just before serving. Puff pastry holds well overnight; just make sure not to seal before completely cooled or it can go soggy.

Serves 10 to 12

Active Time:
25 minutes

Total Time:
4 hours 30 minutes

FOR THE TOMATOES:

16 medium vine-ripened tomatoes (about 3 pounds), cored and halved

¼ cup plus 2 tablespoons olive oil

8 fresh thyme sprigs, plus leaves for garnish

1 teaspoon kosher salt

½ teaspoon freshly ground black pepper

FOR THE TART:

1 standard 9.75 × 10.5-inch puff pastry sheet, defrosted

1 large egg, beaten

1 teaspoon Dijon mustard

½ teaspoon kosher salt, plus more for serving

¼ teaspoon freshly ground black pepper, plus more for serving

½ cup finely grated Parmigiano-Reggiano

2 ounces (½ cup) crumbled feta cheese

1. Make the tomatoes: Preheat the oven to 250°F. Line a large rimmed baking sheet with parchment paper. Arrange the tomatoes, cut sides up, on the lined baking sheet. Drizzle with the ¼ cup olive oil, then scatter the thyme sprigs on top and sprinkle with the salt and pepper. Bake until the tomatoes shrink and wilt and most of the liquid pooled on top of the tomatoes evaporates, 4 to 5 hours (speed up this process by roasting at 350°F for 1 hour 30 minutes to 2 hours; tomatoes will be less dense in texture, but work well nonetheless). Cool completely, then gently layer the tomatoes in a bowl. Drizzle the remaining 2 tablespoons oil over the tomatoes and seal in an airtight container; the tomatoes will keep, refrigerated, for 1 week.

2. Make the tart: Preheat the oven to 400°F. Arrange the puff pastry on a sheet of parchment and roll it out slightly (to about 11 × 12 inches).

RECIPE CONTINUES

Pierce all over with a fork. Whisk the egg and mustard in a small bowl and brush on the tart, season with the salt and pepper, and sprinkle with the Parmigiano-Reggiano. Bake until the pastry is puffed and golden, 18 to 20 minutes. Cool completely.

3. To assemble the tart, layer the tomatoes on top of the pastry, scatter the feta on top, garnish with thyme leaves, and sprinkle with salt and pepper. Use a pizza cutter or sharp knife to cut into squares and serve.

WHITE SHAKSHUKA
with Roasted Crispy Eggplant

Since I've done red, green, and yellow versions of shakshuka (blue seems out of the question), I opted in this case for a white dairy base, something I once tasted at Hedai Offaim's house (see page 368). White is, in fact, the unofficial color of Shabbat in Israel; people wear white shirts and sometimes all-white outfits to signify the holiness and separation of the day from the rest of the week. The yogurt base in this version, seasoned with lemon and herbs, turns almost ricotta-like; it's a surprise I think you'll really enjoy. I layered tomatoes and onions underneath, and while the shakshuka is cooking, eggplant crisps up in the oven to create the tastiest little veggie croutons you've ever had.

Serves 3 or 4

Active Time:
45 minutes

Total Time:
1 hour 15 minutes

1 small eggplant
(1 pound), cut into
½-inch cubes

2 teaspoons kosher salt,
plus more for seasoning

⅓ cup plus
2 tablespoons olive oil

1 large yellow onion,
finely chopped (2 cups)

4 garlic cloves, minced

4 ripe medium Roma or
vine-ripened tomatoes,
thinly sliced

2½ cups Greek yogurt

1 cup plain yogurt
(or more Greek yogurt)

2 tablespoons chopped
Preserved Lemons
(page 15 or
store-bought)*

2 tablespoons finely
chopped fresh thyme

2 tablespoons finely
chopped fresh za'atar
or oregano leaves

2 tablespoons
cornstarch or potato
starch

6 large eggs

¼ cup finely minced red
onion

¼ cup chopped fresh
cilantro

1 small jalapeño,
finely minced

1 lime, cut into wedges

1. Preheat the oven to 425°F. On a rimmed baking sheet, toss the eggplant with 1 teaspoon of the salt and add ⅓ cup of the oil to coat. Spread evenly and roast, shaking once midway through, until crisp and golden, 30 to 35 minutes.

2. While the eggplant is roasting, heat the remaining 2 tablespoons oil in an ovenproof 10-inch skillet over medium heat. Add the yellow onion and cook, stirring, until lightly golden, 8 to 9 minutes. Add 1 tablespoon of the garlic and cook for 1 more minute. Toss the tomatoes with ½ teaspoon of the salt, layer the tomatoes over the onions and garlic, and cook until the tomatoes wilt and release some of their liquid, 10 minutes.

3. While the tomatoes are cooking, whisk together the Greek yogurt, plain yogurt, preserved lemons, thyme, za'atar, cornstarch, and the remaining ½ teaspoon salt and 1 teaspoon garlic in a medium bowl. Pour the yogurt mixture over

RECIPE CONTINUES

the tomatoes and onions, turn the heat to low, and cook until the yogurt bubbles, the sides of the skillet become slightly dry, and the liquid from the yogurt is mostly absorbed, 11 to 12 minutes. Form 6 wells in the yogurt (no need for them to be super distinct), crack the eggs into the wells, and cook, uncovered, until the yogurt begins to bubble around the edges, 5 to 6 minutes. Remove the skillet from the stovetop and preheat the broiler. Transfer the skillet to the broiler and cook until the whites of the eggs are just set but the yolks are runny, 3 to 4 minutes. Remove the skillet from the oven and scatter the eggplant, red onion, cilantro, and jalapeño on top. Serve with lime wedges.

*If you don't have preserved lemons, swap in 1 tablespoon freshly squeezed lemon juice, 1 teaspoon finely grated lemon zest, and 1 teaspoon salt.

APPETIZERS, DIPS & SALATIM

GRAPE, WALNUT & LABANEH TOASTS
with Spicy Thyme Honey

Hors d'oeuvre, first course, or snack? You be the judge. The combination of the juicy grapes, creamy labaneh, toasty walnuts, and crisp sourdough adds up to one of the best bites you've ever had. Drizzle the spicy, thyme-infused honey on just before serving; any extra will make a welcome addition to grilled chicken or fish.

Makes 12 toasts

Active Time:
20 minutes

Total Time:
30 minutes

½ cup chopped walnuts

Six ½-inch-thick slices sourdough bread (preferably from the center of a loaf), cut in half lengthwise

3 tablespoons olive oil

⅓ cup honey

½ teaspoon dried red pepper flakes

4 fresh thyme sprigs, plus thyme leaves for garnish

1¼ cups Labaneh (page 15)

1½ cups (8 ounces) firm red seedless grapes, halved

Flaky sea salt, for sprinkling

1. Arrange two racks in the top and bottom thirds of the oven. Preheat the oven to 350°F. Spread the walnuts out on a small baking sheet.

2. Arrange the bread on another baking sheet and brush one side of each piece of bread with the oil. Place the nuts on the bottom rack and the bread on the top rack and bake until the walnuts are toasted, 5 minutes; remove. Continue to toast the bread until lightly golden but not fully crisp, another 5 to 6 minutes. While the bread is toasting, combine the honey, red pepper flakes, and thyme in a small skillet and warm over medium heat until the honey liquefies and bubbles at the edges, 3 to 4 minutes. Let cool, leaving the thyme in the honey.

3. On each toast, spread 1½ tablespoons of the labaneh, then arrange 8 to 10 grape halves and 2 teaspoons walnuts on top. Drizzle honey on top of the toasts, garnish with thyme leaves, and sprinkle with flaky salt.

ULTIMATE EGG SALAD

Crunchy, creamy, and crowd-pleasing, egg salad is a Shabbat staple that food historian Gil Marks traces back to eleventh-century Franco-German Jews. Some versions contain raw onions, some caramelized; I'm firmly team caramelized, and this version comes courtesy of my friend Nurit Kariv (see page 54), is one for the ages, loaded with scallions and topped with a mound of deeply caramelized onions. Use the serving spoon to drag as many onions into your personal serving as you like (and I predict you'll like a lot).

Serves 6 as an appetizer or side dish

Active Time:
15 minutes

Total Time:
1 hour

¼ cup vegetable oil

3 medium onions, thinly sliced

1 teaspoon kosher salt, plus more to taste

½ cup mayonnaise

1 tablespoon Dijon mustard

¼ teaspoon finely ground black pepper, plus more to taste

10 large eggs

¼ cup thinly sliced scallion greens

1. Heat the oil in a 10- or 12-inch, high-sided skillet over medium heat. Add the onions and ½ teaspoon of the salt and cook, stirring occasionally, until the onions have reduced by two-thirds and are a deep, golden brown but not charred, 35 to 40 minutes.

2. While the onions are cooking, whisk together the mayonnaise, mustard, the remaining ½ teaspoon salt, and the pepper in a small bowl. Chill until ready to use.

3. Make an ice bath by filling a medium bowl with 3 cups ice and add 3 cups cold water; set aside. Place the eggs in a large saucepan, cover with water by 2 inches, season generously with salt, and bring to a boil. Reduce the heat to medium-low and simmer until the eggs are cooked through, 9 minutes. Use a slotted spoon to transfer the eggs to the ice water, deliberately cracking them slightly so some water permeates the shell. Chill for 5 minutes, dry them off, then peel under cold running water. Using the large holes on a box grater, grate the eggs into a large bowl. Gently fold in the dressing and season with more salt and pepper to taste. Transfer to a serving bowl, top with the caramelized onions, and garnish with the scallion greens.

KAVED KATZUTZ
(Chopped Liver)

In Israel, chopped liver isn't something confined to holidays or Ashkenazi homes; you'll see it on a table amid the pantheon of other salads, spreads, and dips served at different points in a meal—or as a meal itself. I'm a huge fan of this sweet, earthy, rich spread that was a major delicacy for me growing up. Enriched with tons of onions and shot through with chopped egg and schmaltz (you can use another oil), I think of it as the poor man's foie gras. I love the chunky texture that results from chopping all of the ingredients by hand.

Makes 3 cups

Active Time:
45 minutes

Total Time:
1 hour

---

8 tablespoons Schmaltz (see page 84), melted if solidified, or vegetable oil

1¾ pounds chicken livers, cleaned*

2 teaspoons kosher salt

1 teaspoon freshly ground black pepper

3 large onions, thinly sliced (6½ to 7 cups)

3 hard-boiled eggs (see page 80)

Shortcut Apple Butter (page 85), Golden Challah (page 20), and Gribenes (page 84), for serving

1. If using a skillet larger than 10 inches in diameter, heat 6 tablespoons of the schmaltz over medium-high heat in the skillet; if not, work in two batches, using half the livers and 3 tablespoons of the schmaltz per batch. Season the livers with 1 teaspoon of the salt and ½ teaspoon of the pepper and cook until they are browned on the outside and just barely blushing pink on the inside, 3 minutes per side.

2. Remove the livers to a plate, leaving any oil and juices in the pan, then add the onions, raise the heat to high, and cook, stirring, until the onions are charred and softened, 13 to 14 minutes. Transfer to a cutting board and chop (somewhere between roughly and finely) the livers, then the onions, then the eggs.

3. Transfer everything to a bowl, add the remaining 2 tablespoons schmaltz, stir gently to combine, and season with the remaining 1 teaspoon salt and ½ teaspoon pepper. Serve with apple butter, challah, and gribenes. Chopped liver can be refrigerated in an airtight container for 4 days.

*To clean the livers, pull out any stringy parts; this is not fun work, but it will result in the smoothest and most delicious experience.

GRIBENES (GRIVALACH) & SCHMALTZ

Today I think of schmaltz as Jewish olive oil or butter, a wondrous ingredient that can work its magic to lighten matzo balls and enhance classic dishes, like the chopped liver recipe on page 82. But the process of rendering chicken skins to extract the fat also has another happy outcome: the creation of gribenes, crispy chicken skins that add deep crunch and flavor to anything they touch. My first encounter with schmaltz and gribenes was at my grandma Mildred's table in Queens, New York. She didn't make them often, but when she did, eating it became a ritualistic experience. A small recycled glass jelly jar of schmaltz would be removed from the fridge to soften, then set on the center of the table with slices of fresh rye bread or challah. The gribenes sat on a small plate alongside, and we would spread the luscious schmaltz on the bread, then top it with gribenes and a sprinkle of salt. (See photo, page 83.)

Makes 2½ cups crispy chicken skins and 1 cup schmaltz

Active Time:
15 minutes

Total Time:
1 hour

---

2 pounds chicken skins*   Kosher salt

1. Line a baking sheet with paper towels. Rinse the chicken skins, pat them dry, and chop them into 1-inch pieces with a very sharp knife. Arrange them in the largest skillet you have, turn the heat to medium, and cook the skins, stirring more frequently as they begin to brown and lowering the heat if necessary, until the fat renders and the skins are deep golden and crisp, 40 to 45 minutes.

2. Lift the skins out of the fat with a spider or slotted spoon, letting any extra fat drip into the pan; drain on the paper towel–lined sheet. Season the skins with salt. Store the gribenes in an airtight container for up to 2 weeks, and refrigerate the schmaltz in an airtight container for up to 3 months.

*When I asked my butcher to save me some chicken skins (this is what you should do), he was more than happy to comply. If you need to remove the skins at home, pat your chicken dry and use dry hands to pull the skins off. You can also collect the skins in a zip-top bag and freeze them, continuing to add more to the bag over time, then defrost the bag when you've reached the full amount needed.

SHORTCUT APPLE BUTTER

I often find myself wanting a sweet touch to cut through the rich funkiness of liver. I came up with a shortcut apple butter that begins with applesauce instead of whole apples and produces a luscious, gently spiced spread you can serve alongside the chopped liver on page 82.

Makes 1 cup

Active Time:
10 minutes

**Total Time
(including cooling and chilling):**
3 hours

2 cups unsweetened applesauce

3 tablespoons granulated sugar

3 tablespoons light brown sugar

1½ teaspoons white wine vinegar

¼ teaspoon kosher salt

Pinch of freshly grated nutmeg

Pinch of ground cloves

1. Combine the applesauce, granulated sugar, brown sugar, 1 teaspoon of the vinegar, and ⅛ teaspoon of the salt in a small (2-quart) saucepan, bring to a boil over medium-high heat, and reduce the heat to maintain a very low simmer. Stir in the nutmeg and cloves and continue to simmer on low heat so the surface is just bubbling, not at a full rolling boil, stirring occasionally, until the liquid is concentrated and reduced, 55 to 60 minutes. Remove from the heat, add in the remaining ½ teaspoon vinegar and ⅛ teaspoon salt, let cool for at least 1 hour, then transfer to an airtight container and refrigerate at least 1 hour before using. Apple butter will keep, refrigerated, for 1 month.

2. To serve, spread slices of challah (page 20) with apple butter, then top with chopped liver (page 82) and a few crispy gribenes (opposite).

MOCK CHOPPED LIVER

If I'm serving actual chopped liver and we have vegetarians among our guests, I serve this plant-based version alongside the real thing. This is a riff on my mom's very Moosewood-y version, but I swap out the walnuts that she used and instead add ground pecans for a buttery, rich flavor. Lentils replace green beans (less moisture! more density!), and mushrooms add umami meatiness. This makes for excellent weekday leftovers and is just right to spread on a piece of matzo. You might like it better than the real thing, and I wouldn't blame you.

Makes 2 cups

Active Time:
15 minutes

Total Time:
30 minutes

¾ cup pecans

¼ cup dried green lentils, or ½ cup canned and drained cooked lentils

5 tablespoons vegetable oil

1 jumbo onion, thinly sliced (3 cups)

2 garlic cloves, minced

¾ pound button mushrooms, or 10 ounces baby bella (cremini) mushroom caps, thinly sliced

1½ teaspoons kosher salt, plus more to taste

¼ teaspoon freshly ground black pepper, plus more to taste

2 hard-boiled eggs, quartered (see page 80)

1 radish, grated or sliced into thin matchsticks

Matzo or challah, for serving

1. Place the pecans in a bowl, cover with very hot water, and let sit for 15 minutes; drain. If using dried lentils, place the lentils in a small microwave-safe bowl, cover with 3 inches of water, and microwave on high until the lentils are tender, 13 to 14 minutes; drain.

2. In a large skillet, heat 3 tablespoons of the oil over medium-high heat. Add the onions and cook, stirring, until golden and slightly charred around the edges, 10 to 11 minutes. Reduce the heat to medium, add the garlic, and cook, stirring, 1 minute. Add the mushrooms and ½ teaspoon of the salt and cook, stirring often, until they release their water and are deeply golden in color, 6 to 7 minutes. Remove from the heat, cool slightly, and transfer to a food processor. Add the pecans, lentils, the remaining 2 tablespoons oil and 1 teaspoon salt, and the pepper. Process until grainy but on the way to smooth, making sure not to overprocess, 15 to 20 pulses. Add the eggs and pulse until the eggs are finely chopped, an additional 5 to 10 pulses. Season with more salt and pepper and garnish with radishes. Serve with matzo or challah. Refrigerate in an airtight container for up to 1 week.

TOMATO JAM

I couldn't resist yet another way to use the bumper crop of tomatoes I always have on hand, and got to thinking about the tomato chutneys in Indian restaurants that I love. I began to play around with this recipe, whose sweetness can adhere to a variety of applications, from lavishing on top of salmon (see page 230) to piling into a little bowl to go alongside some goat cheese and crackers. I have really tried to streamline the number of spice blends in my pantry and find myself returning again and again to baharat, whose warm, sweet, savory, and spicy notes yet again work perfectly. I also suggest this as a spread for challah, especially around Rosh Hashanah, where the confluence of peak tomato season and the custom of serving sweet foods as a symbol of good luck benefits any table.

Makes 3 cups

Active Time:
15 minutes

Total Time:
1 hour 15 minutes

2 pounds ripe, red tomatoes, cored and chopped

¾ cup sugar

1 tablespoon grated lemon zest plus 4 tablespoons freshly squeezed lemon juice (from 1 very large or 2 small lemons)

1 tablespoon freshly grated turmeric root, or 1 teaspoon ground

1½ teaspoons ground cumin

1½ teaspoons kosher salt

1 teaspoon Baharat Spice Blend (page 14 or store-bought)

1 teaspoon dried red pepper flakes

1 teaspoon black mustard seeds

1 teaspoon sweet paprika

In a large (3-quart) heavy saucepan, combine the tomatoes, sugar, 3 tablespoons of the lemon juice, the turmeric, cumin, salt, baharat, red pepper flakes, mustard seeds, and paprika. Bring to a low boil over medium heat, then reduce the heat to a simmer and cook until the tomatoes are thick and jammy, darken in color, and reduce to 3 cups, 50 minutes to 1 hour. Remove from the heat, cool for 15 minutes, and stir in the remaining 1 tablespoon lemon juice and the lemon zest. Let cool to room temperature, then refrigerate in sealed jars for up to 1 month.

HUMMUS MASABACHA

This has become my preferred way to eat hummus: chunky as opposed to creamy, bathed in tahini, and topped with even more melt-in-your-mouth chickpeas rendered silky by their cooking process. For Arabs and Jews alike, hummus is a Friday food; most hummus places are closed on Saturday, and a wonderful late-Friday morning can be made of sitting at a restaurant to enjoy a full portion, which will more than tide you over until dinner is served that evening.

Serves 8

Active Time:
20 minutes

**Total Time
(including soaking time):**
10 hours

---

2 cups (12 ounces/
360 grams) dried
chickpeas*

3 teaspoons baking
soda

2½ tablespoons kosher
salt

3 garlic cloves

1 cup Tahini Sauce
(page 14), plus more
as needed

Schug (page 16) and
extra-virgin olive oil,
for serving

Paprika, for garnish

Crackers and pita,
for serving

1. In a large bowl, combine the chickpeas, 2 teaspoons of the baking soda, and 1 tablespoon of the salt. Add 8 cups water, cover loosely, and let sit on the counter until most of the water is absorbed into the chickpeas, 8 to 10 hours; drain.

2. Transfer the chickpeas to a large, heavy pot and add the remaining 1 teaspoon baking soda, 1½ tablespoons salt, and the garlic. Cover with 9 cups water, bring to a boil over high heat, reduce the heat to low, and simmer until the chickpeas are very soft and can be easily smashed between two fingers, 1 hour 30 minutes to 2 hours, checking and adding more water if necessary to keep the chickpeas underwater. Drain the chickpeas but keep the cooking water.

3. Reserve 1 cup of the chickpeas and transfer the rest to a large bowl. Add about ¼ cup of the cooking water and use a potato masher to smash the chickpeas until chunky-smooth, adding a little more of the cooking water to achieve your desired consistency; remember, the tahini will firm up a bit as it cools down. Stir in the Tahini Sauce. Spoon into a serving bowl and top with the reserved chickpeas. Garnish with schug, drizzle with olive oil, sprinkle with paprika, and serve with crackers and pita.

*To quick-soak chickpeas, in a large saucepan, cover the chickpeas with water by 5 inches, 2 teaspoons baking soda, and 1 tablespoon salt. Bring to a boil over high heat, boil for 5 minutes, then turn off the heat and let the chickpeas sit in the hot water for 1 hour. Drain and proceed with cooking the chickpeas.

FETA, ARTICHOKE & PEA DIP
with Sumac Pita Chips

More than almost anything else I've created lately, this dip/spread sits right in the Venn-diagram overlap of easy and delicious; I'm almost embarrassed to report just *how* easy. Drain a jar of marinated artichoke hearts, defrost some peas (yes, the sweet and delicious frozen kind), throw in some feta and garlic, and blend. Then, take any chopped herbs you have (though chives and mint really pop here) and use the tangy, sumac-y pita chips to scoop it up. Reimagine any leftovers as a sandwich spread, or fold them into leftover pasta for an impromptu lunch.

Makes 2 cups dip and 32 pita chips

Active Time:
20 minutes

Total Time:
35 minutes

FOR THE PITA CHIPS:

⅓ cup olive oil

1 tablespoon ground sumac

1½ teaspoons ground cumin

½ teaspoon kosher salt

4 pitas, each cut into 8 triangles

FOR THE DIP:

One 12-ounce jar marinated artichokes, drained, or canned and drained or frozen and defrosted*

1 cup frozen peas, defrosted and drained (¾ cup defrosted)

One 4-ounce block (or 1 cup crumbled) feta cheese

¼ cup olive oil

1 small garlic clove

3 tablespoons minced fresh chives, plus more for garnish

2 tablespoons finely chopped fresh mint

1 tablespoon finely minced seeded hot green chili pepper

1. Make the pita chips: Arrange two racks in the top and bottom thirds of the oven. Preheat the oven to 375°F. In a large bowl, combine the oil, sumac, cumin, and salt. Add the pita triangles to the bowl and toss to coat in the sumac oil. Arrange in single layers on two large rimmed baking sheets and bake until golden and crisp, switching them midway through, 13 to 14 minutes. Cool on the baking sheets.

2. While the chips are baking, make the dip: Combine the artichokes, peas, feta, olive oil, and garlic in a food processor and process until grainy-smooth, 25 to 30 seconds. Scrape down the bowl and process until almost smooth, 30 to 45 more seconds. Stir in the chives, mint, and chili. Transfer to a serving bowl and garnish with more chives. Serve the chips with the dip. The dip can be refrigerated in an airtight container for up to 5 days.

*If you're using canned or defrosted frozen artichokes, add 1 tablespoon of your favorite Italian-style vinaigrette when blending.

SHEET-PAN ZA'ALUK

Of the many, many eggplant preparations Moroccans have perfected, za'aluk, which in Arabic means "cooked" or "spread," is a favorite. Morocco had one of the world's richest Jewish communities, with several cities boasting thousands of Jewish residents, most of whom settled in the area known as the Maghreb during the Inquisition when Jews were expelled from Spain in 1492. Most of the Jewish community came to Israel in the 1950s and 1960s in response to increasing persecution and their status as dhimmis, a protected minority but one without equal rights. They brought with them Arabic-Jewish recipes, like this delicious salad, which has a million variations but always contains eggplant. For ease, I turned mine into a broiled, single-sheet-pan affair. After cooking the vegetables together on one pan until charred, they are chopped, then brightened with one last stir of lemon and green herbs.

Makes 3 cups

Active Time:
25 minutes

Total Time:
1 hour 15 minutes

1 medium eggplant
(1 pound), halved

5 medium vine-ripened tomatoes (1 pound), cored

1 small red bell pepper, halved and seeded

1 whole small jalapeño

4 garlic cloves

¼ cup olive oil

1¼ teaspoons kosher salt

1 teaspoon ground cumin

1 teaspoon smoked paprika

½ teaspoon finely grated lemon zest

1 tablespoon freshly squeezed lemon juice

¼ cup chopped fresh cilantro

Water Challah (page 28), for serving

Preheat the oven to 475°F. Arrange the eggplant, skin side down, on a baking sheet along with four of the tomatoes, the bell pepper, jalapeño, and garlic. Bake until the vegetables are charred and softened, watching them to make sure they don't burn, 35 to 40 minutes. Remove the vegetables from the oven, cool slightly, transfer to a cutting board, and finely chop them. Reduce the oven temperature to 400°F. Return the vegetables to the sheet pan, drizzle with the oil and sprinkle with 1 teaspoon of the salt, cumin, and smoked paprika, and gently stir to coat. Bake until fragrant, 5 minutes. Remove from the oven and cool for 10 minutes. Chop the remaining tomato into small pieces and sprinkle with the remaining ¼ teaspoon salt after chopping. Add the chopped tomato to the roasted vegetables and gently fold in the lemon zest and juice and the cilantro. Serve with challah.

SELECTING EGGPLANTS
Most of the time when purchasing produce, we're advised to select fruits and vegetables that are heavy for their size, which means that they're juicy and fresh. When selecting eggplants, you actually want to choose lighter ones; heavier eggplants mean more seeds, more bitterness, and tougher flesh. So in this case, aim for lightness.

MOROCCAN CARROT SALAD

Nearly every Jewish, Israeli, or Moroccan home serves some variation of this salad, and for very good reason. It is easy to make, tastes better the longer it sits around, and is a favorite of kids and adults alike. I try to use carrots that are less than an inch in diameter at their widest point; they cook more evenly and soak up the sauce better. Rather than cutting the carrots into coins first, I cook them whole, which prevents them from getting waterlogged. Dates add a chewy, caramelly sweetness that sets this version apart from the rest; if you're lucky enough to have any salad remaining as leftovers, you'll find that within a few hours the dates melt into the dressing for even more sweetness.

Makes 4 cups

Active Time:
25 minutes

Total Time:
50 minutes

1 teaspoon kosher salt, plus more as needed

1½ pounds medium carrots, trimmed and peeled

1 large lemon

¼ cup olive oil

2 teaspoons Harissa (page 14 or store-bought) or other hot sauce

2 teaspoons honey or silan (date syrup)

1 teaspoon ground cumin

1 garlic clove, grated

½ cup chopped fresh mint

½ cup chopped fresh cilantro

2 Medjool dates, pitted and chopped*

Bring a large pot of generously salted water to a boil. Add the carrots to the pot, return to a boil, and cook until the carrots can be pierced with a fork but aren't mushy, 10 to 11 minutes, depending on the diameter of the carrots. Drain and cool until they're easy to handle, 10 minutes. While the carrots are cooling, finely zest the lemon into a bowl and juice it (you should have 2 teaspoons zest and 3 to 3½ tablespoons lemon juice), then whisk in the olive oil, harissa, honey, cumin, garlic, and the 1 teaspoon salt. Cut the carrots into ¼-inch rounds, add to the bowl with the dressing, and toss to coat. Stir in the mint, cilantro, and dates and refrigerate until ready to use. The salad will keep, covered, up to 5 days in the refrigerator.

*To make the dates easier to chop, freeze them after pitting for 1 hour before chopping.

LACHMAGINE
(Chewy-Crispy Syrian Flatbreads)

After spending the better part of a day cooking with Yvonne Cohen, I realized the most cherished appliance in her kitchen might just be the freezer. Every month or two, she clears her calendar—and her expansive marble countertop—to make and freeze about 200 lachmagine, the irresistible meat-topped flatbreads that are perhaps the most sought-after item in her deliciously expansive repertoire. "I can never make enough," said Cohen.

Initiated at a young age into a coterie of talented female cooks in her tight-knit Syrian-Egyptian-Jewish family in Brooklyn, she began absorbing recipes, almost by osmosis, from her mother, Grace Arking, and grandmother, Yvonne Harari. But it was only after she moved to Israel in 2010 that she became a lachmagine (*lahm* means "meat" in Arabic, *agine* means "dough") expert herself. Homesick for her family—many of whom have since moved to Israel—she would cook with her aunt Kady Harari, who helped her nail down the ideal texture of the chewy-crispy flatbread. "It can never be too thin," she said as we stamped out the circles, spread the meat on top, and slid tray after tray into the oven.

Lachmagine is a labor of love, leading some to make larger "pizzas" to cut down on production time. But Yvonne keeps hers dainty, just like her grandmother's. "She liked everything as small as possible," she said, surmising that in addition to being impressive (more work = more love), things just taste better in small packages. Soon the aroma of the sizzling rounds filled the room, and we cooled and lined them up between layers of parchment. Yvonne packed up a few dozen for me in neat little rows, and within hours of getting home, my husband, stepson, and I had devoured most of them—no freezer required.

Makes fifty 2½-inch flatbreads

Active Time:
1 hour 30 minutes

**Total Time
(including marinating time):**
3 hours

RECIPE AND INGREDIENTS CONTINUE

FOR THE TAMARIND SAUCE
(Makes 1¼ cups, enough for 2 recipes of lachmagine):

¾ cup unsweetened applesauce

¾ cup sugar

⅔ cup tamarind concentrate

⅓ cup freshly squeezed lemon juice

⅓ cup water

FOR THE MEAT:

1¼ pounds 80/20 ground beef

1 medium onion, very finely diced (1½ cups)

⅔ cup tamarind sauce

½ cup ketchup

2 tablespoons freshly squeezed lemon juice

2 tablespoons tomato paste

1½ tablespoons fine sea salt

1 tablespoon ground allspice

¼ teaspoon ground cinnamon

FOR THE DOUGH:

¾ cup (180 grams/ml) plus ¼ cup (60 grams/ml) warm water, plus more as needed

1 teaspoon (3 grams) active dry yeast

1 teaspoon (5 grams) sugar

3¾ cups (488 grams) all-purpose flour, plus more as needed and for flouring the counter

¾ teaspoon (4 grams) fine sea salt

Tahini Sauce (page 14), for drizzling

1. Make the tamarind sauce: Combine the applesauce, sugar, tamarind concentrate, lemon juice, and water in a small (1- or 2-quart) saucepan, bring to a boil over medium-high heat, reduce the heat to medium, and boil, stirring constantly, until the liquid thickens and reduces by half, 20 minutes. Cool completely and transfer to a jar with a tight-fitting lid. The sauce keeps refrigerated in an airtight jar for up to 6 months.

2. Marinate the meat: In a large mixing bowl, combine the beef, onions, ⅔ cup of the tamarind sauce, the ketchup, lemon juice, tomato paste, salt, allspice, and cinnamon, making sure to break up any lumps in the meat, until everything is incorporated and all the meat is darkened. Cover and refrigerate for at least 1 hour and up to 12 hours. When you begin making the dough, transfer the meat to a colander set over a plate or bowl to drain and discard the liquid.

3. Make the dough: In the bowl of a stand mixer, whisk together the ¾ cup/180 ml warm water, yeast, and sugar and let sit until the yeast begins to bloom, 6 to 7 minutes. Fit the mixer with the dough hook and add the flour and salt to the bowl. Knead the dough on medium-low speed until it begins to come together and is no longer dry, adding 1 or 2 additional tablespoons water as needed and stopping and scraping down the sides of the bowl as needed, 3 minutes. Add the remaining ¼ cup/60 ml warm water, 1 tablespoon at a time every minute or so; with each addition, the dough will loosen and get sticky but then absorb the water and become drier again. Once all the water is added and after about 10 minutes of total kneading, the dough will be smooth, supple, easy to handle, and not sticky at all. Divide the dough into two pieces, roll them each into a ball, wrap one of the balls in plastic wrap, and place in the refrigerator.

4. Assemble the flatbreads: Line two large baking sheets with parchment. Preheat the oven to 375°F. Generously flour a clean work surface, then use a rolling pin to roll out the dough, dusting it often with flour, occasionally rotating it and flipping it so it never sticks to the counter, until the dough forms a 15-inch circle. Use a lightly floured 2½-inch cookie cutter to cut 25 circles from the dough (alternatively, you can make 15 or 16 four-inch pizzas).

5. Peel away the dough left between the cut-out circles, wrap in plastic, and refrigerate. Transfer the cut rounds to the prepared baking sheet, leaving ½ inch between rounds.

6. Use a tablespoon measure or cookie scoop to portion a scant tablespoon (2½ teaspoons) of the meat mixture onto each round, then use clean fingertips to spread the meat mixture almost to the very edge of the dough, leaving a sliver of a border. Bake until the edges of the dough are lightly golden and most of the moisture has evaporated from the meat and it appears drier and darkened, 16 to 17 minutes (bake 1 additional minute if you like a very crispy end result). Let cool on the baking sheets. Repeat with the remaining large ball of dough and meat. If there is any meat left over, roll out the refrigerated scraps, top with meat, and bake as directed. Serve hot or at room temperature, drizzled with Tahini Sauce. Lachmagine can be arranged on single layers of parchment, stacked, and frozen in an airtight container for up to 3 months. Arrange straight from the freezer in a single layer on a baking sheet and reheat at 350°F until warmed and crisp, 10 to 12 minutes.

CAULIFLOWER & GREEN BEAN "MASABACHA"

Habasta is a favorite neighborhood restaurant in Tel Aviv, the place where my husband (then boyfriend), Jay, and I ate the first night I moved to Israel, where we take our friends on Fridays for brunch, the bar we slump into for relief as the weekend begins. The chef, Elon Amir, always has a version of this spread on the menu, and it's become a classic. To make it, he blends cooked Jerusalem artichokes with nuts for a modern take on masabacha (see page 90 for the original iteration). I swapped in cauliflower to make it extra simple, and I love how it lightens the dish while still blending up creamy and satisfying. To finish, green beans are braised with mint, then served cold and topped with even more nuts, this time toasted and chopped. It turns this into a salad all on its own, worthy of a small snacky meal alongside plenty of crusty bread.

Serves 4

Active Time:
40 minutes

Total Time:
1 hour

FOR THE MASABACHA:

1 teaspoon kosher salt, plus more to taste

1 pound cauliflower, cored and cut into 1-inch florets (about 4 cups)

1⅓ cups (7 ounces) blanched almonds, slivered or whole

¼ cup olive oil

¼ cup water

3 tablespoons freshly squeezed lemon juice, plus more to taste

1 teaspoon ground cumin

¼ teaspoon ground white pepper

FOR THE GREEN BEANS:

½ pound green beans, trimmed and cut into 2-inch lengths

Finely grated zest of 1 lemon

⅓ cup lemon juice

⅓ cup water

⅓ cup olive oil, plus more for drizzling

3 garlic cloves, chopped

1 tablespoon dried mint

½ teaspoon kosher salt, plus more to taste

¼ teaspoon freshly ground black pepper, plus more to taste

2 tablespoons chopped fresh parsley

¼ cup chopped, toasted almonds

RECIPE CONTINUES

1. Make the masabacha: Bring 1 inch of water and ½ teaspoon salt to a simmer in a 3-quart saucepan. Add the cauliflower and cook over medium heat, partially covered, until very tender, about 15 minutes. Drain the cauliflower and let cool.

2. Place the almonds in the bowl of a food processor and process them to the size of panko bread crumbs, but not superfine, 15 seconds. Add the cauliflower and process until unified and mostly smooth, another 10 seconds. Add the olive oil, water, lemon juice, cumin, the remaining ½ teaspoon salt, and white pepper and process until pureed, stopping the processor and scraping down the sides of the bowl once if necessary, 30 to 45 seconds (the puree will be slightly grainy). Season with more salt and lemon juice to taste.

3. Prepare the green beans: Place the green beans in a 3-quart saucepan and add the lemon zest, lemon juice, water, olive oil, garlic, mint, salt, and pepper. Bring to a boil over medium-high heat, reduce the heat to medium-low, and simmer, partially covered, until the beans are tender, 15 minutes. Cool the beans in the liquid until they reach room temperature (reserve some of the cooking liquid), at least 30 minutes, and season with more salt and pepper. Spread the masabacha on a plate or mound it in a bowl. Lift the beans out of their liquid and pile them on top of the masabacha. Garnish with the chopped parsley, toasted almonds, a drizzle of olive oil, and some of the beans' cooking liquid.

SWEET & SOUR SOUTH AFRICAN CURRIED FISH

Though Lea Laser Silberg has been in Israel for decades, a plate of Cape Malay curried fish transports her directly to the blue summer skies of her youth in Cape Town, South Africa. Shabbat was a time for large family meals hosted by her aunts or uncles, who would greet young Lea with a cheek pinching before sending her off to join her other cousins for games in the garden. In the dining room, an enormous buffet table groaned under the weight of challah, gefilte fish, pickled and oil-cured herrings, rollmops (herring fillets rolled around a savory filling), chopped liver, borscht topped with dill, cucumbers, and smetana (sour cream).

In the midst of this classic Eastern European spread, there was always a crock of sweet-and-sour Cape Malay curried fish, sunshine-yellow from a generous amount of turmeric and fragrant from a raft of pickled onions and whole allspice berries. "It looked totally natural in its environment, even though it came from the other side of the world," said Lea. "South Africa was home to people from all over, so we grew up eating food from all over the place." She believes that a Muslim Cape Malaysian cook must have prepared a fish dish like this one, and it became a permanent part of the local summer table both at shul kiddush (food and drink served after services on Shabbat morning) and at home. Serve with challah and a salad to make the tender, sweet, flaky whitefish a meal on its own.

Serves 4 to 6

Active Time:
15 minutes

**Total Time
(including chilling):**
4 hours 30 minutes

RECIPE AND INGREDIENTS CONTINUE

3 tablespoons vegetable oil

1½ pounds skinless thick whitefish fillets, such as cod or halibut, cut into 2-inch chunks

2 teaspoons kosher salt

½ teaspoon freshly ground black pepper

1 cup white vinegar

⅔ cup plus 2 tablespoons water

⅓ cup sugar

1 tablespoon curry powder

1 teaspoon ground turmeric

¼ teaspoon cayenne pepper

2 medium onions, peeled and sliced into ¼-inch-thick rings

1 teaspoon whole allspice berries

1 tablespoon all-purpose flour

1. Preheat the oven to 300°F. Pour the oil into a 7 × 11-inch or 9 × 13-inch glass or ceramic baking dish. Place the fish in the pan, season with 1 teaspoon of the salt and the black pepper, then turn the fish to coat it with the oil and arrange the fish in a single layer in the dish. Bake until opaque and just cooked through, 25 to 30 minutes.

2. In a large, wide saucepan, combine the vinegar, ⅔ cup of the water, the sugar, curry powder, turmeric, the remaining 1 teaspoon salt, and the cayenne. Bring to a low boil over medium heat, then add the onions and allspice berries and simmer briskly until the onions begin to soften, 5 minutes. While the onions are cooking, dissolve the flour in the remaining 2 tablespoons water, then add it to the onions and cook, stirring constantly, until the sauce is thickened slightly, another 3 to 4 minutes.

3. Pour half of the curry-onion sauce into a 1½-quart serving dish, arrange the baked fish over it, and cover with the remaining sauce. Cover and refrigerate it for at least 4 hours and up to 3 days to deepen the flavor. Serve cold with the sauce. The fish will keep, refrigerated, in an airtight container for up to 1 week.

KIDDUSH HERRING

In his wonderful cookbook *Schmaltz*, Ashkenazi food historian and cook Shmil Holland cites an old joke about herring among Eastern European Jews (allow me the paraphrase here): "When there are no people around, only then shall herring be considered actual fish." Food scholar Gil Marks presents an entirely different perspective. In his *Encyclopedia of Jewish Food*, he writes that herring in barrels was traded heavily and considered a delicacy by Eastern European Jews from the fifteenth century on (the famous painter Marc Chagall's father was a herring merchant in Vitebsk, Belarus, and many believe the iconic flying fish in many of his paintings is in fact a herring).

Herring is most commonly known as a treat offered at kiddush, a meal served either at synagogue or at home after prayers and before lunch (many ritually observant Jews don't eat before praying, resulting in legions of the hungry and devout). The version I developed is similar to the one we ate at the kiddush in my shul in Palo Alto, except I add a fresh hot chili, which rounds out the sweetness of the pickling liquid. My father, Stan, is a major herring devotee; a dream lunch for him is a few slices of herring and a plate of crackers or thinly sliced rye bread, the vehicles of choice. Dad, this one's for you.

Serves 6 to 8

Active Time:
30 minutes

**Total Time
(including cooling time):**
25 hours 30 minutes

---

2 cups water

¼ cup kosher salt

2½ cups ice

1 pound skin-on herring or mackerel fillets, pin bones removed, cut crosswise into 1½-inch pieces

2 cups distilled white or white wine vinegar

¼ cup sugar

2 teaspoons black peppercorns

1 teaspoon yellow mustard seeds

3 bay leaves

1 lemon, thinly sliced

1 small red onion, thinly sliced (1 cup)

1 fresh jalapeño pepper, halved (optional)

1. Bring 1 cup of the water to a boil in a small saucepan. Add the water to a large bowl with the salt, stir to dissolve, then add the ice. Add the herring and chill, covered, overnight in the refrigerator. In a small saucepan, bring the vinegar, sugar, and the remaining 1 cup water to a boil with the peppercorns, mustard seeds, and bay leaves. Simmer for 5 minutes, then remove from the heat and cool to room temperature, 30 minutes.

2. Drain the herring from its brine. In a 1½-quart glass or ceramic jar or bowl, layer the herring with the lemon, onion, and jalapeño, if using. Pour in the cooled pickling liquid, seal tightly, and refrigerate for at least 1 day and ideally 2 before serving. Herring can be kept in the refrigerator for up to 3 weeks.

VEGETABLES & SIDE SALADS

ROASTED KOHLRABI, CHERRY TOMATO & FETA SALAD

This salad employs a kohlrabi-roasting method popularized by Asaf Doktor at his Tel Aviv restaurant, Dok. By cooking the kohlrabies at a high temperature, then letting them cool in their tough skins before peeling, the kohlrabi becomes meltingly tender and sweet. For the brunch at her house (see page 54), Nurit Kariv wisely used the kohlrabi as a foil for tart, roasted cherry tomatoes and sharp feta. The tangy sherry vinaigrette and fresh dill add two more contrasting yet flavorful elements. You can prepare everything for this salad a day in advance and plate it right before serving; it's also wonderful at room temperature.

Serves 4 to 6

Active Time:
15 minutes

**Total Time
(including kohlrabi cooling time):**
2 hours

---

4 medium kohlrabies
(1½ pounds)

8 tablespoons olive oil

½ pound (1½ cups)
orange or yellow cherry
tomatoes

¾ teaspoon kosher salt

1½ tablespoons sherry
vinegar

1 teaspoon honey

4 ounces feta cheese,
cut into ½-inch cubes
(1 cup cubes)

2 tablespoons picked
fresh dill sprigs

1. Arrange a rack in the center of the oven and preheat the oven to 475°F. Arrange the kohlrabies on a baking sheet and drizzle with 3 tablespoons of the oil. Arrange the tomatoes on a small rimmed baking sheet or 9 × 13 inch baking dish; drizzle with 2 tablespoons of the olive oil, and sprinkle with ½ teaspoon of the salt. Place both trays in the oven and roast until the tomatoes begin to shrivel, 15 to 16 minutes. Remove the tomatoes from the oven and cool. Continue to roast the kohlrabies until tender and the outside is dark brown and charred, another hour. Remove from the oven, place in a bowl, seal with plastic, and let cool for 30 minutes. Uncover the bowl, peel, and cut the kohlrabies into ¼-inch-thick slices, then cut the slices into half-moons.

2. Combine the remaining 3 tablespoons olive oil with the sherry vinegar, honey, and remaining ¼ teaspoon salt in a jar with a tight-fitting lid and shake until creamy (or whisk in a bowl).

3. Arrange the sliced kohlrabi on a serving platter and scatter the tomatoes and feta on top. Drizzle with the dressing and garnish with the dill. Dressing can be refrigerated, tightly sealed, in an airtight container for 1 week.

RAINBOW CHARD & ROASTED PINE NUT SALAD

Swiss chard stems usually get short shrift in a recipe. At worst they're discarded; at best, sautéed with the greens, where they tend to get lost. So I reserve some stems for pickling, which leaves them extra crunchy and allows you to taste their earthiness. The leaves get sautéed, and the pickling liquid is used to create a tart dressing that is a beautiful counterpart to the richness of the recipe's olive oil and pine nuts—save any leftover pickling liquid for another use, such as making a salad dressing whisked with olive oil and mustard. I actually prefer this dish at room temperature, and it's great the day after it's made.

Serves 4 to 6

Active Time:
20 minutes

Total Time:
30 minutes

⅓ cup pine nuts

1 large or 2 to 3 small to medium bunches Swiss chard, preferably multicolored (1½ pounds)

¾ cup white wine vinegar

¼ cup honey

1¾ teaspoons kosher salt, plus more for seasoning

1 small jalapeño, sliced into thin rings

⅓ cup olive oil

5 garlic cloves, thinly sliced

1. Preheat the oven to 325°F. Place the pine nuts on a small baking sheet; bake until golden and fragrant, 6 to 7 minutes. Remove from the oven to cool.

2. Using your hands or a knife, separate the leaves from the chard stems. Cut or tear into bite-sized pieces. Trim and discard any dark ends from the stems. Cut the stems into thin half-moons (like celery). Reserve half of the stems (save the rest for another use) and the leaves.

3. In a small saucepan, combine the vinegar, honey, and 1 teaspoon of the salt. Bring to a low boil over medium-high heat, reduce heat to medium-low, and simmer for 2 minutes. Add half the chard stems with half the jalapeño. Transfer to a wide, shallow bowl to cool.

4. In a large (10- to 12-inch) skillet, heat oil over medium-low heat. Add garlic and cook, stirring, until lightly golden, 2 minutes. Raise heat to medium, add reserved chard stems with ¼ teaspoon of the salt, and cook, stirring, until softened, 2 minutes. Raise the heat to medium-high. Working in two batches, add the chard leaves and another ¼ teaspoon salt and cook, stirring, until slightly wilted, 2 minutes per batch. Remove from heat; transfer to a medium bowl.

5. Strain the pickled chard stems, reserving the liquid, and add them along with 3 tablespoons of the pickling liquid to the chard along with the remaining half of the jalapeño, and remaining ¼ teaspoon salt. Sprinkle with pine nuts. Season with pickling liquid and salt to taste.

SEARED BROCCOLI
with Caper Vinaigrette

Ah, broccoli, we *almost* ate you every Friday night. Let me set the scene: In the minutes just before Shabbat came in, my mother would steam some broccoli so we'd have an extra fresh vegetable to enjoy over Shabbat. We would sit schmoozing in the "living room" (where we never lived, except during this precious single hour and a half every Friday). Almost like clockwork, my mom would slap her forehead and say, "I forgot about the broccoli!" Since we didn't turn lights on and off on Shabbat and the microwave had a bulb that activated when its door was opened, the broccoli would sit in isolation until Shabbat ended. And so, no microwave broccoli in my house. Instead, grilled planks of broccoli, where the stem is as much of a treat as the florets. Steam-charring in the skillet turns the vegetable a gorgeous shade of bright green, contributing a wisp of smokiness to the proceedings. The longer I live in Israel, the more I crave salt, spice, and acid, and this zippy caper, shallot, and lemon vinaigrette checks all the boxes. The vinaigrette also works supremely well stirred into pasta or potato salad, and—of course—dolloped on steak, fish, or chicken.

Serves 4 to 6

Active Time:
20 minutes

Total Time:
20 minutes

---

7 tablespoons olive oil

2 tablespoons freshly squeezed lemon juice

2 tablespoons jarred capers (2½ tablespoons if salt-packed), drained, lightly rinsed, and coarsely chopped

2 tablespoons chopped fresh parsley

1 tablespoon finely minced shallots

½ teaspoon finely minced hot chili pepper (seeds optional)

¼ teaspoon kosher salt, plus more for seasoning

⅛ teaspoon freshly ground black pepper

1 large head broccoli (1½ to 1¾ pounds)

6 tablespoons vegetable broth, chicken broth, or water

1. In a medium bowl, combine 4 tablespoons of the olive oil with the lemon juice, capers, parsley, shallots, chili, salt, and black pepper.

2. Use a sharp vegetable peeler to peel the tough outer layer of the broccoli stem to reveal the paler green interior. Cut broccoli through the stem into four 1-inch "steaks," some larger than others. You'll have some stray florets; use them, too.

3. Heat a 9- or 10-inch skillet over medium-high heat. Just before adding the broccoli, add 1½ tablespoons oil to the skillet. Add 2 steaks, season with salt, and sear until the underside is charred on the edges, 3 minutes. Flip, add 3 tablespoons of the broth, cover, and continue cooking until the underside is charred and the broccoli is bright green, 3 to 5 minutes. Remove to a plate; cover with foil to keep warm. Repeat with the remaining oil, steaks, and broth. Transfer to a serving platter and spoon the vinaigrette on top.

SWEET & TART EGGPLANT SALAD

As much as we might try to improve upon some classic techniques, there's really nothing better than frying eggplant. Adding crunchy celery, pine nuts, and onions offers several directions for your taste buds to veer. The tartness the eggplant derives from its vinegary marinade is unusual in a country where lemon reigns supreme, and practically everything required to make it probably resides in your fridge, crisper drawer, or pantry. I happily pile any leftovers onto a piece of challah and drizzle with Tahini Sauce (page 14) and Amba (page 14) for a free-form, open-faced, Shabbat-afternoon sandwich.

Serves 4

Active Time:
30 minutes

**Total Time
(including eggplant sitting
and refrigeration time):**
2 hours 30 minutes

⅓ cup pine nuts

2 pounds (2 medium) eggplant, cut crosswise into ½-inch-thick rounds

3 teaspoons kosher salt, plus more for seasoning

Canola or vegetable oil, for frying

6 tablespoons red wine vinegar

2½ tablespoons honey

1 tablespoon olive oil

½ teaspoon freshly ground black pepper, plus more for seasoning

3 large celery stalks, thinly sliced into half-moons (about 1½ cups), plus 1 cup tender celery greens, for garnish

1 small red onion, very thinly sliced (about 1 cup)

1 small hot chili pepper (seeded if desired), thinly sliced

2 garlic cloves, very thinly sliced

1. Preheat the oven to 325°F. Place the pine nuts on a small baking sheet and bake until golden and fragrant, 6 to 7 minutes. Remove the nuts from the oven to cool.

2. Arrange the eggplant on a wire rack set atop a baking sheet. Season the eggplant on both sides with a total of 2 teaspoons of the salt (use about 1 teaspoon on each side) and let sit for 1 hour, until moisture beads appear. Pat the eggplant dry with clean paper or kitchen towels, pressing to absorb as much water as possible. Cut the large rounds into half-moons and leave the smaller ones whole. Heat ½ inch of oil in the largest, heaviest skillet you have over medium heat. Working in batches, fry the eggplant until lightly golden, flipping midway through, 7 to 8 minutes per side; by the second batch the oil will be very hot and the eggplant may cook a little faster. Drain on paper towels.

3. In a large bowl, whisk together the vinegar, honey, olive oil, the remaining teaspoon salt, and the black pepper. Add the eggplant, celery, onion, chili, and garlic. Toss, cover, and refrigerate at least 1 hour and up to 24 hours. Season with salt and black pepper and toss with the celery greens. Top with the pine nuts.

ROASTED GREEN BEANS & PEPPERS
with Smoky, Nutty Bread Crumbs

Roasting green beans turns them into something magical, shriveled, caramelized, and otherworldly delicious, and bell peppers lend sweet silkiness to the finished dish. I use sweet baby bell peppers, which have few to no seeds, making them easy to slice and incorporate on the sheet pan. This is a vegetable side that tastes equally good at room temperature or even cold out of the fridge; you can top it with the crunchy crumbs just before serving.

Serves 4

Active Time:
20 minutes

Total Time:
35 minutes

1 pound green beans, trimmed

6 multicolored mini bell peppers, seeded and thinly sliced

1 small red onion, cut into 8 wedges

6 tablespoons olive oil

1 teaspoon kosher salt

½ teaspoon freshly ground black pepper

Finely grated zest of 1 lemon

¼ cup sliced almonds

3 garlic cloves, minced

½ cup panko bread crumbs

½ teaspoon smoked paprika

⅛ teaspoon cayenne pepper, or more to taste

1. Preheat the oven to 425°F. Arrange the green beans, bell peppers, and onions together on a large rimmed baking sheet. Drizzle with 3 tablespoons of the olive oil, ½ teaspoon of the salt, and ¼ teaspoon of the black pepper and toss, then spread them into an even layer. Roast the vegetables, shaking the pan once after 10 minutes, until charred and wilted, 20 to 22 minutes. Remove from the oven, cool for 5 minutes, and toss with the lemon zest.

2. While the green beans are roasting, heat the remaining 3 tablespoons olive oil in a large skillet over medium-low heat. Add the almonds and garlic and cook, stirring, until the almonds begin to turn golden and the garlic is fragrant, 3 minutes. Add the panko and the remaining ½ teaspoon salt and ¼ teaspoon black pepper and cook, stirring, until the panko is deeply golden, 6 to 7 minutes. Remove from the heat and stir in the smoked paprika and cayenne. Transfer the bread crumbs to a bowl so they stop toasting. Plate the vegetables and top with the crumb mixture.

QUICK-COOKED AWAZE SWISS CHARD

Ethiopian food is vegetable-forward, and this is a favorite side dish I learned from my friend Fanta Prada (page 37). The primary seasoning is awaze, a spicy, gingery condiment Fanta keeps on hand at all times to punch up any manner of dishes. You'll find yourself with leftover awaze; use it wherever schug is called for.

Serves 4 to 6

Active Time:
15 minutes

Total Time:
35 minutes

FOR THE AWAZE
(makes 1 cup):

6 medium red or green jalapeños, seeded if desired, coarsely chopped

1 small dried chile de arbol

1 garlic clove

1-inch piece fresh ginger, peeled and thinly sliced

1 cup lightly packed fresh cilantro leaves and tender stems

2 tablespoons olive oil

2 teaspoons kosher salt

FOR THE SWISS CHARD:

3 small green jalapeños

¼ cup olive oil

1 jumbo onion, finely chopped (3 cups)

5 garlic cloves, thinly sliced

1 large bunch Swiss chard (1¼ pounds), rinsed, dried, and thinly sliced (about 8 cups sliced), sliced lower stems kept separate

1 teaspoon kosher salt, plus more to taste

Tiny pinch of ground cloves

Tiny pinch of ground cardamom

1 teaspoon ground flaxseed

1 tablespoon freshly squeezed lemon juice

1. Make the awaze: Combine the jalapeños, chile de arbol, garlic, ginger, cilantro, oil, and salt in a small blender or food processor and process until a unified, almost smooth mixture forms, 15 seconds. Seal the awaze in a glass jar and keep refrigerated for up to 2 weeks.

2. Make the Swiss chard: Arrange a rack about 6 inches from the broiler and preheat the broiler. Arrange 2 of the jalapeños on a baking sheet and broil until the skins are puffed and blistered, 10 minutes. Cool completely, remove and discard the stems, and chop.

3. Meanwhile, in a large pot, heat the oil over medium-high heat. Add the onions and cook, stirring, until lightly golden, 8 to 9 minutes. Add the garlic and chard stems and cook until slightly softened, 1 to 2 additional minutes. Add the chard leaves, salt, cloves, cardamom, flaxseed, and 3 tablespoons of the awaze and cook, stirring, until wilted and the stems are soft, 10 minutes. Slice the remaining jalapeño into thin rounds. Stir in the cooked and raw jalapeños, add the lemon juice, and season with salt to taste.

SWEET POTATOES
with Miso Tahini Butter

Called batata in Israel, sweet potatoes have none of the Thanksgiving associations we Americans automatically attach to them. Here, they play savory very, very well. By combining funky miso and creamy, nutty tahini with butter (or a nondairy substitute), you can top all manner of things with an herb-infused flavor bump that takes a dish to a whole other level. After you mix the butter, you can dollop it on top of the sweet potatoes while soft, or roll it up into a tube, chill it, then slice off pieces and use them whenever you want. Extra butter dresses up toast, pasta, or a bowl of rice.

Serves 6

Active Time:
10 minutes

Total Time:
55 minutes

FOR THE SWEET POTATOES:

6 long, thin sweet potatoes (each about 2 inches in diameter, 2¼ pounds total), scrubbed and dried

FOR THE MISO TAHINI COMPOUND BUTTER:

½ cup (1 stick/ 4 ounces) unsalted butter, softened

2 tablespoons thinly sliced scallion greens, plus more for garnish

2 tablespoons pure tahini paste

1 tablespoon blond (shiro) miso

1 teaspoon chopped fresh jalapeño

1 small garlic clove, very finely minced

½ teaspoon kosher salt (optional)

½ teaspoon ground sumac

1. Preheat the oven to 400°F. Arrange the sweet potatoes on a rimmed baking sheet, prick each a few times with a fork, and roast until tight and puffy and the flesh is soft, 45 minutes to 1 hour.

2. While the potatoes are roasting, use a fork to combine the butter, scallion greens, tahini, miso, jalapeño, and garlic in a bowl until smooth. Taste and add the salt, if desired. The butter can be sealed in an airtight container and refrigerated for up to 1 week.

3. When the sweet potatoes are done, split them open, dollop the butter on top, sprinkle with the sumac, and garnish with scallion greens.

GLAZED CRISPY TOFU
with Eggplant & Brussels Sprouts

Deep-frying simply isn't an option in Israel's summery months, so I turn to my baking sheets to help me turn out this crunchy tofu dinner. The glaze contains a surprise ingredient—silan (date syrup)—and has that take-out tang I'm always on the hunt for in my home kitchen. Serve on a Friday afternoon as a holdover meal before a heavier repast later in the day. If you haven't got Brussels sprouts, by all means swap in broccoli.

Serves 4

Active Time:
20 minutes

Total Time:
1 hour 15 minutes

---

1 pound firm tofu

Neutral cooking spray

3 small Japanese eggplants (12 ounces), cut into 1-inch rounds

2 cups (8 ounces) Brussels sprouts, trimmed and halved

5 tablespoons vegetable oil

½ teaspoon kosher salt

½ teaspoon freshly ground black pepper

4 tablespoons soy sauce

3 tablespoons sesame oil

2 tablespoons cornstarch

3 tablespoons water

3 tablespoons silan (date syrup)

2 tablespoons honey

2 tablespoons unseasoned rice vinegar

4 garlic cloves, finely minced

1 tablespoon finely minced fresh ginger

1 teaspoon finely minced hot red chilies

Cooked white rice, for serving

Sliced scallion greens and lightly toasted sesame seeds, for garnish

1. Drain the liquid from the tofu; cut lengthwise into 1-inch slices. Arrange between two clean kitchen towels, cover with a baking sheet, and weigh down with two heavy cans for 30 minutes. Stack the slices; cut into 1-inch-thick logs, then into 1-inch cubes.

2. Arrange racks in the top and bottom thirds of the oven. Preheat the oven to 400°F. Spray 2 large rimmed baking sheets with cooking spray. In a large bowl, toss the eggplant and Brussels sprouts with 3 tablespoons of the oil, the salt, and the black pepper; transfer to one of the prepared baking sheets. In a large bowl, whisk 1 tablespoon each soy sauce and sesame oil with the remaining 2 tablespoons vegetable oil. Add the tofu, toss to coat, scatter 1 tablespoon of the cornstarch on top, and toss to coat again. Arrange on the second baking sheet, leaving room between cubes. Arrange both sheets in the oven. Bake, stirring midway through and switching baking positions, until tofu is golden and vegetables are tender and crisp, 28 to 30 minutes.

3. While the vegetables and tofu are baking, whisk the water and remaining 1 tablespoon cornstarch in a small saucepan. Add the remaining 3 tablespoons soy sauce, 2 tablespoons sesame oil, silan, honey, vinegar, garlic, ginger, salt, and chilies, bring to a boil over medium-high heat, reduce heat to medium-low, and simmer until thickened and bubbly, 2 minutes. Transfer tofu and vegetables to a large bowl; toss with sauce; divide rice among bowls, top with tofu mixture, and garnish with scallions and sesame seeds.

LALE'S SILKY BRAISED SPINACH & BULGUR

Lale Abouaf (see page 61) serves this as a side dish alongside fish and a simple salad for a perfect hot-weather Shabbat meal. The key is to cook the spinach over very low heat—if you need to, raise the pot off direct heat using a diffuser—which renders it silky and tender. A pinch of sugar and a bit of tomato paste are very common in Turkish cooking, and they, along with the carrots, add just the right note of sweetness to the dish.

Serves 4 to 6

Active Time:
20 minutes

Total Time:
1 hour

---

3 tablespoons olive oil

1 large onion, finely chopped (2 cups)

½ teaspoon kosher salt, plus more to taste

2 medium carrots, peeled and diced

2 tablespoons tomato paste

1 pound cleaned spinach leaves

¾ cup water

½ teaspoon dried red pepper flakes

2 teaspoons sugar

¼ cup uncooked coarse bulgur, rinsed and drained

Squeeze of lemon, for serving (optional)

Plain yogurt, for serving

1. In a wide, heavy Dutch oven, heat the oil over medium-low heat. Add the onions and salt, reduce the heat to low, and cook, stirring, until lightly golden, 9 to 10 minutes. Add the carrots and tomato paste and cook, stirring, until the carrots soften, 3 to 4 minutes. Working in batches, add the spinach leaves and cook, stirring, as they wilt.

2. Add the water with the red pepper flakes and sugar, stir, cover, reduce the heat to very low, and cook until the spinach reduces in volume and releases more liquid, 7 to 8 minutes.

3. Uncover, add the bulgur, and cook, uncovered and stirring occasionally, until the bulgur swells, the spinach is soft and silky, and most of the liquid has evaporated, 35 to 45 minutes. (If necessary, raise the pot a bit higher above the heat with a diffuser to prevent scorching or overcooking.) Drain any excess liquid, season with salt, and serve with a squeeze of lemon (if using) and a dollop of yogurt.

BALSAMIC-GLAZED ONIONS & LEEKS

In this allium extravaganza, pretty much every kind of onion plus garlic roast together in one pan. They're bathed in a simple sauce, whose star ingredient is the much-maligned balsamic vinegar, which I believe is ready for its revival. Few condiments have the ability to add as much with one splash, much less the quarter cup called for here. As the vegetables braise and glaze, the sauce thickens; uncovering it for the last few minutes burnishes the color and further deepens the interplay of flavors here. I dare say that these can be a meal in and of themselves, especially if you add a drizzle of tahini or dollop of creamy yogurt.

Serves 6 to 8

Active Time:
20 minutes

Total Time:
2 hours 30 minutes

1½ pounds leeks
(3 medium)

3 or 4 small-medium red onions (1 to 1½ pounds)

6 small-medium yellow onions (2 pounds)

6 to 8 small shallots, peeled and trimmed

10 to 15 large garlic cloves

3 or 4 fresh sage, oregano, and/or thyme sprigs

1½ cups vegetable broth

¼ cup balsamic vinegar

¼ cup olive oil, plus more for drizzling

2 tablespoons pomegranate molasses, honey, or maple syrup

1 teaspoon kosher salt, plus more for seasoning

½ teaspoon freshly ground black pepper

Preheat the oven to 425°F. Bring a large pot of lightly salted water to a boil. Fill a large bowl halfway with ice, then add water to create an ice bath. Trim the root ends off the leeks as well as any tough dark green ends, then score them lengthwise halfway through with a paring knife; do not cut all the way through. Fan the leeks, rinse well with water, and cut into 3- or 4-inch lengths. Peel the papery outer layers from the red and yellow onions, then trim ½ inch off both ends.

Place shallots in boiling water, boil for 2 minutes; use a spider or slotted spoon to remove them to the ice bath. Lower red and yellow onions into the water; boil 5 minutes, then lift out into the ice bath; chill for 3 minutes. Pop shallots out of their skins and remove outer papery skins from the onions. Use a paring knife to cut a 1-inch *X* into the bottoms of the red and yellow onions. Stand the onions up in a 10- or 12-inch skillet or round baking dish, then wedge the leeks in and around the onions. Fit the shallots in (everything should be quite snug in the skillet, but if there's a little space, that's OK), scatter the garlic, and arrange the herb sprigs on top. Whisk together the broth, vinegar, olive oil, pomegranate molasses, salt, and pepper in a bowl, pour it over the vegetables, and drizzle more oil over the top. Seal tightly with foil and bake until the onions are tender and can very easily be pierced with a fork, 1 hour 30 minutes. Uncover, reduce the heat to 400°F, and cook until everything is golden brown and the liquid in the pan thickens slightly, 35 to 40 minutes. Season with salt to taste, then serve the onions and leeks with their liquid.

CHARRED POTATO SALAD
with Mustard & Horseradish Dressing

I make this salad frequently to create a sunny picnic or outdoor bar-becue vibe, regardless of the actual setting or season—not to mention it's an opportunity to revel in the versatility of the simple spud. The idea came to me right after Passover, when I had leftover cooked potatoes and horseradish root from our seder (both are used in different holiday-specific rituals) and was looking to give them new purpose. Precooking the potatoes before throwing them on a hot grill or cast-iron skillet ensures that they're creamy-tender on the inside, crisp and charred on the exterior. I soak the red onions in ice water to give them extra crunch and mitigate their sharpness, and incorporating the horseradish into the lemony, grainy-mustard dressing adds kick and spice.

Serves 4 to 6

Active Time:
20 minutes

Total Time:
45 minutes

½ cup diced red onion

2 pounds small potatoes

5 tablespoons olive oil, plus more for brushing the potatoes

½ teaspoon kosher salt, plus more for seasoning

¼ teaspoon freshly ground black pepper, plus more for seasoning

2 medium whole fresh hot green chili peppers

3 tablespoons freshly squeezed lemon juice

2 tablespoons grainy Dijon mustard

2 teaspoons finely grated fresh horseradish root, or 1 teaspoon bottled prepared white horseradish

4 cups arugula leaves (5 ounces)

1. Combine ½ cup ice and ½ cup water in a small bowl and add the onions.

2. Prick the potatoes a few times with a fork. Wrap in a clean kitchen towel; microwave on high until just tender, 10 to 11 minutes. (Or steam them, covered, in a pot with 1 inch of water, 13 to 14 minutes.) Cool for 15 minutes, then halve.

3. Preheat a grill, grill pan, or large heavy skillet over medium-high heat.

4. Working in two batches, brush the potatoes with oil, season generously with salt and black pepper, and grill, cut side down, along with the whole chilies, until the potatoes are charred and cooked through and the chilies are blistered (you can turn the chilies once), 7 to 8 minutes.

5. Remove the potatoes and chilies to a plate to cool. Whisk together the olive oil, lemon juice, mustard, horseradish, salt, and black pepper. Once cooled, cut the potatoes into chunks. Seed the chilies and chop them.

6. Drain the onions and pat them dry. Arrange the arugula on a platter and top with the potatoes, chilies, and onions. Drizzle dressing on top, toss to coat, and season with more salt and black pepper to taste. Dressing can be refrigerated in an airtight container for 1 week.

CHERRY TOMATO, FETA & KALAMATA SALAD

Easy to assemble, crowd-pleasing to the max, and warm-weather perfect, this salad is all about the sum of its parts. If you like, prep all the elements in advance, then throw it together just before serving. Or, if you're like me, wait to serve it until the salad releases its juices just so you can take a spoon to the salty, deeply flavorful liquid that pools at the bottom of the platter. Make it a bit in advance and refrigerate for a little while before serving.

Serves 6

Active Time:
15 minutes

Total Time:
15 minutes

FOR THE DRESSING
(makes ½ cup):

¼ cup freshly squeezed lemon juice (from 2 small lemons)

¼ cup olive oil

¼ teaspoon kosher salt, plus more for seasoning

¼ teaspoon freshly ground black pepper, plus more for seasoning

¼ teaspoon ground coriander (optional)

FOR THE SALAD:

1 large or 2 medium heirloom, beefsteak, or vine-ripened tomatoes (¾ pound), sliced into rounds

¾ pound multicolored cherry tomatoes, halved

½ small red onion, sliced into half-moons

4 ounces (1 cup) feta cheese, crumbled

½ cup lightly packed whole fresh cilantro leaves

¼ cup whole pitted kalamata (or other) olives, halved

1 hot green chili pepper, seeded and cut into thin rounds (optional)

1. Make the dressing: In a jar with a lid, combine the lemon juice, olive oil, salt, black pepper, and coriander (if using). Cover and shake until emulsified, 5 seconds. Dressing can be refrigerated, tightly sealed, in an airtight container for 1 week.

2. Assemble the salad: In a salad bowl or on a platter, arrange the heirloom and cherry tomatoes, red onion, feta, cilantro, olives, and chili (if using). Dress to your liking (I generally use it all), then season with salt and black pepper and add more dressing if needed.

CUCUMBER & APPLE SALAD

"Appele falt nisht fein fun beimele" ("The apple doesn't fall far from the tree") was a Yiddish aphorism my grandma Mildred would use often when complimenting someone's progeny. You could say the same about this salad, which hews close to the original I grew up eating. Why mess with success? The way the sweet, crunchy, and mildly spicy elements come together in the bowl begs for it to be made again and again. It's the perfect contrast to a rich meat dish like brisket, or you can create a light meal out of it by adding chickpeas or a chunk of feta. I like to use red apples, because the skin color contrasts with the salad's mostly green ingredients, and Persian cucumbers, which are super crunchy and contain less water than other varieties, work great here. If you can't find them, though, any cuke will do.

Serves 6 to 8

Active Time:
10 minutes

**Total Time
(including chilling time):**
45 minutes

⅓ cup apple cider vinegar

¼ cup sugar

1½ teaspoons kosher salt, plus more to taste

¼ cup olive oil

12 Persian or 2 small English cucumbers (1½ pounds), thinly sliced on the bias

1 medium crispy, tart red apple (such as Pink Lady), cored, quartered, and thinly sliced

½ small red onion, thinly sliced

½ cup finely chopped dill

1. In a small, microwave-safe bowl, microwave the vinegar on high for 30 seconds. Transfer to a medium salad bowl, add the sugar and salt, whisk to dissolve, and let cool to room temperature, 10 minutes. Whisk in the oil, then add the cucumbers, apple, onion, and dill, toss, and chill at least 30 minutes before serving.

2. Before serving, season with more salt if desired.

SPINACH SALAD
with Oranges & Pine Nuts

Serve this wintery salad when you want something fresh and crunchy to present alongside richer dishes. The sharpness of raw onion, juiciness courtesy of orange segments, and crunch from bell peppers and roasted pine nuts combine with spinach for a felicitous pairing (add feta or goat cheese if you like). In Israel, I use so-called Turkish spinach, which has thicker leaves that hold up to dressing without wilting; look for the heartiest variety in your neck of the woods.

Serves 6

Active Time:
20 minutes

Total Time:
20 minutes

---

1 tablespoon olive oil

⅓ cup pine nuts

⅛ teaspoon plus ¼ teaspoon fine sea salt

One large 9- to 10-ounce bunch spinach, preferably large-leaved

1 medium orange, rind removed, segmented,* and 1 tablespoon juice reserved

½ small white onion, finely chopped

½ small red bell pepper, seeded and thinly sliced

¼ cup olive oil

2 tablespoons white wine vinegar

1 tablespoon finely chopped shallots

1 tablespoon honey

2 teaspoons Dijon mustard

¼ teaspoon freshly ground black pepper

1. Combine the oil, pine nuts, and ⅛ teaspoon of the salt in a small saucepan. Toast the nuts over medium heat, shaking often, until golden, 5 to 6 minutes. Transfer to a plate to cool. Stack the spinach leaves and slice them crosswise into ½-inch strips.

2. Arrange the spinach in a salad bowl and top with the pine nuts, orange segments, onions, and bell pepper. Combine the oil, vinegar, reserved orange juice, shallots, honey, mustard, the remaining ¼ teaspoon salt, and the pepper in a jar, seal tightly, and shake until creamy. Pour the dressing over the salad and toss to coat. Dressing can be refrigerated, tightly sealed, in an airtight container for 1 week.

*To cut orange segments, slice off the top and bottom ends of an orange so it can sit flat on the counter. Using a sharp knife and starting from the top, cut away the zest and white pith beneath, leaving the flesh exposed. Hold the orange in your hand over a bowl. Release the segments by cutting the flesh away from the white membrane surrounding each segment. Squeeze the membrane to release any juice; reserve 1 tablespoon of the juice for this salad.

DOUBLE MANGO SALAD
with Amba Dressing

My love affair with amba—the Iraqi-Jewish condiment that's a less-chunky riff on Indian mango chutney—was well documented in *Sababa*, and I was incredibly honored to have Tejal Rao write about it in the *New York Times Magazine*. A few years later and I'm still as besotted with its funky, salty, briny, and mildly fruity qualities, and find myself looking for inventive ways to use it. This is a new favorite: a salad that takes inspiration from amba's main ingredient—mango—by incorporating both unripe and juicy, ripe mango into a tangled contrast of sweet, crunchy, spicy, and herby elements. It's a little Asian, a little Middle Eastern, and all irresistible.

Serves 4 to 6

Active Time:
15 minutes

Total Time:
15 minutes

FOR THE DRESSING:

6 tablespoons freshly squeezed lime juice (from 2 large or 3 small limes)

3 tablespoons vegetable oil

1½ tablespoons Amba (page 14 or store-bought)

1 tablespoon honey

FOR THE SALAD:

1 small or ½ large unripe, green mango (1¼ pounds), peeled*

1 medium ripe, juicy mango (10 ounces)

1 cup fresh cilantro leaves

½ small red jalapeño, or more or less to taste, seeded and sliced into thin rings

½ cup toasted sunflower seeds

1. Make the dressing: In a small bowl, whisk the lime juice, oil, amba, and honey (alternatively, combine the ingredients in a jar and shake); reserve. Dressing can be refrigerated, tightly sealed, in an airtight container for 1 week.

2. Make the salad: Use a julienne peeler or grater to shred the unripe mango into a medium salad bowl. Carefully peel the ripe mango with a sharp vegetable peeler, then slice it into ¼-inch wedges and add to the bowl along with the cilantro leaves. Just before serving, add the jalapeño and dressing to the bowl, toss, and sprinkle with the sunflower seeds.

*If you can't find unripe mango, substitute shredded green cabbage or carrots.

GRILLED HALLOUMI, FIG & TOASTED HAZELNUT SALAD

Grilling firm, salty Halloumi adds a slight charred texture to its exterior and softens the interior, while still maintaining its shape and bite. I find that Halloumi is a great foil for all kinds of salad fixings, or, as my husband, Jay, calls them, "toys." In this case, the things I am playing with are figs, roasted hazelnuts, and a dressing that gets a lift from sherry vinegar and mustard. I purposely chose tender, malleable butter lettuce here; if you ever saw me eating this salad, you might find me building little lettuce wraps and happily eating them with my hands.

Serves 4 to 6

Active Time:
20 minutes

Total Time:
30 minutes

½ cup hazelnuts

7 tablespoons olive oil, plus more for grilling

1 teaspoon kosher salt, plus more for seasoning

2 tablespoons sherry vinegar

1 tablespoon honey

1½ teaspoons Dijon mustard

¼ teaspoon freshly ground black pepper, plus more for seasoning

Two 8-ounce packages Halloumi, halved lengthwise and then cut crosswise to form 16 equal-sized rectangles

4 cups butter lettuce leaves (from 1 large lettuce head)

5 large or 8 medium ripe figs

1. Preheat the oven to 350°F. Arrange the nuts on a small rimmed baking sheet, drizzle with 1 tablespoon of the oil, sprinkle with ¼ teaspoon of the salt, toss to coat, and toast until lightly golden and fragrant, 9 to 10 minutes. Allow the nuts to cool and coarsely chop them; set aside.

2. In a jar with a tight-fitting lid, combine the remaining 6 tablespoons olive oil with the vinegar, honey, mustard, ¼ teaspoon of the salt, and the pepper; cover and shake until creamy.

3. Preheat a grill or grill pan over medium-high heat. Pat the Halloumi dry and season lightly with the remaining ½ teaspoon salt and pepper, or to taste. Toss the Halloumi with a light drizzle of oil, then grill the cheese until deep-golden grill marks form, 3 to 4 minutes per side; remove to a plate. Tear the lettuce into large pieces, then tear the figs into large chunks and scatter them on top of the lettuce. Arrange the Halloumi on top, drizzle with the dressing, scatter with the nuts, and season with lots of pepper. Dressing can be refrigerated, tightly sealed, in an airtight container for 1 week.

CRUNCHY SLAW
with Chickpeas & Creamy Sesame Dressing

This dressing is a reminder of just how versatile tahini really is. Here, it assumes a more Asian inclination, shaken with ginger, sesame oil, and rice vinegar into a creamy, dreamy dressing that also steps up as a dip for crudités or as a sandwich spread. Using hot water helps loosen the tahini, which can seize when it comes in contact with liquid; if you find your dressing a bit thick, just add a drop more water. It's rare you'll find a savory salad from me without a sweet addition, and in this case I add either dried mango or pineapple, things I keep in the house for snacking or a cheese plate but often find myself using in recipes. Of course, swap in any dried fruit of your choice.

Serves 8 to 10

Active Time:
25 minutes

Total Time:
25 minutes

FOR THE DRESSING:

⅓ cup pure tahini paste

1½ tablespoons soy sauce

1½ tablespoons maple syrup

1½ tablespoons unseasoned rice vinegar

1 tablespoon finely grated fresh ginger

2 teaspoons toasted sesame oil

1½ tablespoons boiling water, plus more as needed

1 teaspoon Harissa (page 14 or store-bought), sriracha, or other hot sauce of your choice

FOR THE SLAW:

4 scallions (green and white parts), trimmed

1 medium kohlrabi*

3 cups thinly shredded green cabbage (from a 6-ounce piece)

3 cups thinly shredded red cabbage (from a 6-ounce piece)

1 large carrot, shredded

One 15-ounce can chickpeas, drained and rinsed (about 1¾ cups)

¼ cup finely chopped dried mango or dried pineapple

½ cup chopped fresh parsley

2 teaspoons thinly sliced hot red chili

1. Make the dressing: In a jar with a tight-fitting lid, combine the tahini, soy sauce, maple syrup, rice vinegar, ginger, toasted sesame oil, water, and harissa. Cover and shake until creamy, 10 seconds, loosening with additional water if necessary. Dressing can be refrigerated, tightly sealed, in an airtight container for 1 week.

2. Make the slaw: Cut the pieces lengthwise into thin shreds. Add to a large salad bowl. Use a sharp knife to cut the green outer layer and white, fibrous underlayer from the kohlrabi. Cut it into ¼-inch-thick rounds, stack the rounds, and slice into thin strips. Add to the bowl with the scallions, then add the green and red cabbage, carrot, chickpeas, dried mango, parsley, and chili. Pour the dressing over the salad and toss to coat.

*If you can't find kohlrabi, a crunchy vegetable in the cabbage family, swap in jicama or peeled broccoli stems.

SUMAC-ROASTED CORN SALAD
with Smoky Dressing

Galia Schipper is a Mexico City transplant who's a whiz with a knife and a pleasure to be around and who often works with me in my kitchen. Together we developed this roasted corn salad that fuses her Mexican upbringing and her penchant for Israeli spices. We blended chipotle en adobo—an ingredient now very popular in Tel Aviv, thanks to a recent explosion in the popularity of tacos—into a simple, spicy dressing that brings the whole salad together beautifully.

Serves 4 to 6

Active Time:
15 minutes

Total Time:
55 minutes

FOR THE CORN & CHILIES:

2 dried pasilla or ancho chilies, stemmed and seeded

4 tablespoons olive oil

4 large ears fresh corn

1 tablespoon ground sumac

½ teaspoon kosher salt

FOR THE DRESSING
(makes 1 cup):

½ cup mayonnaise

5 tablespoons olive oil

4 tablespoons fresh lime juice (from 2 small limes)

1 tablespoon honey

1 tablespoon very finely chopped canned chipotle chile in adobo sauce

¾ teaspoon kosher salt

FOR THE SALAD:

6 cups (4½ ounces) arugula leaves

½ small red onion, thinly sliced (½ cup)

1 large avocado, diced

1. Prepare the corn and chilies: Arrange two oven racks in the top and bottom thirds of the oven and preheat to 425°F. Use sharp kitchen shears to thinly cut the chilies; toss with 1 tablespoon of the oil and arrange them on a small rimmed baking sheet. Fit a cutting board inside a large rimmed baking sheet (to catch runaway kernels). Stand the ears of corn on the cutting board and use a sharp knife to cut off the kernels. Go around a second time to shave off any you missed; you should have 2½ to 3 cups of kernels. Transfer to a large bowl and toss with the remaining 3 tablespoons olive oil, the sumac, and salt. Transfer back to the large rimmed baking sheet. Place the chilies on the bottom rack and the corn on the top rack and roast, stirring each once midway and removing the chilies once crisp, 10 minutes. Continue to roast the corn until some is browned and shriveled, another 20 to 25 minutes.

2. Make the dressing and assemble the salad: In a jar with a tight-fitting lid, combine the mayonnaise, oil, lime juice, honey, chipotle, and salt. Cover and shake until creamy, 10 seconds.

3. Assemble the salad: Toss the arugula, corn kernels, onion, and avocado in a bowl, add ½ cup of the dressing and the crispy chilies, and gently toss. Refrigerate any extra dressing in an airtight container for up to 5 days. Use on other salads or as a dip for crudités.

KUGELS

COLORFUL VEGETABLE KUGEL

This is our family's California take on a starchier kugel, lightened up with garden vegetables and often served cold or at room temperature for Shabbat lunch. The combination of onions, carrots, and zucchini lends a touch of earthy sweetness, and garlic adds a little zing. Since the zucchini and potatoes are quite watery, squeezing out most of the liquid is key, as is adding a bit of potato starch, which helps lend the kugel a light creaminess. If you have leftovers, try stuffing a piece of the kugel into a mini pita with lettuce and tomato for a filling vegetarian lunch. For an extra-special-looking kugel, spiralize the vegetables or use a julienne peeler to create longer strands.

Serves 10 to 12

Active Time:
30 minutes

Total Time:
1 hour 30 minutes

⅓ cup plus 1 tablespoon vegetable oil

1 pound russet potatoes (2 large potatoes), peeled and shredded

1 pound green, yellow, or a combination zucchini (3 medium), shredded

1 tablespoon kosher salt

¾ pound carrots (2 large or 3 medium), peeled and shredded

1 large onion, very thinly sliced

4 garlic cloves, minced

4 large eggs, lightly beaten

¼ cup olive oil

½ cup potato starch or all-purpose flour

½ teaspoon freshly ground black pepper

1. Preheat the oven to 400°F.

2. Grease a 9 × 13-inch baking dish with the 1 tablespoon vegetable oil. Place the shredded potatoes and zucchini in a large bowl with ½ teaspoon of the salt, toss, and let sit for 5 minutes. Arrange a clean kitchen towel on a work surface and place a large handful of the potato-zucchini mixture on the towel. Wrap the towel around the mixture and squeeze out and discard as much excess liquid as you can. Transfer to a large bowl and repeat with the remaining potatoes and zucchini. Add the carrots, onions, garlic, eggs, olive oil, the remaining ⅓ cup vegetable oil, the potato starch, the remaining 2½ teaspoons salt, and the pepper until everything is incorporated. Pour into the prepared pan and bake until the top is golden, 1 hour. Cool slightly and cut into squares.

BUBBE'S EXTRA-CRISPY POTATO KUGEL

Whenever she came to visit us in Palo Alto, my grandma Mildred would make her incredibly delicious potato kugel. It served as a powerful magnet for my friends, who were on "kugel alert," especially on Fridays, when she would make a fresh batch. My dear friend Heather Henriksen had a particularly close relationship with my grandmother, who would summon her to our house with just a few words: "Heather, I made kugel, come over, I saved you a corner." The two of them would sometimes sit in the backyard kibitzing for hours, and later Heather would recount stories that some of us in the family had never heard ourselves.

One in particular has become the stuff of family legend. Mildred and my grandfather Jack Sussman, who died before I was born, lived a modest, hardworking life. Jack was a printing "jobber," serving as a middleman for anyone needing triplicate receipts and business cards, and my grandmother worked as a bookkeeper. Money was tight, and when they became engaged in 1933, an engagement ring was out of the question. As my grandma told Heather, on their twenty-fifth anniversary, they went out for dinner and, as he always did, Jack came around to help her out of the car on the passenger side. He opened the door, then promptly dropped to one knee, proffering a modest diamond ring. "Mildred," he said. "It's been twenty-five years since we got married. Isn't it about time we got engaged?" My grandmother's special gift was just that: She had a special story, an inside joke, and a somehow endless supply of crispy kugel corners for those who wanted—and needed—them the most.

Serves 12

Active Time:
25 minutes

Total Time:
2 hours

---

8 medium russet potatoes (4½ pounds), peeled

2 large onions, halved

6 large eggs

⅔ cup vegetable oil (not olive oil)

¼ cup all-purpose flour or potato starch

1½ tablespoons kosher salt, plus more if needed

½ teaspoon freshly ground black pepper

1. Preheat the oven to 400°F.

2. Grate the potatoes and onions on the large holes of a box grater or using the large shredding disc of a food processor. Place the grated potatoes and onions on a clean kitchen towel and squeeze out as much liquid as you can. Transfer the

RECIPE CONTINUES

grated vegetables to a large bowl and mix with the eggs, ⅓ cup of the oil, the flour, salt, and pepper, ensuring the potatoes are evenly coated. If you don't mind tasting raw egg, taste the batter to make sure the salt level is to your liking.

3. Place a 9 × 13-inch or 10 × 14-inch ceramic or metal baking dish on top of a rimmed baking sheet. Add the remaining ⅓ cup oil to the baking dish, place it in the oven, and heat until the oil is very hot, 10 minutes. Using oven mitts, carefully remove the baking dish from the oven, stir the batter, gently spoon the batter into the dish, and

spread it out evenly, making sure not to splash the hot oil. If some of the oil comes up the sides, use a spoon to carefully spread the hot oil over the top of the kugel. Return the kugel to the oven and bake until the exterior is very crisp and deep golden brown, 1 hour 30 minutes to 1 hour 45 minutes. (It might seem like it's taking forever for the top to brown, but it will!) Remove from the oven, cool slightly, and sprinkle with more salt, if desired. Serve hot, warm, or cold out of the fridge the next day, when it might remind you slightly of a piece of Spanish tortilla española.

Yapchik: Kugel by Another Name (with Meat)

When we had our Havdalah service at Hedai Offaim's home (see page 368), he made a delicious yapchik—essentially a potato kugel studded with flanken (short-rib meat) and cooked for hours and hours in a low oven. My grandma Mildred used to make something very similar she called "potato cholent," baked overnight in her aluminum Magnalite pot, so I was delighted to have Hedai talk me through the recipe. To turn my potato kugel into Hedai's yapchik, season 1½ pounds of 2-inch cubes of flanken with kosher salt and freshly ground black pepper, heat 2 tablespoons vegetable oil over medium-high heat in a large skillet, and brown it on all sides, 8 minutes total. Cool slightly, then add the meat to the prepared, unbaked kugel mixture (use a minimum 10 × 14-inch baking dish), and bake according to the instructions above. Next, reduce the oven temperature to 200°F, seal the kugel tightly in two layers of heavy-duty foil, and bake for at least another 6 hours and up to 12. When done, you will have the deep brown, meat-studded kugel of your dreams.

CARAMEL APPLE NOODLE KUGEL RING

When I was two years old, my mother met another young mother named Bette Hootnick in the tiny kosher food aisle at a local supermarket near Palo Alto. A decades-long friendship was forged, one cut short only by my mother's untimely death from ovarian cancer in 2006. Bette, who at that point was divorced, was a great source of comfort to my father, and within a year and a half they were married (and one of my close childhood friends, her daughter Michelle, is now my stepsister). Seventeen years into this second chapter, they have created new traditions, including beautiful Shabbat meals of their own (now in Israel, where they recently moved).

One of Bette's best desserts is a delicious cinnamony apple cake, whose flavors I co-opted here for an apple-crowned noodle ring. Sweet kugels like these may seem incongruous with a savory meal but have long been a staple of Shabbat tables, reinforcing the festive nature of the day. It's important to grease your tube pan generously so the kugel pops out after baking. In a pinch, use a nonstick Bundt pan or a shallow 3-quart baking dish. This would also make a fabulous side dish (or dessert) for Rosh Hashanah, when apples are traditionally used in cooking.

Serves 8 to 10

Active Time:
25 minutes

Total Time:
1 hour 25 minutes

¾ cup vegetable oil

1 teaspoon kosher salt, plus more for salting the water

One 12-ounce bag wide egg noodles

⅔ cup lightly packed dark brown sugar

2 teaspoons water

1½ teaspoons ground cinnamon

Generous pinch of freshly grated nutmeg

⅛ teaspoon ground cloves

1 pound tart apples (3 medium), such as Granny Smith or Pink Lady, cored and cut into 1-inch pieces (about 4 cups)

2 teaspoons pure vanilla extract

4 large eggs

½ cup granulated sugar

⅓ cup golden raisins

Flaky sea salt, for finishing

1. Set a rack in the center of the oven and preheat the oven to 350°F. Grease a 10-inch (10- to 12-cup) tube cake pan with 1 tablespoon of the oil, making sure to grease all the way up the sides and the center.

2. Bring a large pot of generously salted water to a boil and cook the noodles according to the package directions. (I like to add 1½ teaspoons kosher salt per quart of water. So if you fill an 8-quart pot halfway, add 2 tablespoons salt.) Rinse well with cold water and drain well.

RECIPE CONTINUES

3. In a large 12-inch skillet, heat 3 tablespoons of the oil over medium heat. Add the brown sugar with the water, ½ teaspoon of the cinnamon, the nutmeg, cloves, and ¼ teaspoon of the kosher salt and stir until the mixture liquefies and begins to bubble, 2 to 3 minutes. Add the apples and cook, stirring occasionally, until tender, 8 to 10 minutes. Add 1 teaspoon of the vanilla. Spoon the apples with the caramel into the bottom of the prepared tube pan and cool while preparing the noodle mixture.

4. In a large bowl, whisk together the eggs, the remaining ½ cup oil, the granulated sugar, raisins, the remaining teaspoon each cinnamon and vanilla, and the remaining ¾ teaspoon salt. Stir the noodles into the mixture and spoon them evenly into the pan over the apples.

5. Bake until the top is golden and crusty, 35 to 40 minutes. Cool for 15 minutes, then loosen the sides of the pan with a thin, sharp knife, invert the kugel ring onto a serving plate with a lip, and sprinkle with flaky sea salt.

Kugel Is King

"Kugel is the king of the Sabbath meal," Joan Nathan writes in her wonderful book *Kugels, Quiches, and Couscous: My Search for Jewish Cooking in France.* According to Nathan, the word *kugel* is derived from the German word for "ball," meaning the terra-cotta vessel it was baked in. In his book, *Schmaltz,* Shmil Holland posits that it's a derivation of the German word *kuchen,* or "cake." No matter its etymology, Jewish food historian Gil Marks writes in his *Encyclopedia of Jewish Food* that most kugels have the following in common: ". . . starch base, eggs, and fat, without the addition of water or other liquids." Originating in France's Alsace-Lorraine region and the Rhineland of Germany, kugel eventually made its way to Poland and Russia—countries better known now as standard-bearers of the dish. Though today the most popular kugels contain potatoes and noodles, the original ones were devised as a way to use scraps of bread, bound with fat and studded with fruit. Like cholent (see page 304), kugel was often cooked overnight in a community's communal oven, to be eaten on Sabbath morning. Today, most kugels are baked in an hour or two, though the sweet, peppery Yerushalmi Kugel (see my cookbook *Sababa* for a recipe) is often cooked overnight, as is meat-studded yapchik (see page 154). Easy, homey, and satisfying, kugels are a worthy counterpart to a main-course protein, requiring little else other than a salad to round out a meal.

MUSHROOM & APPLE MATZO KUGEL

It is the tradition of some families to eat matzo only during the eight days of Passover, but if my sister, Sharon, has an extra box lying around, she makes this delicious, sweet-and-savory kugel on any given day of the year. It was a favorite of our mother's, and she makes it for Thanksgiving—just after we finish our annual bake sale to raise money in my mother's memory to support women living with ovarian cancer. The combination of mushrooms, celery, apples, and dried fruit is hard to beat, and the kugel freezes and reheats beautifully.

Serves 8

Active Time:
15 minutes

Total Time:
1 hour

Neutral cooking spray

2 tablespoons olive oil

1 medium white onion, roughly chopped

1 medium red onion, roughly chopped

2 celery stalks, sliced

2 pounds button mushrooms, tough stems removed and discarded, sliced

½ cup golden raisins

1 large apple, cored and chopped

½ cup chopped fresh parsley

3 matzos, crushed into bite-sized pieces

2 large eggs, beaten

Finely grated zest of 1 lemon

1 teaspoon honey

¼ teaspoon dried red pepper flakes

½ teaspoon paprika

½ teaspoon kosher salt, plus more to taste

½ teaspoon ground cinnamon, or to taste

1. Preheat the oven to 350°F. Coat an 8 × 10-inch baking dish with cooking spray.

2. In a large (at least 6-quart) pot, heat the oil over medium heat. Add the onions and celery and sauté, stirring occasionally, until translucent and just beginning to caramelize, 8 to 9 minutes. Add the mushrooms and cook until they release their water and are reduced in size by half, 5 to 6 minutes. Stir in the raisins, apples, and parsley and cook, stirring, until the apples just begin to soften, 3 to 4 minutes.

3. Remove from the heat, add the matzo, and stir thoroughly until incorporated; if there is not enough liquid to hydrate the matzo, add water a few tablespoons at a time until the matzo is soft but not mushy. Let cool, stirring occasionally to help release heat, 15 to 20 minutes.

4. Stir in the eggs, lemon zest, honey, red pepper flakes, paprika, salt, and cinnamon; mix well. Transfer the mixture to the prepared pan and bake until the top begins to brown, 45 to 55 minutes. Kugel can be covered tightly and frozen in its casserole dish for up to 1 month. To reheat, defrost on the counter, then reheat for 20 minutes in a 325°F oven.

PASTA & GRAINS

P'TITIM RISOTTO

I first encountered this genius "risotto" at Igra Rama, a short-lived yet very beloved restaurant near the Carmel Market that only used ingredients made or grown in Israel. Rice, which isn't grown in significant quantities in Israel, was out of the question, so chef Aner Ben Refael-Furman turned to p'titim, little round pasta balls that were invented in Israel in the 1950s and went on to be known all over the world as pearl or Israeli couscous.

The recipe takes on a gorgeous deep-green hue courtesy of tbecha, a crispy confit of greens that Ben Refael-Furman cribbed from his half-Libyan wife's family. Made by reducing a mountain of Swiss chard leaves in oil, tbecha is more commonly used in a long-cooking Sabbath stew his sister-in-law makes for family gatherings (see page 307 for a similar Tunisian variation).

Since Libya was a colony of Italy between 1911 and 1943, pasta plays prominently in its cuisine, another reason Aner felt like p'titim was the right choice here. The additions of sage, butter, and white wine tie the Israeli and Italian elements together perfectly.

Serves 8

Active Time:
50 minutes

Total Time:
1 hour 5 minutes

---

1 large bunch Swiss chard (about 1 pound)

3 tablespoons vegetable oil, plus more if needed

2 teaspoons kosher salt, plus more for boiling the p'titim

4 to 5 small zucchini (1 pound)

1 pound p'titim (Israeli couscous; about 3 cups)

3 tablespoons olive oil

4 large garlic cloves, thinly sliced

6 fresh sage leaves

1¾ cups dry white wine

4 tablespoons (½ stick) unsalted butter (or more olive oil)

2 ounces (1½ cups) finely grated Parmigiano-Reggiano cheese, plus more for garnish

1. Separate the leaves from the stems on the chard; discard the stems or reserve them for another purpose. You should have about 8 cups (½ pound) leaves.

2. In a medium saucepan, heat the vegetable oil over medium-high heat. Add the chard in batches, letting each batch wilt a bit before adding more, then continue to cook the chard, stirring occasionally, lowering the heat and adding an extra tablespoonful of oil if needed, until it gets really dark, greenish black in color and almost crispy but not burnt, 25 to 35 minutes.

3. While the chard is cooking, fill a large pot more than halfway with water, then season the water generously with salt (I like to add

RECIPE CONTINUES

1½ teaspoons kosher salt per liter of water, so if you fill an 8-quart pot halfway, add 2 tablespoons kosher salt) and bring to a boil over high heat. Add the zucchini, return to a boil, lower the heat to medium-low, and cook until tender, 20 to 25 minutes. Lift the zucchini from the water with a spider or slotted spoon and transfer to a colander to cool; tear the zucchini into free-form chunks. Add the p'titim to the pot of water and cook until al dente, 5 minutes. Drain the p'titim, reserving 1 cup of the cooking water.

4. In a large, high-sided skillet, heat the olive oil over medium-low heat. Add the garlic and sage and cook, stirring, until the garlic is softened and the sage is fragrant, 2 to 3 minutes. Add the wine, reserved cooking water, butter, and the 2 teaspoons salt, bring to a boil, then reduce the heat and cook, stirring, until reduced slightly, 2 to 3 minutes. Add the p'titim, most of the crispy chard, and the zucchini and cook, stirring, until the p'titim absorb some of the liquid but the dish is still brothy, 3 to 4 minutes. Stir in the cheese. Season with more salt, divide among bowls, and garnish with a generous raft of Parm and the reserved crispy chard.

KRESCH FAMILY CABBAGE NOODLES

After high school, I spent time on a gap-year program at Jerusalem's now-defunct Gold College for Women (I was only seventeen at the time, so the name was a bit of a reach). It was there that I met Amy Klein, a sassy, funny Brooklynite who was much smarter than me in almost every way. She could recite verses of the Talmud from memory, hop on the back of a motorcycle like she'd done it a million times before, and read novels at a pace that dizzied the mind. Perhaps because we were so different—me from Palo Alto, with my Birkenstocks, tie-dyed shirts, and wide-eyed friendliness—we hit it off immediately and remain close friends to this day. Once we returned to the United States for college, I would often travel from Boston to Amy's parents' home in Flatbush and spend Shabbat there. Her mother, Dorothy Kresch, would make these very simple, very delicious noodles, which we would devour down to the last bites of slightly caramelized cabbage and onions. Amy, who now lives in Harlem with her husband, Eyal, and their sweet daughter, Lily, told me she had never codified the recipe. So we went back and forth, sharing photos and methods until we were both satisfied that our taste memories and culinary standards aligned. Now, Amy can pass the recipe on to Lily, and the Kresch cabbage noodles can live on for at least another generation.

Serves 6 to 8

Active Time:
20 minutes

Total Time:
40 minutes

2 teaspoons kosher salt, plus more for the pasta water and seasoning

¾ pound wide egg noodles

4 tablespoons plus 1 teaspoon olive oil

2 medium onions, sliced (4 cups)

4 garlic cloves, sliced

½ medium white cabbage (1½ pounds), sliced into ½-inch-thick strips

½ cup chicken or vegetable broth, plus more as needed

½ teaspoon freshly ground black pepper, plus more as needed

½ cup chopped fresh parsley

Sour cream or crème fraîche, for dolloping (optional)

1. Bring a large (8-quart) pot of generously salted water to a boil over high heat. (I like to add 1½ teaspoons kosher salt per quart of water. So if you fill an 8-quart pot halfway, add 2 tablespoons salt.) Add the noodles and cook until al dente, according to the package directions; transfer to a colander, rinse, drain well, and toss with the 1 teaspoon oil to prevent sticking.

2. Dry the pot, heat 3 tablespoons of the oil over high heat, then add the onions and 1 teaspoon

RECIPE CONTINUES

of the salt and cook, stirring, until the onions are slightly charred and softened, 6 to 7 minutes.

3. Reduce the heat to medium-high, add the garlic, and cook for 1 additional minute. Add the remaining 1 tablespoon oil to the pot. A few cups at a time, add the cabbage, wilting it for a minute or two between additions, then add the broth, the remaining 1 teaspoon salt, and the pepper and cook until the cabbage is soft but not mushy and some of the pieces maintain their green color, 4 to 5 minutes. If desired, add a splash more broth if you like a wetter mixture (I like mine more dry).

4. Stir in the noodles and parsley, cook to warm everything through, and season with more salt and pepper to taste. Dollop with sour cream, if desired.

CREAMY CORN PASTA

By using pasta water to cook the corn in this recipe, you save yourself from cleaning another pot, and a food processor makes quick work of transforming the kernels into a sinfully creamy sauce that needs no dairy or cream. I add heat, herbs, and garlic to tame the corn's sweetness, and a curly pasta, like radiatore or fusilli, best captures the sauce. This one's also great served cold or at room temperature, making it excellent for a warm-weather Shabbat lunch.

Serves 4 to 6

Active Time:
35 minutes

Total Time:
35 minutes

---

1 teaspoon kosher salt, plus more for the pasta water and seasoning

5 large ears fresh corn, husked (about 2½ pounds)

¾ pound pasta, such as radiatore or fusilli

6 tablespoons olive oil

1 small garlic clove

1 pint multicolored cherry tomatoes (about 10 ounces), halved

½ teaspoon freshly ground black pepper

1 fresh small hot red or green chili pepper, finely minced (1 tablespoon)

½ cup chopped fresh parsley, finely shredded basil, or a combination, plus more for garnish

1. Bring a large (8-quart) pot of generously salted water to a boil over high heat. (It may sound like a lot, but I like to add 1½ teaspoons kosher salt per quart of water. So if you fill an 8-quart pot halfway, add 2 tablespoons kosher salt.) Carefully drop the corn into the boiling water and cook until the kernels darken in color and soften slightly, 3 to 4 minutes. Using tongs, transfer the corn to a colander and rinse under cold water until cool enough to handle. Use a slotted spoon or spider to remove any corn silk that may be floating in the water.

2. Add the pasta to the pot and cook until al dente, following the package instructions. Reserve 1 cup of the pasta water, then drain the rest (but don't rinse the pasta).

3. While the pasta cooks, fit a cutting board inside a rimmed baking sheet (this helps catch runaway kernels). Stand a cooked ear of corn on the cutting board and use a sharp knife to cut off the kernels. Go around a second time to shave off any strips you missed; you should have about 4½ cups.

4. In a blender, combine 3 cups of the corn kernels, ¼ cup of the olive oil, ½ teaspoon of the salt, and the garlic clove. Blend on high speed until creamy, 1 to 2 minutes. Transfer the puree to the empty pasta pot and stir in the pasta along with the tomatoes, the remaining 2 tablespoons olive oil and ½ teaspoon salt, the black pepper, and the chilies, and warm through over medium-low heat, adding the reserved pasta water in splashes to achieve the desired creaminess. Toss in the chopped herbs and the remaining corn, reserving a few kernels. Divide the pasta among bowls and garnish with more herbs and corn kernels.

COLD & CRUNCHY RICE SALAD

If you have leftover plain white rice, using it can be not just a concession but a celebration of the rice itself. When cold, it takes on a different kind of sweetness and texture, not to mention its unique ability to soak up any flavor thrown its way. It is important to start with a good basmati or jasmine rice, one that holds its shape after cooking. A mustardy lemon dressing coats this bowl of rice, studded with raw zucchini, almonds, radishes, celery, and pomegranate seeds—basically every crunchy thing I could think of. I recommend tossing the salad just before serving to let the dressing have maximum impact.

Serves 6

Active Time:
15 minutes
(if you have cooked rice)

Total Time:
15 minutes

FOR THE DRESSING:

Finely grated zest
and juice of 2 lemons
(1 tablespoon zest and
6 tablespoons juice)

¼ cup olive oil

1 tablespoon Dijon
mustard

¾ teaspoon kosher salt,
plus more to taste

½ teaspoon dried basil

¼ teaspoon freshly
cracked black pepper

FOR THE SALAD:

½ cup whole almonds

5 cups cold cooked
basmati or jasmine rice

4 baby (2 inches long ×
½-inch diameter)
or 1 small zucchini
(4 ounces), thinly sliced
into rounds

3 small radishes,
thinly sliced

1 large celery stalk,
finely diced

½ cup pomegranate
seeds

½ cup finely chopped
fresh parsley

1. Make the dressing: In a jar, combine the lemon zest and 4 tablespoons of the juice, the olive oil, mustard, salt, basil, and pepper and shake until creamy. Dressing can be refrigerated, tightly sealed, in an airtight container for 1 week.

2. Preheat the oven to 350°F. Arrange the almonds on a small rimmed baking sheet and toast until fragrant, 9 to 10 minutes. Remove from the oven, allow them to cool, and coarsely chop them.

3. Make the salad: In a large salad bowl, combine the rice, zucchini, ⅓ cup of the almonds, the radishes, celery, pomegranate seeds, and parsley and gently toss to combine. Just before serving, add the dressing and toss; taste and add more lemon juice and salt to taste. Top with the remaining almonds and serve immediately.

SPICY BUTTERNUT SQUASH PASTA
with Crispy Sage Bread Crumbs

Butternut squash is considered a fall and winter vegetable in the United States, but as my friend and chef Snir Eng-Sela points out, it's actually grown in the summertime. Here in Israel, people relate to it differently, considering it a year-round kitchen workhorse. Snir and I both lived in New York for many years but didn't become friends until we both ended up back in Israel permanently. At Gouje & Danielle, the restaurant about forty-five minutes north of Tel Aviv where Snir is the chef, I always look forward to ordering this pasta, which makes me see butternut squash in a whole new light. 'Nduja, the spicy Italian charcuterie spread made with several highly unkosher ingredients, is Snir's inspiration for this vegetarian alternative. He taught me how to grind the butternut squash in the food processor, then add lots of spice, butter, and cheese to make the dish not just vegetarian, but main-course-worthy. Those sage bread crumbs really take this one over the top; save any extra crumbs and put them on absolutely everything.

Serves 6 to 8

Active Time:
45 minutes

Total Time:
1 hour

---

3 slices stale white bread (crusts included), torn into bits

One 2¾-pound butternut squash, peeled, seeded, and cubed (about 6½ cups/1¾ pounds cubes)

1 small habanero or Scotch bonnet pepper (or half, if you're spice-sensitive), seeded if desired

2 teaspoons kosher salt, plus more for the pasta water and seasoning

1 pound dry linguine pasta

3 tablespoons olive oil

6 garlic cloves, minced (2 tablespoons)

2 tablespoons thinly sliced fresh sage leaves, plus more whole leaves for garnish*

2½ ounces (1¾ cups) finely shredded Parmigiano-Reggiano cheese

½ cup (1 stick) unsalted butter

1 cup half-and-half

½ teaspoon freshly ground black pepper

RECIPE CONTINUES

1. Process the bread in a food processor until fine crumbs form, 15 seconds. Remove the crumbs to a bowl and set aside. Place the squash and the habanero in the food processor and process in 5-second bursts until the squash appears like very small bread crumbs but isn't pureed, about 45 seconds total. Bring a large (8-quart) pot of generously salted water to a boil over high heat. (I like to add 1½ teaspoons kosher salt per quart of water, so if you fill an 8-quart pot halfway, add 2 tablespoons kosher salt.) Cook the pasta according to the package directions until very al dente; before draining, reserve 2 cups of the pasta water.

2. Dry the pot and heat the oil in the pot over medium heat. Add 1 tablespoon each of the garlic and sage, the bread crumbs, and ½ teaspoon of the salt and cook, stirring, until toasty and crisp, 6 to 7 minutes total. Transfer to a bowl, cool for 10 minutes, then stir in ½ cup of the shredded cheese. Add the butter to the pot and heat until foamy, then cook until the butter develops golden-brown flecks and smells toasty, 2 to 3 minutes. Add the remaining tablespoon each of garlic and sage and cook, stirring, until the garlic is fragrant, another 1 to 2 minutes. Add the squash mixture and cook, stirring, until it begins to soften, 4 to 5 minutes. Add the half-and-half and ½ cup of the reserved pasta water, stir, bring to a simmer, then add the pasta, ¾ cup of the cheese, the remaining 1½ teaspoons salt, and the black pepper. Cook until warmed through, adding as much of the remaining pasta water as needed to achieve your desired consistency. Season with more salt and black pepper to taste, divide among bowls, and top with the bread crumbs and the remaining ½ cup shredded cheese.

*CRISPY SAGE LEAVES

To make crispy sage leaves, heat ¼ inch of olive oil in a small skillet over medium heat. Add whole sage leaves and fry until crisped and the color darkens slightly, 10 to 15 seconds. Drain on paper towels.

ROASTED VEGETABLE & BARLEY SALAD
with Charred Lemon Dressing

In his *Encyclopedia of Jewish Food*, the late Gil Marks wrote extensively about the history of barley as a prized commodity. In ancient Israel, it was so cherished that it was used as currency, and the value of land was estimated by how much barley could be grown on it. Only after the Roman Empire collapsed did wheat supplant barley as the grain of choice. Still, it's one of the seven species identified with the land of Israel since biblical times, so why not reconsider how to use it beyond the more expected soup or stew? Cook it, drain it, and have it on hand to make all kinds of salads just as you would with pasta, quinoa, or farro. It's got a lovely sweetness and texture, and it cooks up faster than wheat berries or farro but has similar applications. This salad is an interplay of bitter and sweet, with golden raisins ably standing up to shards of charred lemon and radicchio.

Makes 6 cups

Active Time:
30 minutes

Total Time:
1 hour

---

1 teaspoon kosher salt, plus more for cooking the barley and seasoning

1¼ cups pearl barley

½ pound zucchini (1 large or 2 smallish), unpeeled, cut into ½-inch cubes (1¼ cups cubed)

1½ pounds assorted root vegetables (carrots, parsnips, beets, etc.), peeled and cut into ¾-inch cubes (about 4½ cups cubed)

½ cup olive oil

½ teaspoon freshly ground black pepper, plus more to taste

1 large lemon, preferably thin-skinned, cut into ⅛-inch-thick rounds, seeds removed

4 long scallions (green and white parts), cut into 2-inch lengths

¼ cup golden raisins

½ small radicchio head, or 2 red or white endive heads, thinly sliced

1. Cook the barley: Fill a 3- or 4-quart saucepan halfway with generously salted water and bring it to a boil over high heat. (I like to add 1½ teaspoons kosher salt per quart of water, so if you fill a 3-quart pot halfway with water, add 2¼ teaspoons.) Add the barley, return the water to a boil, and cook, skimming off any foam during the first few minutes, until the barley is cooked just past al dente, 25 to 30 minutes. Drain the barley.

2. While the barley is cooking, arrange two racks in the top and bottom thirds of the oven. Preheat the oven to 400°F. Drain the barley well, then spread it out on a towel-lined baking sheet to absorb more moisture.

RECIPE CONTINUES

3. Roast the vegetables: Place the zucchini and root vegetables on a large rimmed baking sheet, drizzle ¼ cup of the olive oil over the vegetables, add the salt and pepper, and stir to coat.

4. On a smaller rimmed baking sheet lined with parchment or foil, gently toss the lemons, scallions, and 1 tablespoon of the olive oil, seasoning with salt and pepper to taste. Arrange the lemons and scallions in a single layer.

5. Place both baking sheets in the oven at the same time. Roast the lemons and scallions until the lemon rinds and scallions are partially charred, 20 to 22 minutes. Remove from the oven and cool. When you take the lemons out, remove the vegetables, stir them, return to the oven, then stir them again 10 minutes later and roast until the vegetables have shrunk and some of the edges are charred, 35 minutes total.

6. To finish the salad, scrape the lemons and scallions, including any flesh and pulp from the lemon, to a cutting board (discard any errant seeds you find) and finely chop them. Transfer to a large bowl and whisk in the remaining 3 tablespoons olive oil.

7. Add the barley, roasted vegetables, and raisins to the bowl and toss to coat, seasoning with more salt and pepper if desired. Fold in the radicchio and serve.

SOUPS

My mother's soups were the stuff of legend, delicious and impossible to replicate because they never started with a recipe. To her, a soup was jazz, rife with interpretation and a bit of mystery. If she used a can of corn, the liquid would get thrown into the pot along with a leftover piece of kugel, a few carrots from the bottom of the crisper, the chopped scraps of onions she'd saved from a week of cooking, and maybe an ingot of last week's chicken soup broth she'd frozen for just this very moment of potage creation. Soup was a constant on our Shabbat table, be it a thick mushroom puree, classic chicken–matzo ball, lentil, or any of the other recipes that were in my mother's prolific rotation. Soup on Shabbat just made sense for her busy schedule, as it could be easily prepared in advance, kept warm without destroying its essence, and often fed a crowd, and took well to freezing in many instances. At my sister's home, Shabbat dinner will sometimes be—at her husband's request—a pot of chicken soup, available for seconds, accompanied by pieces of matzo to be broken directly into the bowl. Inspired by her, my repertoire is varied, and in this book includes a couple of different chicken-based varieties and a whole lot of veg-etable versions, which I often carry over into the week's beginning to provide working lunches at home on Sunday (when our workweek starts in Israel) and Monday. Since Jay and I don't usually finish a pot on our own and don't always have guests, I will often freeze the leftovers in 2-cup portions (I use silicone freezer molds by Souper Cubes), perfect for a midweek dinner or the following Shabbat.

MATZO BALL SOUP

This is the classic, comforting bowl of soup you want for a Friday night dinner: plush, tender matzo balls and a rich, super-chicken-forward broth that, when eaten together, can truly serve as a full meal. This one is a departure from my mother's famous Overnight Chicken Soup from *Sababa*, requiring less cooking time but still bringing that deep soulfulness. A bonus: The broth, meat, and vegetables all taste great right out of the pot and for a few days after. It's important to let the matzo ball mix rest in the fridge; it moistens the batter, resulting in light, fluffy matzo balls every time; in my book, there is no other kind. Make the little soup croutons (recipe follows) in advance or while the soup is simmering; they're the crowning glory to this perfect bowl of Shabbat goodness.

Makes 16 matzo balls,
2 generous quarts of broth,
and 1 generous quart of meat,
plus vegetables;
serves 6 to 8

Active Time:
60 minutes

Total Time:
4 hours 30 minutes

FOR THE MATZO BALLS:

5 tablespoons vegetable oil or Schmaltz (page 84)

4 large eggs

2 teaspoons kosher salt

¼ teaspoon freshly ground black pepper

½ cup cold plain seltzer or club soda

1 cup matzo meal

FOR THE SOUP:

One whole 4-pound chicken, giblets removed

8 medium carrots, trimmed

3 large celery stalks, trimmed and halved crosswise

1 medium parsnip, trimmed and peeled

2 medium or 1 jumbo onion, peeled but left whole

4 garlic cloves

3 tablespoons kosher salt, plus more for the matzo ball water

Mini Israeli Soup Croutons (page 184), for serving

Parsley or celery leaves, for garnish

1. Mix the matzo ball batter: In a medium bowl, vigorously whisk together the oil, eggs, salt, and pepper until the color lightens, 30 seconds. Pour in the seltzer, followed by the matzo meal, and stir with a wooden spoon until the matzo meal is fully moistened and no clumps remain. (The mixture will be a thick pancake-batter consistency and will continue to thicken as it rests.) Press plastic wrap onto the surface of the mixture and chill in the fridge while you make the soup, at least 3 hours and up to 24.

2. Make the soup: While the matzo ball mix is chilling, place the chicken, carrots, celery, parsnip, onion, and garlic in a large (at least 8-quart) pot, cover with water almost to the top (about 3½ quarts), add the salt, and bring to a boil over medium-high heat. Boil, skimming off and discarding any foam that rises to the surface, 10 to 15 minutes.

RECIPE CONTINUES

3. Reduce the heat to low and simmer gently, uncovered, until the soup deepens in color and the broth is flavorful and rich, about 3 hours. During the last 45 minutes of cooking, fill a large, wide, lidded pot halfway with water and season it very generously with salt. (I like to add 1½ teaspoons kosher salt per quart of water. So if you fill an 8-quart pot halfway, add 2 tablespoons salt.) Bring it to a boil over medium-high heat.

4. Remove the matzo ball mix from the fridge. Fill a small bowl with water. Dip a tablespoon into the water, scoop out a heaping tablespoon of the batter, use moistened hands to form a walnut-sized ball, and set it on a plate. Continue to make the balls; you should have about 16. Lower the balls into the boiling water, cover, reduce the heat to medium-low, and simmer until the matzo balls are fluffy, tender, and cooked through, 40 to 45 minutes.

5. Turn off the heat and leave the pot covered. (You can also make these a few hours early and leave them hanging out in the pot and liquid until you're ready to use them, then reheat over medium-low until just heated through, 10 to 15 minutes.)

6. To assemble the soup, gently break the vegetables in the soup into pieces using tongs. Ladle some of the hot soup and vegetables into a bowl, then add 2 or 3 matzo balls and some shredded chicken. (You can also shred the dark meat from the whole chicken if you like dark-meat chicken better.) Sprinkle with the croutons and garnish with parsley or celery leaves.

Out of the Box

My mother's matzo balls, or kneidlach, were always perfectly light and fluffy, and she unashamedly told anyone who asked that hers came from a boxed mix. A well-calibrated blend of matzo meal (ground matzo), spices, and baking powder, the mix was blended with eggs, oil, and water to yield great results every time. Joan Nathan, my friend and the godmother of Jewish food writers, writes that matzo balls can trace their beginning to knoedel, bread dumplings with origins in twelfth-century Alsace and Germany. Eventually, they found their way east to Jewish communities in Poland, where they were renamed kneidlach in Yiddish and adapted for Passover with matzo. Kosher food manufacturer Manischewitz began manufacturing a prepared mix for something called "Alsatian Feathery Balls" in the 1930s, and the matzo ball mix was born. While some other cooks stigmatized convenience products, my mother loved them, and if I'm in a time crunch, I will certainly use them too. Boxed mix is found in practically every supermarket in the postage stamp–sized kosher section.

MINI ISRAELI SOUP CROUTONS
(Shke'dei Marak)

Known as "soup almonds" in Hebrew, these tiny, crunchy, bright-yellow croutons (shown at right before baking) are an etymological relative of mandlach, the Yiddish name for baked croutons. Osem, a major food manufacturer in Israel, introduced them to the market when food was scarce during Israel's austerity period in the 1950s. Soup was often an entire meal, and croutons were an inexpensive way to fill both bowl and belly. Traditionally, shke'dei marak are left on the table, and people spoon in as many as they want to customize their personal bowl of soup; some eat them as a crunchy snack even when no soup is involved. You can use a paring knife to slice the dough, but a pizza cutter really saves the day here.

Makes 2 cups

Active Time:
15 minutes

**Total Time
(including dough resting time):**
1 hour 15 minutes

¾ cup potato starch

¾ cup all-purpose flour

¼ cup vegetable oil

1½ teaspoons ground turmeric

1 teaspoon fine sea salt

¼ cup ice water, plus more as needed

1. In a food processor, pulse the potato starch, flour, oil, turmeric, and salt until large crumbs form, 15 to 20 pulses. Add the ice water, 1 tablespoon at a time, pulsing just until a loose dough comes together. Gather the dough, form it into a ball, wrap it in plastic, and refrigerate for 30 minutes.

2. Preheat the oven to 350°F. Unwrap and place the dough between two 12 × 18-inch sheets of parchment and roll it out to ⅛-inch thickness (the dough will come close to the edges of the parchment on all sides). Transfer to a baking sheet, peel off the top layer of parchment, and use a pizza cutter (preferably) or very sharp paring knife to cut tiny ¼-inch (or less) strips of dough, then cut the strips crosswise to form tiny ¼ × ¼-inch squares. Bake until the squares separate, shrink, and are fragrant and toasty, 23 to 24 minutes. Store in an airtight container for up to 3 days; to retoast, warm on a baking sheet in a 350°F oven for 4 to 5 minutes.

COLD YOGURT, CHICKPEA & CUCUMBER SOUP
with Toasted Cumin Oil

Yogurt is a kitchen staple in Israel, one I often find myself slipping into a sauce, dressing, or topping. In this chilled soup, I let it stand on its own as the star ingredient. Inspired by cold, refreshing, yogurt-based Bulgarian tarator, the soup only improves as it sits in the fridge. By warming ground cumin in a bit of olive oil, I created an entirely new seasoning component, which I add to both the soup and use as a drizzle on top. Tender chickpeas, crisp garlic chips, and a hint of mint elevate this one. I used cow's milk yogurt, but a mild sheep or goat yogurt would be wonderful here too.

Serves 4 to 6

Active Time:
20 minutes

**Total Time
(including oil cooling time):**
1 hour 20 minutes

---

4 cups full- or low-fat plain yogurt

Zest and juice of 1 lemon (3 tablespoons juice and 1½ teaspoons zest), plus more to taste

One 15-ounce can chickpeas, drained (about 1¾ cups)

3 or 4 Persian cucumbers (½ pound), finely diced (about 1¾ cups)

1 teaspoon kosher salt, plus more to taste

½ teaspoon freshly ground black pepper

½ cup olive oil

6 large garlic cloves, very thinly sliced

1 teaspoon ground cumin

Chopped fresh mint, for garnish

1. In a large bowl, combine the yogurt, lemon juice and zest, 1½ cups of the chickpeas, 1½ cups of the cucumbers, the salt, and pepper. Cover and chill for 1 hour.

2. While the soup is chilling, warm the oil over medium heat in a small saucepan. Add the garlic and fry, stirring, until golden and crisp, 3 minutes. Remove the garlic with a spider or fork to a paper towel–lined plate to drain, then season lightly with salt. Remove the oil from the heat, then add the cumin and let the oil come to room temperature, 10 to 15 minutes.

3. Once cool, stir 3 tablespoons of the cumin oil into the soup, then thin the soup with a little water or lemon juice to achieve your desired thickness. Season with salt, then divide the soup among bowls, garnish with the remaining ¼ cup each cucumbers and chickpeas, drizzle with the cumin oil, and top with the crispy garlic and mint.

DILLY CHICKEN & RICE SOUP

The goal here was a soup that achieves maximum chicken flavor without extended cooking time, and this one meets the mark. Searing skinless, boneless chicken breasts right in the pot saves time and adds flavor; when you add aromatics and liquid and then scrape up those delicious brown bits, you're reinvesting the soup with even more depth. Starting with the best chicken broth you have access to goes a long way here, so if you have some stashed away in the freezer, pull it out. The kickers here are the dill and jalapeño peppers for flavor, and of course, that rice, which, over time, thickens the soup in the most pleasing way. If the soup becomes too thick (though is there ever such a thing?), just stir in a little water or broth to loosen it.

Serves 6

Active Time:
20 minutes

Total Time:
1 hour

---

2 pounds skinless, boneless chicken breasts (about 2 medium)

1 tablespoon kosher salt, plus more for seasoning

¾ teaspoon freshly ground black pepper, plus more for seasoning

4 tablespoons olive oil

1 large leek, pale green and white parts only, thinly sliced*

2 large carrots, diced

2 celery stalks, diced

2 garlic cloves, minced

1 small jalapeño, seeded if desired, chopped

8 cups chicken broth, plus more if needed

1 cup uncooked long-grain white rice

½ cup chopped fresh dill, plus more for garnish

1. Season the chicken with ½ teaspoon of the salt and ¼ teaspoon of the black pepper. In a large (at least 5-quart) pot, heat 3 tablespoons of the oil over medium heat. Place the chicken in the pot, cover, and brown, flipping once, until deeply golden and just barely cooked through, 5 to 6 minutes per side. Transfer to a bowl to cool.

2. Add the remaining tablespoon oil to the pot, then add the leeks and cook, stirring, until translucent, 6 to 7 minutes. Add the carrots, celery, garlic, jalapeño, and another ½ teaspoon of the salt and cook, stirring, until the vegetables begin to soften, 4 to 5 minutes. Add the chicken broth, rice, and the remaining 2 teaspoons salt and ½ teaspoon black pepper. Bring to a boil, reduce the heat to medium-low and simmer until the rice softens and releases its starch and the soup turns cloudy and thickens, 25 to 30 minutes, adding additional broth by the ½ cup if the soup is too thick. During the last 5 minutes of cooking, shred the chicken into bite-sized chunks. Return the chicken and any juices to the soup, stir in the dill, season with more salt and black pepper to taste, and divide among bowls. Garnish with dill.

*To clean the sliced leeks, place in a bowl and cover with ice water. Swirl for a few seconds, then lift the leeks out of the water, leaving any sand and grit behind.

HEARTY VEGAN MULTI-MUSHROOM SOUP

My recipe for this soup has evolved over time to accommodate a variety of mushrooms, and I promise you that, no matter which varieties you use, this soup will come out irresistibly stellar. A little miso enhances the experience without overpowering the mushrooms' flavor. The crispy shiitake topping adds a nice contrast to the silky-chunky texture underneath. Serve this in large bowls for a heartier, more filling meal, or in small bowls or espresso cups for a starter or hors d'oeuvre.

Serves 4 to 6

Active Time:
35 minutes

Total Time:
1 hour

---

2 pounds button mushrooms, baby bellas, or a combination, stems removed and discarded, caps cleaned, and roughly chopped (about 12 cups chopped)

1 pound large portobello mushroom caps (about 5), cleaned, gills removed with a spoon, and coarsely chopped (6 cups)

6 tablespoons olive oil

1 large onion, diced (2 cups)

1 tablespoon picked fresh thyme leaves, plus more finely chopped for garnish

3 garlic cloves, minced

6 ounces fresh shiitake mushroom caps, sliced (2 cups)

4 cups vegetable or mushroom broth*

1 tablespoon blond miso

1 tablespoon soy sauce

1½ teaspoons kosher salt, plus more as needed

½ teaspoon freshly ground black pepper, plus more as needed

½ teaspoon smoked paprika

¼ teaspoon dried red pepper flakes, plus more as needed

1. In a food processor and working in batches, combine the button and portobello mushrooms and pulse until finely processed but not liquidy, 15 to 20 pulses, scraping down the mixture in between pulses.

2. In a large (at least 6-quart) pot, heat 3 tablespoons of the oil over medium heat. Add the onions and thyme and cook, stirring occasionally, until lightly golden, 8 to 9 minutes. Add the garlic and cook for 1 additional minute. Add the pulsed mushrooms and 1½ cups of the sliced shiitakes and cook, stirring, until the mushrooms wilt and begin to release their liquid, about 5 minutes.

3. Pour in the broth, miso, soy sauce, salt, pepper, smoked paprika, and red pepper flakes, bring to a boil, reduce the heat to medium-low, and cook, stirring, until the soup thickens, the liquid reduces, and the mushrooms darken, 15 to 20 minutes. Season with salt and pepper. Transfer 2 cups of the soup to a blender and puree, then stir it back into the soup.

RECIPE CONTINUES

4. Meanwhile, heat the remaining 3 tablespoons oil in a large skillet over medium-high heat, add the remaining ½ cup shiitakes, and cook, stirring as little as possible, until they become browned and crispy, 4 to 5 minutes. Season with salt and pepper.

5. Divide the soup among bowls and top with shiitakes, thyme, and, if desired, more red pepper flakes.

*To make mushroom broth, rehydrate 1 ounce dried mushrooms of your choice in 4 cups boiling water for 30 minutes. Strain the broth before you add it to the pot, discard any sand, then squeeze any liquid from the mushrooms, chop them, and add to the soup.

LENTIL, WHITE BEAN & CAULIFLOWER SOUP

Lentil soups have been a staple since biblical times when, as the story goes, Esau had his entire birthright sold out from under his nose in exchange for a bowl of the stuff. Here, I add white beans (not mentioned in the Bible, but versatile, creamy, and delicious) to turn this into a greatest-hits-of-the-pantry kind of proposition, one that transforms stuff you have around the kitchen into a dal-ish delight. Indian and Israeli spices have a great deal of overlap; both regions were stops on the ancient Silk Road.

Serves 8

Active Time:
35 minutes

Total Time:
1 hour

---

5 tablespoons olive oil

1 large onion, chopped (2 cups)

4 garlic cloves, minced

1 teaspoon ground turmeric

1 teaspoon sweet paprika

½ teaspoon ground cumin

½ teaspoon dried red pepper flakes, plus more to taste

2 tablespoons tomato paste

6 cups low-sodium vegetable or chicken broth, plus more as needed

1 medium cauliflower (1½ pounds), separated into florets (about 6 cups), chopped into very small florets

Two 15.5-ounce cans cannellini beans, drained and rinsed (about 3 cups)

1 cup red lentils, picked over

2½ teaspoons kosher salt, plus more to taste

1½ cups frozen peas, defrosted

Zest and juice of 1 large lemon (about 1½ teaspoons zest and 3 tablespoons juice)

¼ cup chopped fresh chives, for garnish

1. In a large (at least 5-quart) soup pot, heat 2½ tablespoons of the oil over medium heat. Add the onions and cook, stirring, until lightly golden, 8 to 9 minutes. Add the garlic, turmeric, paprika, cumin, and red pepper flakes and cook, stirring, 1 additional minute. Add the tomato paste and cook, stirring, until lightly caramelized, 2 minutes. Add the broth, 4 cups of the cauliflower, 1¾ cups of the beans, the red lentils, and 2 teaspoons of the salt, bring to a boil, reduce the heat to medium-low, and simmer until the cauliflower is tender and the liquid has reduced by about one-quarter, 30 minutes.

2. While the soup cooks, preheat the oven to 425°F. Scatter the remaining 2 cups cauliflower on a large rimmed baking sheet, toss with the remaining 2½ tablespoons oil and ½ teaspoon salt, and roast, stirring once halfway through,

RECIPE CONTINUES

until the cauliflower begins to brown in parts, 12 to 13 minutes. Stir in the remaining 1¼ cups beans and continue to roast until the beans and cauliflower are golden and crisp, another 14 to 15 minutes.

3. When the soup is ready, use an immersion blender to blend the soup as smooth as you like, adding additional broth to achieve the desired consistency. Stir in the peas and warm through for 3 to 4 minutes. Stir in the lemon zest and juice, season with salt, divide among bowls, and top each bowl with some of the crispy cauliflower and beans. Garnish with the chives.

BEET KUBBEH SOUP

Like French baguettes, I always thought marak kubbeh—the semolina-wrapped-meatball-dumpling soup with Kurdish and Iraqi roots—was something best left to the experts, but Sarah Walter, an olah (immigrant to Israel) from Boston and married mother of two, whom I met through an online Israeli cooking group for English speakers, persuaded me to meet her Iraqi mother-in-law, Heli, and put my fears aside. I hopped on a train to the Krayot, a series of Haifa suburbs with a combined population of 200,000, where Sarah picked me up and whisked me off to Heli's house. We climbed some stairs and were welcomed with warm hugs, milky coffee, and cookies before we got to work. As we flattened knobs of semolina dough into disks on moistened palms, then sealed the dough around a highly spiced meat mixture, Heli's warm conversation and encouragement made the process feel special, rather than difficult.

One of seven children of parents who emigrated from Iraq along with about 125,000 other Jews between 1951 and 1952, Heli and her family were placed in an absorption camp in the city of Binyamina along with immigrants from other countries Jews had fled. They eventually left the camp and built a house nearby, and it was there she learned to cook from her mother and older sisters.

Along with a full table of other traditional dishes, Heli makes kubbeh soup for Shabbat every week, hosting family and sending everyone home with leftovers. As much as I loved the process of making the kubbeh, I was equally moved by Sarah and Heli's loving relationship, and how much they enjoyed each other's company.

Once the broth was simmering, we gently lowered the dumplings in and watched as they plumped up and took on a gorgeous vermillion hue. It's important not to expect anything like a matzo ball here; kubbeh is slightly chewy, and deliberately so. If done properly—and with even half the amount of love Heli puts into the process—the shell and the meat become one, a dumpling of memory, preservation, and family unity, all swimming in a delicious bowl of soup.

Serves 10

Active Time:
2 hours

Total Time:
2 hours 30 minutes

RECIPE AND INGREDIENTS CONTINUE

FOR THE KUBBEH SEMOLINA SHELL:

3 cups plus
2 tablespoons
(500 grams) semolina

½ teaspoon (3 grams)
fine sea salt

¼ teaspoon baking soda

1⅓ cups (314 grams/ml)
water, plus more
as needed

1½ tablespoons
(21 grams/ml)
vegetable oil

FOR THE KUBBEH FILLING:

¾ pound 85/15 ground
beef*

¼ pound ground chicken
(dark meat, light meat, or
a combination)* or more
ground beef

1 small onion,
very finely chopped

1½ cups fresh parsley
leaves, very
finely chopped
(½ cup chopped)

1 teaspoon sweet
paprika

1½ teaspoons Baharat
Spice Blend (page 14
or store-bought)

1 teaspoon kosher salt

½ teaspoon finely
ground black pepper

1 large egg yolk

¼ teaspoon baking soda

FOR THE SOUP:

4 large beets
(2¼ pounds)

¼ cup vegetable oil

1 medium onion, diced
(2 cups)

4 medium carrots,
cut into ¼-inch rounds

3 celery stalks,
cut into ¼-inch slices

2 teaspoons Baharat
Spice Blend (page 14
or store-bought)

1 teaspoon sweet
paprika

½ teaspoon finely
ground black pepper

12 cups (3 quarts)
low-sodium chicken,
vegetable, or beef broth

1 tablespoon kosher salt,
plus more to taste

6 tablespoons freshly
squeezed lemon juice
(from 2 large lemons)

2 tablespoons sugar

1. Make the shell: In a large, wide bowl, combine the semolina, salt, and baking soda and begin to add 1 cup of the water and the oil slowly, letting the semolina absorb the water and working out any lumps with your hands as you go. Add the remaining ⅓ cup water and continue to knead until the dough is sticky but unified and a lightly moistened hand can be pressed into the dough, then pulled away without any dough sticking. Press plastic wrap onto the surface of the dough while you make the filling.

2. Make the filling: In a large bowl and using your hands, gently combine the ground beef, ground chicken, onion, parsley, paprika, baharat, salt, pepper, egg yolk, and baking soda until everything is incorporated. Shape the filling into 20 balls about the size of walnuts (2 tablespoons or just shy of 1 ounce; use a small pastry scoop to portion it evenly) and arrange them on a large plate or small sheet pan. Cover and chill the meat while you get the broth ready.

3. Make the soup: Peel the beets, halve them, then cut each half crosswise into ¼-inch half-moons. In a very large (at least 6-quart) soup pot, heat the oil over medium heat. Add the onions and cook, stirring, until lightly golden, 6 to 7 minutes. Add the carrots, celery, baharat, paprika, and pepper and cook, stirring, until the vegetables begin to soften, 3 to 4 minutes. Add the beets, broth, and salt, bring to a boil over high heat, reduce the heat to medium-low, and cook, uncovered, until the broth turns very pink and the beets have softened partially (they'll continue to cook when you add the kubbeh), 25 to 30 minutes. Once the broth is ready, add the lemon juice and sugar, and season with more salt to taste. (If you are still forming the kubbeh after the broth simmers for 30 minutes, reduce the heat to low to keep it warm until you are ready to add the kubbeh.)

4. While the soup cooks, form the kubbeh: Check the kubbeh dough; it should feel moist and pliable. (Imagine wrapping a meatball with this dough! If you can't, add water by the tablespoonful and mix thoroughly.)

5. Arrange a bowl of cold water for moistening your hands next to the semolina and meatballs. Using moistened hands, pull a piece of dough about one and a half times the size of a meatball (approximately golf ball sized or 1⅜ ounces), roll it into a ball, then place it on the palm of one hand and press and pat it into about a thin 4-inch disk. (If you try to peel the dough circle away from your hand, it should come off in one piece and not tear or fall apart.) Place the meatball in the center of the disk, then gather the dough up and around the meatball and pinch and press it closed, making sure no meat is visible through the dough and the meatball seems totally covered. Pinch off any excess dough at the top of the closed kubbeh to prevent the top from being dense and doughy.

6. Arrange the kubbeh on a clean plate or baking sheet and continue with the remaining dough and meatballs. If there are a few extra meatballs, gently lower them into the soup along with the kubbeh, return the soup to a boil, reduce the heat to medium-low, and simmer until the meatballs are cooked through and the semolina has formed a harder shell around the meatballs, 20 to 25 minutes.** Divide the kubbeh, broth, and vegetables among bowls. Enjoy hot.

*To make the dish vegetarian, the ground beef and chicken can be replaced with 1 cup cooked lentils and 1 pound button mushrooms, cleaned, stemmed, and finely chopped.

**Filled, formed kubbeh dumplings can be frozen in a single layer, then stored in a zip-top bag or airtight container for up to 3 months; to use, drop directly into soup from frozen.

DUSHPARA
(Uzbeki-Jewish Dumpling Soup)

On a cool autumn night, I took the elevator up to Doris Haimov's spar-
kling home in the Tel Aviv suburb of Holon, to find a kitchen deep in
motion. Doughs were resting, soups were simmering, and bunches of
herbs rested on the counter as Doris, immaculately dressed and sport-
ing a gorgeous wig (religious Jewish women cover their own hair), welcomed me warmly before we set out to cook. Her husband, David, a
professionally trained cook in his own right, hit Pause on *Squid Game*
before joining us. Married at seventeen and twenty, respectively, after
Doris immigrated to Israel from the central Asian country of Uzbekistan
(David had come years before), the couple have created a successful catering business based on the Jewish foods of Bukhara, one of
two cities in Uzbekistan with Jewish communities. Jews in Uzbekistan
trace their history back to ancient times, when Israelites came to the
area to seek work and trade opportunities. They have a distinct culture and cuisine with many Asian inflections, especially a dazzling ar-
ray of dumplings. Though we made several that night, this dushpara,
adapted from a traditional Asian-Muslim dish called joshpara, stole my
heart. Doris rolled out her dough on an industrial-sized electric pasta
maker, then cut out circles, filled them with ground meat, and sealed
and shaped them into tortellini-like orbs. After many practice folds, I
managed to form a few successful dumplings on my own, making me
feel like an actual Pasta Granny. Later that night, after my husband, Jay,
joined us, we sat down to dinner with her children and grandchildren,
enjoying the fruits of our labor and reveling in their warm company and
delicious food. The soup makes a wonderful first course—or even main
course, if you load up on the dumplings—for a Shabbat dinner.

Serves 6 to 8

Active Time:
1 hour 30 minutes

Total Time:
2 hour 30 minutes

RECIPE AND INGREDIENTS CONTINUE

FOR THE BROTH:

1 medium onion, peeled and halved

5 garlic cloves

2 pounds beef chuck, cut into 2-inch pieces

2 beef soup bones

½ cup dried chickpeas, soaked for 12 hours, or 1 cup cooked chickpeas

3 celery stalks, halved

3 carrots, trimmed, peeled, and halved

9 cups water

1 tablespoon kosher salt

4 medium potatoes (1½ pounds), peeled and quartered

FOR THE DOUGH*:

3½ cups (455 grams) all-purpose flour, plus more as needed

½ teaspoon (3 grams) fine sea salt

1 large egg, beaten

¾ cup (176 grams/ml) water, plus more as needed

FOR THE FILLING:

1 small onion

¾ pound fattier (at least 75/25) ground beef

¼ cup chopped fresh cilantro, plus more for serving

1 teaspoon kosher salt

1 teaspoon coarsely ground black pepper

1. Make the broth: Combine the onion, garlic, beef, bones, soaked and drained chickpeas (if using canned, wait until later), celery, and carrots in a 6-quart soup pot. Add the water, bring to a boil over high heat, and boil, skimming off and discarding any scum for the first 5 to 6 minutes of boiling. Add the salt, reduce the heat to medium-low and simmer, partially covered, until the meat is tender, 2 hours. Add the potatoes (and canned chickpeas, if using), return the broth to a boil, then reduce the heat and cook until the potatoes are tender, another 30 minutes. Skim off any fat from the surface.

2. While the broth is cooking, make the dough: Combine the flour and salt in a medium bowl. Add the egg, then add the water and knead the dough in the bowl for 1 minute, until everything comes together but is still firm. Turn it out onto a lightly floured surface and knead, adding water by the tablespoonful if the dough feels cracked and dry, or flour by the tablespoonful if the dough is too wet, until a smooth, firm dough is formed, 8 to 9 minutes. Divide the dough into two pieces, completely wrap each in plastic wrap, and let the dough rest on the counter while you prepare the filling, 30 to 45 minutes.

3. Make the filling: Grate the onion into a medium bowl, then add the ground beef, cilantro, salt, and pepper.

4. To form the dumplings, line a baking sheet or plate with parchment paper and lightly dust the parchment with flour. Lightly flour a work surface, unwrap one piece of the dough, and roll it out as thinly as possible into a 20-inch circle. Use a 3-inch cookie cutter to cut 20 to 24 circles from the dough. Peel off the dough around the circle, rewrap it, and refrigerate it (if you have extra filling at the end, you can make more dumplings; otherwise you can discard it). Place about 1½ teaspoons filling on the center of each circle, then moisten the edges of the circle with water using a pastry brush. Fold the dough over the filling and seal it tightly with your fingers into a half-moon, pinching the dough above the meat to leave ¼ inch of sealed dough around the top and sides of the meat. Holding a sealed dumpling, fold the top over so the fold meets the top of the sealed meat, then bring the edges of the folded dumpling together on the bottom of the dumpling, using a finger to leave a small gap above where you pinch and then pinching one side over the other. Arrange on the baking sheet and cover with a clean kitchen towel. Repeat with the remaining filling and dough, using the second piece of dough and rerolling the scraps. The dumplings can be used immediately or frozen in a single layer on a lined baking sheet, then stored in an airtight container for up to 3 months.

5. Remove and discard the celery and soup bones from the broth. Reheat the broth to a simmer over medium-low heat, then add the dumplings, return the broth to a simmer, and cook until tender, 6 to 7 minutes. Ladle some of the broth, dumplings, potatoes, onion, and meat into bowls and garnish with lots of fresh cilantro.

*Instead of making the dough, you can swap in twenty-four 3½-inch round dumpling wrappers, then cook the dumplings for 5 or 6 minutes—2 minutes less than the recipe calls for.

MAIN COURSE SALADS

OYSTER MUSHROOM, PICKLED ONION & KALE SALAD

This mushroom salad, topped with a sunny egg, borrows from the flavor profile of a falafel bar to create a vegetarian dish worthy of any meal, day or night. In the past, I've been ambivalent about massaging raw kale leaves, but it really does tenderize them and mellow their some-times aggressively raw flavor. The pickled onions, tahini dressing, and shawarma-spiced mushrooms add up to something meaty and sub-stantial. Skip the egg and double the recipe for a salad that can stand on its own on any Shabbat table.

Serves 4

Active Time:
25 minutes

Total Time:
30 minutes

FOR THE ONIONS:

1 large red onion, thinly sliced

Juice of 1 large lemon

1 tablespoon ground sumac

¼ teaspoon kosher salt

FOR THE DRESSING:

¼ cup pure tahini paste

¼ cup lemon juice

2 tablespoons water, plus more as needed

2 tablespoons olive oil

¼ teaspoon kosher salt, plus more to taste

FOR THE MUSHROOMS, KALE & EGGS:

8 ounces (8 cups lightly packed) kale leaves (dinosaur, curly, or a combination)

6 tablespoons olive oil

1 teaspoon ground cumin

¼ teaspoon cayenne pepper

¼ teaspoon ground turmeric

½ teaspoon kosher salt

1 pound oyster mushrooms, trimmed (about 10 ounces trimmed)

½ cup cherry tomatoes, halved

4 large eggs

Flaky sea salt

1. Pickle the onions: In a bowl, toss together the onions, lemon juice, sumac, and salt. Let sit at room temperature until the onions change color, about 10 minutes. Refrigerate until ready to use (you will have extra onions, which is a good thing). Sealed in an airtight container, the pickled onions can be refrigerated for up to 1 month.

2. Make the dressing: In a large bowl, combine the tahini, lemon juice, water, olive oil, and salt and whisk until creamy, adding water by the tablespoon if the dressing feels too thick. Leftover dressing can be refrigerated, tightly sealed, in an airtight container for 5 days.

3. Prepare the mushrooms and salad: Remove and discard the stems from the kale, then tear the kale into bite-sized pieces and place it in a large bowl. Add 1 tablespoon of the olive oil and, using your hands, massage the kale until it is evenly

RECIPE CONTINUES

coated with oil and the leaves become more tender, 2 to 3 minutes. Pour the tahini dressing over the kale and toss to evenly coat the leaves.

4. In a large bowl, combine 3 tablespoons of the olive oil with the cumin, cayenne, turmeric, and kosher salt. Add the mushrooms and toss to coat. Heat a large nonstick skillet over medium-high heat. Working in batches, if necessary, cook the mushrooms, flipping them midway through, until crisped and golden, 3 to 4 minutes per side.

5. Divide the kale among four plates, then top it with the mushrooms and cherry tomatoes. Using the skillet you used for the mushrooms, add 1 tablespoon of the oil to the skillet and warm over medium-high heat, then crack in 2 of the eggs and fry until the whites are set and lacy but the yolks are runny, 3 to 4 minutes. Place the cooked eggs on top of two of the plates and repeat with the remaining 1 tablespoon oil and 2 eggs. Garnish each salad with some of the pickled onions and flaky sea salt.

SKIRT STEAK & STONE FRUIT SALAD
with Grated Tomato Vinaigrette

The simplest of Yemenite-Jewish condiments, resek, or grated tomatoes—traditionally served with breads like kubaneh and jachnun (see page 34)—helps lift this dressing. The steak soaks up the garlicky pomegranate marinade quickly, then grills up in a flash before being sliced into the ultimate salad topper. Stone fruit (named as such because pits are known as "stones" in the King's English) adds juicy sweetness, and herbs, tossed into the salad leaves, lend freshness. This one has "make ahead" written all over it: You can make the dressing, cut the fruit, and prep the greens in advance. Then grab the steak right off the grill and slice it, or throw the cooked meat in the fridge, then let it come to room temperature any time during the next day (or two) and assemble the rest of the salad.

Serves 4 to 6

Active Time:
20 minutes

**Total Time
(including minimum marinating time):**
1 hour 10 minutes

FOR THE MARINADE & STEAK:

¼ cup extra-virgin olive oil

4 garlic cloves, smashed

2 tablespoons tamarind paste

2 tablespoons pomegranate molasses or honey

½ teaspoon kosher salt

¼ teaspoon freshly ground black pepper

1½ pounds skirt steak*

FOR THE TOMATO VINAIGRETTE:

3 small, ripe, juicy tomatoes
(about ½ pound)

¼ cup extra-virgin olive oil

2 tablespoons red wine vinegar

1 tablespoon pomegranate molasses or honey

Finely grated zest and juice from ½ small lime (juice the whole lime if you're using honey)

2 scallions (green and white parts), finely chopped

¾ teaspoon kosher salt, plus more to taste

¼ teaspoon freshly ground black pepper, plus more to taste

FOR THE SALAD:

5 cups salad greens, such as arugula, endive, radicchio, or a combination

½ cup assorted herb leaves, such as mint and basil, coarsely chopped

4 medium, ripe stone fruits, such as plums, apricots, or nectarines, pitted and cut into ½-inch wedges

2 small, ripe tomatoes, cored and cut into wedges

RECIPE CONTINUES

1. Marinate the steak: In a 9 × 13-inch baking dish, whisk the olive oil, garlic, tamarind paste, pomegranate molasses, salt, and pepper. (Alternatively, smush it all together in a large, resealable zip-top bag.) Add the steak and move it around to coat it in the marinade. Let the meat marinate on the counter at room temperature for 30 to 45 minutes before grilling or for a few hours or overnight in the refrigerator (if marinated in the refrigerator, remove to the counter 30 minutes before grilling).

2. Make the vinaigrette: Halve the tomatoes horizontally. Grate the cut sides of the tomatoes on the large holes of a box grater directly into a medium bowl. Discard the skins. Whisk in the olive oil, vinegar, pomegranate molasses, lime zest and juice, scallions, salt, and pepper until a unified dressing forms. Dressing can be made ahead and will keep, refrigerated, in an airtight container for up to 1 week.

3. Heat a grill or grill pan over medium-high heat (if using a grill pan, cut the steak into large pieces that will fit). Grill the meat until it is cooked but still pink on the inside, 3 to 4 minutes per side. Let rest 5 minutes before slicing it against the grain.

4. Assemble the salad: Arrange the salad greens and herbs on a platter, then scatter the fruit and tomatoes around the platter. Top with the steak, season generously with salt and pepper, and drizzle it with some of the dressing. Serve with additional dressing on the side.

*If you're using kosher skirt steak, which tends to be very salty, soak the steak in ice water for 1 hour, changing the water once midway through. Drain, pat dry, and proceed.

SPICY SCHNITZEL SALAD
with Cracked Pepper Dressing

A schnitzel-salad combination isn't exactly a new concept, but as my friend Lee Schrager always says, even the *Mona Lisa* can use the occasional touch-up. Milanese, the Italian classic, is essentially salad piled atop a whole fried breaded cutlet. Here, I flip the equation, first jacking up the spice level in the breading on a crispy thin-cut chicken cutlet, then slicing it and scattering it over crunchy lettuce. The kicker here is the creamy, dairy-free black-pepper dressing, which marries the two main elements of the salad like an expert matchmaker. I've eaten this salad with the schnitzel right out of the skillet, and I've also had it cold, and I must tell you I'm torn about which I like better. A leftover piece of the schnitzel is a delicious, guilty pleasure, best enjoyed here by swiping directly into the dressing. To make ahead, you can prepare the salad and bread the schnitzel in advance, then just fry it when guests arrive. And, of course, you can treat the schnitzel recipe as a new spicy classic and serve it hot, unsliced, as the main course at any meal.

Serves 4

Active Time:
40 minutes

**Total Time
(including minimum resting time):**
1 hour 15 minutes

FOR THE DRESSING:

½ cup mayonnaise

¼ cup freshly squeezed lemon juice

¼ cup olive oil

1 teaspoon coarsely cracked black pepper, plus more for seasoning

1 teaspoon sugar

½ teaspoon kosher salt

FOR THE SCHNITZEL:

2 tablespoons plus ½ teaspoon Harissa (page 14 or store-bought)

2 tablespoons vegetable oil, plus more for frying

2 large garlic cloves, finely minced

2 teaspoons sweet paprika

1½ teaspoons kosher salt, plus more for seasoning

1 teaspoon freshly ground black pepper, plus more for seasoning

¼ teaspoon cayenne pepper

4 thin-cut boneless, skinless chicken breasts (about 1 pound)

1 cup panko bread crumbs

½ cup all-purpose flour

2 large eggs

FOR THE SALAD:

2 romaine lettuce hearts (about ¾ pound total), smaller leaves left whole, larger ones roughly chopped

1 cup cherry tomatoes, halved

2 tablespoons chopped fresh chives

RECIPE CONTINUES

1. Make the dressing: In a jar with a tight-fitting lid, combine the mayonnaise, lemon juice, olive oil, black pepper, sugar, and salt and shake until creamy, 10 seconds. Refrigerate until ready to use. Dressing can be refrigerated, tightly sealed, in an airtight container for 1 week.

2. Make the schnitzel: In a medium bowl, combine 2 tablespoons of the harissa with the oil, garlic, 1 teaspoon of the paprika, ½ teaspoon of the salt, ¼ teaspoon of the black pepper, and the cayenne. Add the chicken and rub the paste all over; let it rest while you prepare the flour and breading (the paste can be applied and the chicken refrigerated up to 24 hours in advance).

3. In a wide, shallow bowl, toss the panko with ¼ teaspoon of the paprika, ½ teaspoon of the salt, and ¼ teaspoon of the black pepper.

4. In another wide, shallow bowl, combine the flour and ¼ teaspoon each of the paprika, salt, and black pepper.

5. In another bowl, whisk the eggs with the remaining ½ teaspoon harissa, ½ teaspoon paprika, and ¼ teaspoon each salt and black pepper.

6. Dip the chicken in the flour, shaking off the excess, then in the egg mixture, letting the excess drip off, and finally press the chicken firmly into the panko on both sides. Transfer to a plate, cover with plastic wrap, and refrigerate for at least 30 minutes and up to 8 hours to allow the crumbs to adhere to the chicken. Heat ½ inch of vegetable oil in a large skillet over medium heat until a panko crumb sizzles on contact. Fry the schnitzels two at a time until golden and crisp, 2 to 3 minutes per side. Transfer to a towel-lined plate to cool slightly and repeat with the remaining 2 schnitzels. Slice them each across the grain.

7. Assemble the salad: Combine the lettuce and tomatoes on a serving platter and arrange the schnitzel slices on top of the salad. Drizzle with the dressing and top with the chives and more cracked black pepper.

NUTTY '90S ROASTED BEET & SWEET POTATO SALAD

I spent five years in Jerusalem after college and an inordinate amount of my free time then playing cards, drinking iced coffee, and eating French fries at any number of cafes in the German Colony, the "it" neighborhood of the day. It was lined with cafes housed in old buildings left over from the time when German Templars established a religious community in the holiest city on earth (join the club!). At cafes named Caffit, Kapulsky, and Aroma, there was almost always a salad consisting of roasted sweet potatoes and beets, copious lettuces, tons of greens, a raft of deeply roasted nuts, salty feta, and a delicious sweet dressing. It disappeared around the beginning of the aughts, so I nostalgically refer to it as the '90s Salad. On days when I want healthy, filling, nostalgic comfort food, I make this salad, which my friends and I would sometimes split three ways, especially on months when we could barely make our rent. I present you with the closest facsimile I could reproduce from taste memory.

Serves 4

Active Time:
20 minutes

**Total Time
(including cooling time):**
2 hours 20 minutes

**FOR THE NUT MIX
(makes 2 cups):**

2 cups assorted nuts, such as pecans, walnuts, pistachios, almonds, pumpkin seeds, and/or sunflower seeds

2 teaspoons olive oil

½ teaspoon kosher salt

FOR THE ROASTED VEGETABLES:

½ pound beets
(3 smallish or 1 medium), peeled

4 tablespoons olive oil

1 teaspoon kosher salt

1 pound (1 large or 2 small) sweet potatoes, peeled

FOR THE SALAD & DRESSING:

5 tablespoons walnut oil or olive oil

3 tablespoons sherry or red wine vinegar

1 tablespoon maple syrup

2 teaspoons Dijon mustard

¼ teaspoon kosher salt

¼ teaspoon freshly ground black pepper

4 cups crisp salad greens, such as romaine, Little Gems, or a combination

½ cup thinly sliced red onion

½ cup crumbled feta

1. Roast the nuts: Preheat the oven to 350°F. Arrange the nuts on a large rimmed baking sheet, drizzle with the oil, sprinkle with the salt, and stir to coat. Bake until fragrant, 10 minutes; cool on the baking sheet. Nuts can be stored in an airtight container for up to 2 weeks.

2. Roast the vegetables: Increase the oven temperature to 400°F. Cut the beets crosswise into ½-inch-thick rounds and toss in a medium bowl with 2 tablespoons of the oil and ½ teaspoon of the salt. Arrange in a single layer on a large baking sheet. Cut the sweet potatoes crosswise into ½-inch-thick rounds and toss in a medium bowl with the remaining 2 tablespoons oil and ½ teaspoon salt. Add to a second baking sheet in a single layer; roast both trays until the

RECIPE CONTINUES

vegetables are tender and the undersides are crisped on the edges, 25 to 30 minutes for the sweet potatoes (remove them at this point) and 40 minutes for the beets. Remove from the oven and cool.

3. Make the dressing: In a jar with a tight-fitting lid, combine the walnut oil, vinegar, maple syrup, Dijon mustard, salt, and pepper and shake until creamy.

4. Arrange the greens on a serving platter. Scatter the onions over the greens, arrange the roasted vegetables on top, crumble the feta over them, and drizzle with dressing to taste. Scatter with ½ cup of the nut mix. Extra dressing can be refrigerated in an airtight container for up to 1 week.

SPRINGY VEGGIES
with Creamy Basil Dressing & Runny Eggs

This one's all about the eggs. Oh, wait—it's about the super-herbaceous dressing. No! It's the amazingly crisp, perfectly blanched veggies. I guess what I'm getting at here is that there are just so many parts to this salad that I love. The conceit of using the same water to cook the eggs and the veggies is a time- and dish-saving wonder. The dressing itself, which coats the salad in a layer of green goodness, would be enough, but when the runny egg yolks mingle with that said dressing, it takes each individual serving to a whole new level.

Serves 6

Active Time:
15 minutes

Total Time:
25 minutes

½ teaspoon kosher salt, plus more for the water and to taste

6 large eggs

¾ pound pea pods, shelled (1¼ cups shelled), or 1¼ cups frozen peas

¾ pound green beans, trimmed

¾ pound snow peas, trimmed

2 cups lightly packed basil leaves

⅓ cup freshly squeezed lime juice (from 2 medium or 3 small limes)

⅓ cup olive oil

4 garlic cloves

¼ teaspoon freshly ground black pepper, plus more to taste

3 Little Gem lettuce heads, halved lengthwise, or 2 cups chopped romaine hearts

1. Bring a medium saucepan of generously salted water to a boil. Gently lower the eggs into the saucepan and boil for exactly 4 minutes.

2. While the eggs are boiling, fill a large bowl with ice, then add enough water to make a very cold ice-water bath. Remove the eggs to the ice-water bath with a slotted spoon (leaving the saucepan on the heat), chill them for 2 minutes, and transfer them to a plate.

3. Drop the shelled peas, green beans, and snow peas into the boiling water and let them sit in there for 1½ minutes; any longer and you risk overcooking. Drain them in a colander, then drop them into the ice water briefly (a minute will do), drain again, and arrange them on a large kitchen towel–lined baking sheet to absorb moisture. In a bullet-style blender or the small bowl of a food processor, combine the basil, lime juice, olive oil, garlic, salt, and pepper. Blend until smooth, creamy, and bright green, 30 seconds. Carefully peel the eggs. Arrange the lettuce in a large salad bowl, then add the blanched vegetables. Drizzle with the dressing, arrange the eggs on top, and gently split them with a knife. Season with more salt and pepper. Leftover dressing can be refrigerated, tightly sealed, in an airtight container for 1 week.

LIME-GRILLED CHICKEN
with Melon & Cucumber Salad

Skinless, boneless chicken breasts get a bad rap, so let me extol their virtues. They're a flavor sponge, able to take on any acid, herbs, and spice you throw their way. They cook fast, a benefit for busy cooks getting ready for a relaxing Shabbat. When marinated (with a mix that also doubles here as dressing), sliced thin, and grilled over high heat, they dispel any concerns about dryness. I like to pile the grilled chicken pieces on top of one another to keep them warm, then drizzle any pooled juices on top just before serving. Melon and cucumber are in the same plant family, and the sweetness of the melon and the vegetal crunch of the cucumbers play beautifully off each other.

Serves 4 to 6

Active Time:
35 minutes

Total Time:
35 minutes

FOR THE CHICKEN:

3 small or 2 medium limes

½ cup olive oil

1½ tablespoons honey or maple syrup

1½ tablespoons Dijon mustard

¼ teaspoon kosher salt

¼ teaspoon freshly ground black pepper

2 garlic cloves, smashed

1 small fresh red hot chili pepper, seeded and thinly sliced

1½ pounds thin-cut chicken cutlets (5 or 6 cutlets)

FOR THE SALAD:

½ ripe medium orange or yellow melon, such as cantaloupe, Crenshaw, or Canary

4 Persian cucumbers

1 cup purslane, watercress, or other tender greens

1. Prepare the chicken: Finely grate the zest of the limes into a large bowl or zip-top plastic bag, then juice the limes (you should have about 6 tablespoons juice) into the bowl. Whisk in the oil, honey, mustard, salt, and pepper; you should have about 1 cup dressing/marinade. Transfer ½ cup to another bowl and reserve. Add the garlic cloves, half of the sliced chili, and the chicken to the bowl, toss to coat, and marinate on the counter for 15 minutes.

2. Prepare the salad: While the chicken is marinating, remove and discard the seeds from the melon half and cut it in half lengthwise. Remove the rind from the melon pieces, then cut each piece crosswise into ¼-inch slices. Cut the cucumbers on the diagonal into ¼-inch slices. Arrange the melon, cucumbers, and purslane on a serving platter and scatter with the remaining sliced chili.

3. Heat a grill or grill pan over high heat. Remove the chicken from the marinade, let any excess liquid drip off, season with salt and pepper, and grill until cooked through and grill marks form, 2 to 3 minutes per side.

4. Drizzle the reserved ½ cup dressing on the salad, season with salt and pepper, and serve with the chicken.

FISH MAIN COURSES

SUMAC-DUSTED SEA BASS & ASPARAGUS
with Garlicky Mayo

That little jar of sumac in your spice drawer? It was born to be used right here. I turn to sumac for an extra pop of acidity, and sprinkling it on fish fillets is like squeezing an extra lemon on top, with much less effort. Not that lemons don't make an appearance here; I roast slices along with asparagus, then create a bed of extra-garlicky homemade mayonnaise to tie the whole dish together. You won't use all the mayo when serving this dish, which is a great thing; you'll find yourself using it absolutely everywhere—try it on a juicy, ripe tomato sandwich in season (or on any other sandwich, for that matter) or folded into tuna, hard-boiled eggs, or cooked potatoes.

Serves 4

Active Time:
15 minutes

Total Time:
25 minutes

FOR THE FISH & VEGETABLES:

Four 6- to 7-ounce center-cut fish fillets, such as cod, halibut, or bass (between 1¾ and 2 inches thick), patted dry

4 tablespoons olive oil

1¼ teaspoons kosher salt

1 tablespoon ground sumac

¾ pound asparagus, trimmed

1 lemon, thinly sliced

½ teaspoon freshly ground black pepper

FOR THE GARLICKY MAYO
(makes 1½ cups):

1 large egg

1 tablespoon Dijon mustard

1 tablespoon freshly squeezed lemon juice

1 garlic clove

¾ teaspoon kosher salt

Pinch of cayenne pepper

¾ cup neutral oil, such as canola or sunflower

¼ cup olive oil

1. Prepare the fish and veggies: Arrange two racks in the bottom and top thirds of the oven. Preheat the oven to 425°F. Arrange the fish on a small rimmed baking sheet and brush with 2 tablespoons of the olive oil. Sprinkle with ¾ teaspoon of the salt and then with the sumac. Arrange the asparagus and lemon slices on a larger rimmed baking sheet, drizzle with the remaining 2 tablespoons olive oil, and shake to coat. Season with the remaining ½ teaspoon salt and the black pepper. Arrange the asparagus sheet on the top rack of the oven and roast for 4 to 5 minutes, rotate the asparagus sheet, then place the fish on the lower rack and roast both until the fish is just cooked through, the asparagus is slightly wilted, and the lemons have some charred edges, another 15 minutes.

RECIPE CONTINUES

2. Make the mayonnaise: Place the whole egg (still in its shell) in a glass, fill it with warm (not hot) water, and let the egg warm up for 5 minutes. In the bowl of a food processor, crack the egg and process it for 15 seconds, then, with the motor running, add the mustard, lemon juice, garlic, salt, and cayenne and process for another 20 seconds. In a measuring cup with a spout, combine the two oils and very (very!) slowly drizzle the oil into the food processor through the feed tube (this requires patience*) until you see and hear the mayo begin to emulsify; it will lighten in color and the processor will sound like it's working a bit harder (it will require about half of the oil and a good, slow-drizzly 3 to 4 minutes to make this happen). Then you can begin to add the oil in a bit of a larger stream until it's all incorporated and you have 1½ cups of the best mayo you've ever tasted.

3. Spread about half of the mayonnaise on the bottom of a large serving tray, then arrange the lemons and asparagus, followed by the fish, on the platter.

*If you look at the feed tube pusher on some food processors, there may be a tiny hole at the bottom to release air pressure while processing. This is the ideal slow-drip vehicle for your oil, so if your processor has one, pour half the oil into the tube at a time and watch as it slowly drips into your mayonnaise in a tiny stream—the perfect pace for wonderfully emulsified mayonnaise.

COOKING & RESTING

What does "work" actually mean? I find myself delving into this question often when cooking on Shabbat, a time when, according to Jewish tradition, I'm not supposed to. The ancient Jewish laws prohibiting cooking on Shabbat come from a variety of Jewish sources, beginning with the Old Testament itself and continuing with other written works that, when combined, comprise what is known as the oral law. They're all meant to prevent anything that could lead us to toil, and growing up that meant absolutely no active cooking—only assembling and reheating dishes. There was sometimes a last-minute scramble to get everything cooked before we lit candles on Friday night, and we had a well-calibrated routine that set us up to enjoy hot food over the weekend. The oven was preset, we left a burner lit on the top of the stove, we used a slow cooker for our cholent, and we filled a giant urn with hot water that we would use to make coffee and tea.

These days, as someone who does not observe Shabbat in the traditional sense of the word, I interpret it in a looser, more spiritual fashion centered around ideas of mindfulness and stillness. Shabbat mornings are a time for me to meditate over my mise en place, and I chop a little more lazily and breathe a little more deeply, sometimes pulling up one of my barstools to the counter so I can sit while shelling peas or peeling carrots. I talk to my husband or a friend over the counter as I stir, sauté, and sear. I spontaneously call friends to come over for a late lunch. I just let things happen; it's pure Shabbat cooking joy and, for me personally, the opposite of work. As someone who cooks for a living, the concept of doing so at my own pace is the ultimate form of self-indulgence.

POACHED SALMON
with Zucchini Salad

I always thought of poached salmon as a bit too precious, something reserved for Ladies Who Lunch. But then I realized that cold, perfectly cooked salmon has Ladies Who *Shabbat* Lunch written all over it. By filling a pot with aromatics and liquid and simmering ever so gently (a technique the French call *smile*, something I learned from Laurie Colwin's beautiful book *Home Cooking*), you produce tender, silky salmon that is actually better cold, making it a perfect, no-reheat main course. The accompanying zucchini salad is a breeze to put together and turns the poached fish into an ideal warmer-weather meal. Any leftover salmon can be mixed with mayo and chopped celery for a quick salmon salad.

Serves 6

Active Time:
20 minutes

Total Time:
45 minutes

FOR THE SALMON:

5 cups water

½ cup freshly squeezed lemon juice (from 2 large or 3 medium lemons)

3 celery stalks

2 teaspoons black peppercorns

2 teaspoons kosher salt

1 jalapeño, halved lengthwise, seeded if desired

2 shallots, halved

2 fresh thyme sprigs

Six 6-ounce center-cut skinless salmon fillets

1 recipe creamy basil dressing (see page 218)

FOR THE ZUCCHINI SALAD:

3 large or 4 medium zucchini (1½ pounds), trimmed

3 tablespoons freshly squeezed lemon juice

3 tablespoons olive oil

1 teaspoon ground sumac

½ teaspoon kosher salt

½ cup picked fresh mint leaves

½ cup picked fresh basil leaves

1. Prepare the salmon: In a large, wide pot, combine the water, lemon juice, celery, peppercorns, kosher salt, jalapeño, shallots, and thyme sprigs and bring to a boil over high heat. Add the salmon, cover gently with a piece of parchment, reduce the heat to very low, and simmer (the water should be bubbling just ever so slightly) until the salmon turns pale pink on the exterior, 10 minutes. Turn off the heat, let it sit another 5 minutes, then use a fish spatula to gently remove the salmon to a plate and discard the poaching liquid.

2. While the salmon is cooling, make the salad: With a T-peeler, cut wide, thin ribbons from the zucchini, using as much of each zucchini as you can and saving any unused part for vegetable broth or another use. In a large bowl, gently toss the zucchini in the lemon juice and let it sit for 10 minutes, then add the oil, sumac, and salt and toss to coat. Gently fold in the mint and basil leaves. Serve the zucchini salad with the salmon and dressing.

TOMATO JAM ROASTED SALMON

For my entire childhood, zemirot, or "table hymns" sung on Shabbat, created a lyrical component that enhanced our meals and were an integral part of our tradition. It might sound strange if you've never experienced it, but to me breaking out in song between the appetizer and the main course felt as normal as lighting candles on Friday night. Mostly written by kabbalists (Jewish mystics) during the medieval era, zemirot celebrate the otherness and beauty of Shabbat, including its food. One of my favorites, "Ma Yedidut," written in the tenth century by Menachem Ibn Saruq, is a paean to rest and indulgent meals. "How friendly your rest is, Queen Shabbat, so we run to meet you," the song goes. "Wearing beautiful clothes, lighting and blessing the candles, all work stops . . . to enjoy delicacies, swans [yes, people ate them back then], quail, and fish."

The song inspired this salmon topped with my sweet-and-spicy tomato jam and accompanied by a burst of roasted tomatoes. It creates a centerpiece dish most definitely worth a song.

Serves 6

Active Time:
10 minutes

**Total Time
(including marinating time):**
1 hour 25 minutes

One 2-pound skin-on salmon fillet, patted dry

1 tablespoon plus ½ teaspoon ground cumin

1 tablespoon sweet paprika

1½ teaspoons kosher salt, plus more to taste

1 teaspoon dried red pepper flakes

½ teaspoon freshly ground black pepper, plus more to taste

Finely grated zest of 1 lemon

1 cup Tomato Jam (page 88)

⅔ pound multicolored cherry tomatoes (2 cups)

3 tablespoons olive oil

6 fresh thyme or oregano sprigs

1. Line a large baking sheet with foil; center the salmon on the sheet. In a small bowl, combine 1 tablespoon of the cumin, the paprika, 1 teaspoon of the salt, the red pepper flakes, black pepper, and lemon zest and spread it all over the salmon. Cover with plastic wrap; let sit on the counter for 1 hour or in the fridge for up to 24 hours; if chilled, remove from fridge 1 hour before roasting.

2. Preheat oven to 425°F. Arrange a rack in the top third of the oven. Spread the tomato jam evenly over the salmon. In a medium bowl, combine the tomatoes, olive oil, and the remaining ½ teaspoon salt and ½ teaspoon cumin and gently toss to coat. Arrange the tomatoes around the salmon. Scatter the herb sprigs on top and bake until the jam is slightly caramelized and the tomatoes begin to soften, 26 to 27 minutes. Remove from the oven; turn on the broiler. Return to the top third of the oven; broil until the top darkens slightly and the tomatoes burst, 2 to 3 minutes. Season with salt and black pepper to taste.

BAKED SEA BASS
with Olives, Capers & Lemon

Simplicity, speed, and supplies are all the keys here. Capers and olives add salt and punch, panko adds crunch, and lemon slices baked right on top help keep the fish tender and infused with a sunny zinginess. This is a recipe I would try to serve either immediately or at room temperature; if you do decide to reheat it, add a drop of liquid to the pan, cover, and heat gently just to warm it through.

Serves 4

Active Time:
10 minutes

Total Time:
25 minutes

---

1 medium lemon, preferably thin-skinned, plus more lemon wedges for serving

4 tablespoons olive oil, plus more for drizzling

Four 5- to 6-ounce whitefish fillets, such as sea bass or trout

1 teaspoon kosher salt, plus more to taste

1 teaspoon freshly ground black pepper, plus more to taste

¼ cup pitted green olives, such as Castelvetrano, halved

1 small hot green chili pepper, thinly sliced, seeded if desired

2 teaspoons capers, drained and rinsed (optional)

2 tablespoons chopped fresh parsley, plus leaves for garnish

¼ cup panko bread crumbs, or more if desired

1. Arrange a rack in the top third of the oven and a second rack in the center of the oven and preheat the broiler. Using a sharp knife, slice the lemon in half. Slice one half into very thin rounds, stack the rounds, and quarter them. Reserve the remaining half.

2. Drizzle the bottom of a 9 × 13-inch baking dish with 2 tablespoons of the oil. Arrange the fish in the dish and season with ½ teaspoon each of the salt and black pepper. Scatter the lemon quarters, olives, chili slices, capers (if using), and the parsley on top.

3. In a small bowl, toss the panko with the remaining 2 tablespoons oil and ¼ teaspoon of the salt and ¼ teaspoon of the black pepper. Sprinkle the fish evenly with the panko mixture and season it with the remaining ¼ teaspoon salt and ¼ teaspoon black pepper. Broil on the higher rack until the lemons begin to char and the panko mixture turns golden, 2 to 3 minutes. Move the fish to the lower rack, reduce the oven temperature to 300°F, and bake until the fish is cooked through and flaky, 7 to 8 minutes. Squeeze the remaining lemon half over the fish, drizzle with more olive oil, season with salt and black pepper, and serve with more lemon wedges.

CACCIUCCO LIVORNESE
(Italian Fish Stew)

I first met Italian-Israeli chef Emanuela Panke in the shuk, just two immigrant cooks shopping for ingredients in our relatively new homeland. Emanuela left behind a vibrant life as a restaurateur in Sicily to start a new one in Israel with her husband, and now she hosts Italian dinners at her home in Tel Aviv, as well as serving as a liaison to Italian cultural organizations in Israel.

One time she told me about cacciucco, and on a Friday she came over to teach me how to make this soothing, deeply flavorful Italian fish stew, bringing fresh fish and market-fresh produce with her. To make it, whole snappers are simmered in a tomatoey, mildly spicy, olive oil–rich, sage-and-wine-infused fish stock, then served with crusty bread lavished in olive oil.

Like many traditional Italian dishes, this one has Jewish history. After being expelled from Spain and Portugal in the late 1400s, Jews eventually found their way to the coastal Italian city of Livorno, where they experienced relative economic, financial, and legal freedom, thanks to the protection of the Medici family. The dish is believed to have been brought to Livorno by Portuguese Jews, and it eventually became part of the Livornese cooking canon. It's perfect for a Friday-night dinner and can also be gently rewarmed the next day. Make sure to use the freshest fish you can get your hands on, and don't skimp on the olive oil for the toasts, which are as much a selling point as the fish itself.

Serves 6

Active Time:
30 minutes

Total Time:
1 hour

FOR THE FISH BROTH*:

2 tablespoons olive oil

1 medium onion, coarsely chopped

1 medium carrot, chopped

1 large celery stalk, chopped

1 bay leaf

5 whole black peppercorns

¾ pound fish bones (ask your fishmonger for these)

6½ cups water

FOR THE STEW:

10 tablespoons olive oil

9 fresh sage leaves

7 garlic cloves, halved

1 hot chili pepper

¼ cup tomato paste

1 cup red wine

2½ to 3 pounds whole red snapper (4 small, 3 medium, or 1 large snapper), cleaned

1 teaspoon kosher salt, plus more for seasoning

1 cup water, as needed to cover the fish

8 thick slices crusty bread, such as sourdough or country loaf

RECIPE CONTINUES

1. Make the broth: In a 3- or 4-quart saucepan, heat the oil over medium-low heat. Add the onion, carrot, and celery and cook, stirring, until the vegetables begin to soften, 6 to 7 minutes. Add the bay leaf, peppercorns, fish bones, and water, increase the heat to high, bring to a boil, and boil for 5 minutes, skimming and discarding any scum that gathers on top. Reduce the heat to low and simmer, uncovered, for 25 minutes. Strain, discarding the solids; you should have about 6 cups broth.

2. Make the fish stew: In a large pot, heat ¼ cup of the olive oil over medium-low heat. Add the sage leaves, 6 of the garlic cloves, and the chili and cook until fragrant, 2 minutes. Add the tomato paste and cook, stirring, for 1 minute. Add the wine, scrape the pot to bring everything together, bring to a boil, then turn off the heat and scrape the mixture into a bowl. Pat the fish dry and season it generously with salt on both sides. Add another 3 tablespoons of the oil to the pot,

increase the heat to high, add the fish, and sear until golden, 2 to 4 minutes per side. Add the red wine–tomato liquid, the fish broth, and the salt; use a spatula to shift the fish to make sure the liquid gets in between all the fish, adding the water, if necessary, to cover the fish, and bring to a boil. Reduce the heat to medium-low and simmer until the liquid thickens slightly and the fish cooks through, 15 to 17 minutes.

3. While the fish is cooking, make the toasts: Arrange a rack in the top third of the oven and preheat the broiler. Rub one side of the bread with the cut sides of the remaining garlic clove, arrange the slices on a baking sheet, brush one side generously with the remaining 3 tablespoons oil, and broil until golden and toasty, 2 to 3 minutes. Season with salt and serve with the fish stew.

*If you like, substitute 6 cups of store-bought fish stock for the fish broth.

CHEN'S CHRAIMEH
(North African Shabbat Fish)

"This is often what we serve on Friday night," Chen Koren (see page 270) told me as she unpacked fresh grouper fillets and steaks that she had picked up at the Machane Yehuda shuk in Jerusalem. Typically, chraimeh—a North African dish that varies depending on the provenance of the cook—is made with tomato paste and cumin, but Koren opts for a presentation based entirely on fresh tomatoes. Soon she began to prepare a rich, spicy sauce in her spacious, well-lit kitchen, cooking garlic, blooming paprika, and simmering tomatoes until a fragrant swirl of steam rose from the pot, the building blocks of a rich, yet simple, sauce. At the same time, she heated a pot of vegetable oil to fry whole green hot chili peppers and potato wedges, which were eventually placed right into the skillet. And so a delicious skillet of starch and protein was born.

Serves 6

Active Time:
30 minutes

Total Time:
1 hour 35 minutes

---

1 pint ripe red cherry tomatoes (2 cups)

9 large vine-ripened tomatoes (about 2 pounds)

½ cup olive oil

1 large head garlic, peeled and minced (about ⅓ cup)

2 tablespoons sweet paprika

2 teaspoons kosher salt, plus more to taste

½ teaspoon cayenne pepper (optional)

Vegetable oil, for frying

2 medium waxy yellow potatoes (such as Yukon Gold, 1¼ pounds total), each cut into 8 wedges

1 or 2 large whole jalapeños

Six 6-ounce center-cut, skin-on grouper or snapper steaks (about 2 pounds)

Fresh lemon wedges, for seasoning and serving

1. Finely chop the cherry and vine-ripened tomatoes by hand, or place them in a food processor and pulse until finely chopped, 15 to 20 pulses; set aside. In a 10- or 12-inch high-sided skillet, heat ¼ cup of the olive oil over low heat. Add the garlic and cook, stirring, until fragrant and softened but not crisped or darkened, 4 minutes. Add the paprika, salt, and cayenne (if using) and cook, stirring, scraping the pot so the bottom doesn't burn, until the flavors bloom, 1 to 2 minutes. Add the tomatoes, turn the temperature to high, and cook, stirring, until the sauce thickens and the color deepens, 10 minutes. Reduce the heat to medium-low and cook until the sauce reduces and thickens, 40 to 45 minutes, adding water by the quarter cup if the skillet appears to dry out and covering it during the last 10 minutes.

RECIPE CONTINUES

2. While the sauce is cooking, heat 3 inches of vegetable oil in a medium saucepan to 350°F, or until a small piece of bread sizzles and turns golden upon contact but doesn't burn. Line a plate with paper towels and have nearby. Working in batches, lower the potatoes into the oil and fry them, turning occasionally, until the exteriors are golden and crisp and the centers are cooked, 11 to 12 minutes; drain on a paper towel–lined plate. Lower in the jalapeño(s) and fry until softened and slightly shriveled, 2 to 3 minutes; add to the paper towel–lined plate. Uncover the sauce, stir in the remaining ¼ cup olive oil, and simmer for 5 minutes. Gently add the fish to the skillet, making sure the fish is covered by the sauce (if not, add up to ¼ cup water). The sauce should be bubbling but not boiling vigorously. Cover the skillet and gently shake the pot occasionally until the fish is just cooked through and opaque, 7 to 8 minutes. Uncover, nestle the jalapeño(s) and potatoes into the skillet, squeeze in lemon to your liking, and season with salt. Divide the fish, sauce, and potatoes among plates. Serve with small pieces of the fried jalapeño(s) and more lemon wedges.

FRICASSEE

In the pantheon of sandwiches, fricassee (pronounced frick-UH-say) ranks close to the top. Luscious poached fresh tuna and a host of strong supporting players are layered onto a savory, donut-like roll, resulting in something that's as beautiful to look at as it is to eat.

I first tasted this sandwich at the home of Ron and Leetal Arazi, the founders of beloved Middle Eastern spice company New York Shuk and undisputed fricassee royalty in Brooklyn (and beyond). A few times a year, the Arazis host a fricassee party at home, and it's always a stylish and delicious affair. Last year they were visiting family in Israel and were kind enough to come over to show me the process from start to finish.

It started with homemade, yeasty dough that Ron rolled into torpedoes, letting them rise before shallow-frying them to golden perfection. Then we poached a chunk of tuna in olive oil with harissa, herbs, and spices, yielding confit fish I couldn't believe we'd just pulled off at home. Potatoes and eggs were boiled and cooled. We piled everything onto the rolls smeared with harissa and preserved lemon paste, then garnished with olives and scallion greens for springy freshness. Each bite was a study in contrasts, squishy and crunchy and heavenly in every sense of the word. "We've given all our secrets," Ron joked as he and Leetal headed out. "Do us proud."

Serves 6 to 8 (with extra rolls)

Active Time:
1 hour 30 minutes

**Total Time
(including rising time):**
3 hours

FOR THE ROLLS*:

3½ cups (455 grams) all-purpose flour

1 tablespoon (9 grams) instant yeast

1½ teaspoons (6½ grams) sugar

2½ teaspoons (15 grams) fine sea salt

1¼ cups (295 grams/ml) water

⅓ cup (73 grams/ml) vegetable oil, plus more for frying

FOR THE TUNA*:

1½ pounds sushi-grade tuna

3 cups olive oil, or enough to completely cover the tuna

Thick strips of zest, peeled from 1 orange

1 lemon, cut into rounds

Fresh thyme, oregano, or za'atar sprigs

4 garlic cloves

2 bay leaves

1½ tablespoons kosher salt

½ teaspoon dried red pepper flakes

½ teaspoon cumin seeds

FOR THE SANDWICHES:

2 medium waxy potatoes (1 pound), such as Yukon Gold

6 large eggs

Kosher salt

Preserved Lemon Paste (page 15 or store-bought)

3 medium vine-ripened tomatoes, sliced crosswise into rounds

Harissa (page 14 or store-bought)

Pitted Moroccan salt-cured olives, halved

Thinly sliced scallion greens

Freshly ground black pepper

RECIPE CONTINUES

1. Make the rolls: In the bowl of a stand mixer fitted with the dough hook, combine the flour, yeast, sugar, and salt. Add the water and oil. Mix first at low speed, then raise the speed to medium-low. Mix until the dough pulls away from the sides and is smooth and not sticky, 5 to 6 minutes. Remove from the mixer bowl, lightly flour the bowl, return the dough to the bowl, cover it with plastic wrap, and let rise in a warm place until doubled in size, 30 to 40 minutes.

2. Uncover, deflate the dough, and fold the dough over on itself twice. Cover and let rise again for 30 minutes. Divide into 20 equal-sized balls. Use your hands to gently press the air out of the dough; roll each one into a 4 × 2-inch log.

3. Arrange the buns on a clean work surface, cover them lightly with a clean garbage bag or large plastic bag, and let them rise again for 30 minutes. In a wide pot, heat 1½ inches of oil to 360°F. Line a baking sheet with paper towels and have nearby. Gently lower the buns, four or five at a time, into the oil and fry until golden, 1 to 2 minutes per side. Drain on the paper towel–lined sheet. Repeat with the remaining dough. The rolls can be individually wrapped and frozen for up to 3 months. To defrost, remove from the freezer and let thaw on the counter.

4. Prepare the tuna: Place the tuna in a pot that just fits the fish, with about an inch around on all sides (if the pot is too large, you will need to use more olive oil). Add the olive oil, orange peel, lemon, thyme, garlic, bay leaves, kosher salt, red pepper flakes, and cumin. Set over very low heat until you see tiny bubbles form on the surface of the oil and cook the tuna until it turns opaque and can be flaked into pieces, 20 to 25 minutes. Remove the pot from the heat and let the tuna cool in the oil. (If you're not using the tuna immediately, or if you don't use all, store the tuna in its poaching oil in an airtight container and refrigerate for up to 1 week. The oil can be strained, then refrigerated, for up to 3 months and reused to poach more tuna.) Flake the tuna into bite-sized pieces.

5. Fill a medium bowl with 3 cups ice and add 3 cups cold water. Place the potatoes and eggs in a large saucepan. Cover with water by 2 inches, season generously with kosher salt, bring to a boil over medium-high heat, reduce the heat to medium-low, and simmer until the eggs are cooked through, 9 minutes. Leaving the potatoes in the pot to continue cooking, use a slotted spoon to transfer the eggs to the ice water, deliberately cracking them slightly so some water permeates the shell. Chill for 5 minutes, then peel them under cold running water. Continue to cook the potatoes until they can be pierced with a fork, another 7 to 8 minutes. Drain and cool until easy to handle, then slice both the potatoes and eggs into ½-inch-thick rounds.

6. To assemble the sandwiches, split a roll and spread one side with preserved lemon paste and cover it with tomato slices, then spread harissa on the other side. Layer on some tuna, potatoes, and eggs and top with a couple of olives and some scallion greens. Sprinkle with kosher salt and black pepper to taste. Repeat with the remaining rolls and ingredients.

*If you're short on time and can't make the rolls, any simple, small sandwich buns will do (if you can convince your local donut shop to sell you plain fresh hole-free donuts with no icing, those work great, too). Same goes for the tuna; use any good-quality tuna in olive oil, such as Ortiz; their ventresca (tuna belly) is pricey, but it's the best there is.

MEXICAN GEFILTE FISH
in Spicy Tomatillo Sauce

Upon completing her military service in Israel, Leah Stoffer traveled to Oaxaca, Mexico, to study Spanish while living with her host family, the Cruzes. After returning home, she lost touch with the family until, two years later, a message arrived via a newfangled social network called Facebook. "Hi from your family in Oaxaca," wrote the Cruz's elder son, Luis. A friendship developed, and shortly after, Luis packed his bags to explore the Big Apple with Leah. It didn't take long for a romance to bloom. Eventually Luis and Leah married and moved back to Israel with dreams of launching an authentic taqueria.

In 2018, along with Leah's sister, Yittie Stoffer-Lawson, they opened Tacos Luis, Israel's best, most authentic, happens-to-be-kosher taqueria. Living blocks from one another, the Cruz–Stoffer–Lawson clan often eats together on Shabbat, and they've taken to making this Mexican-inspired version of gefilte fish cooked in a thick, spicy tomatillo broth, a departure from the better-known gefilte veracruzana, which involves tomato sauce. They keep the dish gluten-free by binding it with almond flour, serving it with avocado and tostadas fritas (fried whole-corn tortillas) from the restaurant. You can make your own or easily swap in good-quality store-bought chips.

Serves 6 to 8 as a main course, 8 to 10 as an appetizer

Active Time:
45 minutes

Total Time:
1 hour 45 minutes

RECIPE AND INGREDIENTS CONTINUE

FOR THE GEFILTE FISH BALLS
(makes 20 balls):

2½ pounds skinless whitefish fillets, such as carp, snapper, flounder, lemon sole, tilapia, or a combination

1 large onion, coarsely chopped (2 cups)

½ cup almond flour

2 large eggs, beaten

4 teaspoons kosher salt

2 teaspoons ground coriander

1 teaspoon finely ground black pepper

FOR THE SALSA VERDE:

3 tablespoons vegetable oil

1 large onion, finely chopped

6 fresh large jalapeños (10 to 12 ounces total), seeded if desired, chopped

One 28-ounce can tomatillos (2 cups), coarsely chopped, plus ¼ cup brine from the can

1 cup water

5 garlic cloves

2 cups fresh cilantro leaves and tender stems

2 teaspoons kosher salt, plus more to taste

1 cup fish broth (see page 234 or store-bought)

FOR FINISHING:

¼ cup chopped fresh cilantro, plus leaves for garnish

¼ cup chopped pickled jalapeños, plus more pickled jalapeño rings for garnish (optional)

1 avocado, peeled, pitted, and cut into 1-inch pieces

Baked or fried whole corn tortillas or tortilla chips

1 lime, cut into wedges

1. Make the gefilte fish balls: Pat the fish fillets dry. Cut them into chunks and pulse them (in two batches, if necessary) in a food processor until finely chopped but not pasty, 5 to 10 seconds, or more as needed. Transfer to a large bowl. Add the onion, almond flour, eggs, salt, coriander, and black pepper to the processor bowl and pulse until the onions are very finely chopped or minced, scraping down the sides of the processor if necessary, 20 to 30 pulses. Add the onion mixture to the fish and combine thoroughly with your hands. Chill, covered, while you make the salsa verde.

2. Make the salsa verde: In a large (5-quart) heavy Dutch oven, heat the oil over medium heat. Add the onion and cook, stirring, until tender and translucent, 6 to 7 minutes. Add the fresh jalapeños, tomatillos and brine, water, garlic, cilantro, and salt, bring to a boil, then reduce the heat to a simmer, cover, and cook until the garlic is soft, 20 minutes. Add the fish broth to the cooked vegetables, warm through for 1 minute, then remove the pot from the heat and use an immersion (stick) blender or conventional blender to blend until smooth, 15 to 20 seconds.

3. Cook the fish: Using moistened hands, use ⅓ cup of the mixture to form each gefilte fish ball. Gently lower the gefilte fish balls into the salsa verde and shake the pot slightly to ensure they are coated in the sauce. Bring to a low boil over medium heat, then reduce the heat to medium-low and simmer, partially covered, until the fish balls are firm and opaque and the sauce has thickened, 20 to 25 minutes. Stir in the chopped cilantro and pickled jalapeños and season the sauce with salt to taste. Divide among bowls and garnish each serving with pickled jalapeño rings (if using), cilantro leaves, and chopped avocado. Serve with corn tortillas and lime wedges.

CHICKEN & MEAT MAIN COURSES

BAGHDADI CHICKEN CURRY
with Sweet & Nutty Shabbat Rice

To enter Idit Katz's home in the southern Israeli suburb of Omer is to instantly enter the spiritual presence of her late mother, Mathilde, who moved to Israel from Kolkata, India, as a teenager. "These are all her paintings and sculptures," Idit, a college professor, told me, motioning to a room filled with colorful canvases and abstract metal figures. In India, Mathilde's father worked in the large tobacco factory owned by the legendary Sassoon family. Her life in Kolkata—a major trading hub with a Jewish community founded by Iraqi Jews in the late eighteenth century—was upended when, at age fifteen, a shaliach (emissary) convinced her and other teenagers to relocate to Kibbutz Gal Ed, a predominantly German-Jewish agriculture-based community. Raven-haired, dark-skinned, and feeling out of place, Mathilde was subjected to racism, making her even more eager to begin her life as an adult. She enrolled in the army, where she met her future husband, married, and raised six children in the suburb of Ramat Hasharon.

"Only when my mother married did she learn how to cook," said Idit, who remembers Shabbat as a time when Mathilda and Moshe opened their home to guests for lavish meals that combined her mother's Indian and father's Eastern European heritages. After the British left India in 1947, most of Kolkata's remaining Jews immigrated to England or, as was the case with Idit's grandmother Chana, to Israel. "I think my mother's cooking really improved when my savta [grandmother] arrived," she told me with a laugh. This chicken curry, which is creamy without the addition of cream and benefits from a lavish blanket of caramelized onions, was always on the table. With the accompanying green "chutney" and a bowl of rice (of my invention), it's a deliciously different Indian-Israeli meal.

Serves 6

Active Time:
50 minutes

Total Time:
1 hour 5 minutes

RECIPE AND INGREDIENTS CONTINUE

6 large onions
(3½ to 4 pounds),
peeled and quartered

8 garlic cloves

2 pounds skinless,
boneless chicken thighs

3 teaspoons kosher salt,
plus more to taste

½ teaspoon freshly
ground black pepper,
plus more to taste

½ cup plus
2 tablespoons
vegetable oil

¾ cup good-quality
tomato paste, such as
Redpack or Muti brand

3 tablespoons curry
powder

1 teaspoon ground
cumin

1 teaspoon dried red
pepper flakes, or
½ teaspoon cayenne
pepper

¾ cup water, plus more
as needed

Sweet & Nutty Shabbat
Rice and Chutney,
for serving
(recipes follow)

1. In the bowl of a food processor, place half of the onions and pulse until finely chopped, trying to avoid making the onions liquidy, 15 to 20 pulses. Transfer to a bowl and repeat with the remaining onions and the garlic. Pat the chicken dry and season it generously with 1 teaspoon of the salt and the black pepper.

2. In a large, high-sided skillet (or a wide soup pot), heat 2 tablespoons of the oil over medium-high heat. Add the chicken and brown until golden, 3 to 4 minutes per side, working in two batches if needed to not overcrowd the pan. Transfer the chicken to a plate, then add the remaining ½ cup oil to the skillet, heat for 2 minutes, carefully add the tomato paste and the remaining 2 teaspoons salt, and cook, stirring often, until the tomato paste caramelizes slightly, 1 to 2 minutes. Add the onions and garlic and cook, uncovered, stirring often and reducing the heat as needed, until the mixture thickens, becomes jammy and caramelized, and has reduced by about half, 35 to 40 minutes. Add the curry powder, cumin, and red pepper flakes and cook, stirring frequently, until fragrant, 3 to 4 minutes. Add the water, bring to a boil, then reduce the heat to medium-low and simmer for 2 to 3 minutes.

3. Transfer the mixture to the food processor and process until smooth, 15 to 20 seconds, then return the sauce to the pan. Cut the cooled chicken into 2-inch chunks, add it to the skillet along with any juices, bring to a boil, then reduce the heat to medium-low and cook, stirring occasionally, until the chicken is cooked through and the sauce thickens, another 7 to 8 minutes. Season with more salt and black pepper to taste. Serve with rice and chutney.

CHUTNEY

Makes 1 cup

Active Time: 5 minutes

Total Time: 5 minutes

3 cups packed fresh parsley leaves and tender stems

3 cups packed fresh cilantro leaves and tender stems

3 tablespoons vegetable oil

1 teaspoon kosher salt, plus more to taste

½ teaspoon ground cumin

1 jalapeño, chopped, with seeds

½ cup freshly squeezed lemon juice (from 2 or 3 large lemons)

Pinch of sugar

In a blender or the bowl of a food processor, place the parsley, cilantro, oil, salt, cumin, jalapeño, lemon juice, and sugar and process until smooth, 20 to 25 seconds. Season with additional salt to taste. Refrigerate in a sealed container for up to 1 week.

SWEET & NUTTY SHABBAT RICE

Makes 5½ cups

Active Time: 20 minutes

Total Time: 40 minutes

1½ cups basmati rice

1 teaspoon cumin seeds

¼ cup vegetable oil

½ cup whole cashews

1 large onion, thinly sliced

1 teaspoon ground turmeric

1 bay leaf

1 teaspoon kosher salt

2¼ cups water

½ cup chopped dried apricots

½ cup thinly sliced scallion greens

1. Rinse the rice in a colander until the water runs clear, 1 minute; drain. Heat a large, dry saucepan over medium-high heat. Add the cumin seeds and cook until fragrant and one or two seeds pop, 1 to 2 minutes. Transfer to a small bowl, then add the oil and cashews to the pot and cook, stirring, until toasted and lightly golden, 2 to 3 minutes.

2. Use a slotted spoon to transfer the cashews to another small bowl, then add the onions to the pot and cook, stirring occasionally, until lightly golden, 8 to 9 minutes. Add the rice along with the cumin seeds, turmeric, bay leaf, and salt, stir, and cook until the rice is glossy, 1 minute. Add the water, bring to a boil, cover, reduce the heat to low, and simmer until the rice is tender and fluffy, 16 to 17 minutes. Remove from the heat, uncover, remove and discard the bay leaf, and fluff the rice. Stir in most of the apricots and scallions, transfer the rice to a serving platter, and top with the cashews, the reserved apricots, and more scallions.

CHICKEN THIGHS
with Roasted Figs & Grapes

Figs and grapes—two of the seven ancient species associated with the land of Israel—are romanticized in ancient Jewish texts that I learned in school growing up. In the Song of Songs, also known as the Song of Solomon, a seductive verse reads: "The fig tree forms its early fruit; the blossoming vines spread their fragrance. Arise, come, my darling; my beautiful one, come with me." I invite you to make this luscious recipe, which harnesses the sweetness of both fruits by roasting them in the skillet with the chicken.

Serves 6

Active Time:
15 minutes

Total Time:
45 minutes

¾ cup chicken broth

1 tablespoon cornstarch

2 tablespoons grainy Dijon mustard

2 tablespoons silan (date syrup)

1 tablespoon honey

1 tablespoon freshly squeezed lemon juice

1 teaspoon kosher salt, plus more for seasoning the chicken

¼ teaspoon freshly ground black pepper

¼ teaspoon chili flakes

6 bone-in, skin-on chicken thighs (2¼ pounds), patted dry

2 tablespoons olive oil

2 small onions, each cut into 8 wedges

¼ cup white wine

6 large or 8 medium whole figs

½ pound red grapes

6 thyme sprigs, plus chopped thyme for garnish

1. Arrange a rack 6 inches from the broiler. Preheat the oven to 400°F. In a bowl, whisk the chicken broth and cornstarch until dissolved, then whisk in the mustard, silan, honey, lemon juice, salt, pepper, and chili flakes.

2. Season the chicken generously with salt. Heat the oil in a large (12-inch) heavy skillet over medium-high heat. Add the chicken, skin side down, and brown until chicken skin is crisp and rendered, 5 minutes. Flip and cook 1 additional minute. Remove to a plate and cover with foil.

3. Add the onions to skillet and brown until undersides are golden, 2 to 3 minutes. Flip and cook 1 additional minute. Remove to the plate with the chicken. Add the wine to the skillet and cook, stirring and scraping up the bits from the pan, until wine reduces by half, 2 minutes. Add the broth mixture, bring to a boil, reduce heat to medium, and cook until mixture thickens and reduces slightly, 3 to 4 minutes. Return chicken and onions to the pan; nestle figs and grapes among the chicken pieces. Scatter the thyme sprigs around the skillet, spoon some of the sauce over the chicken, cover with foil, and cook until sauce begins to thicken and the figs and grapes begin to soften, 20 minutes. Remove the chicken from the oven, uncover, and raise temperature to 425°F. Spoon sauce from the pan on top of chicken, return to oven, and roast until figs and grapes are slightly caramelized and chicken skin is crisped and deep mahogany in color, 15 minutes. Season with more salt and pepper to taste; garnish with chopped thyme.

ROAST CHICKEN OVER SCALLOPED POTATOES

This chicken becomes guest-worthy with the additions of roasted garlic paste (don't worry, there's a swap-in) and a bed of thinly sliced potatoes. The potatoes that rest directly under the chicken get soft and tender, while the concentric layers on the outside crisp up, veering pretty close to potato chip territory. It's a choose-your-own experience dinner that pleases all of the people, all of the time. If you have time, let the chicken chill, uncovered, in the fridge for at least 4 hours and up to 24 hours and remove 30 minutes before roasting; this deepens the flavors. I like to carve the chicken right in the roasting pan so every last bit of the juices melds with the potatoes.

Serves 4 to 6

Active Time:
30 minutes

Total Time:
1 hour 45 minutes

⅓ cup Garlic Confit cloves (recipe follows), or 7 large garlic cloves*

6 tablespoons Garlic Confit oil (recipe follows) or olive oil

2 tablespoons finely grated lemon zest (from 4 lemons)

2 tablespoons finely chopped fresh thyme leaves or 1 tablespoon dried

4 teaspoons kosher salt

1 teaspoon paprika

1 teaspoon freshly ground black pepper

1¼ pounds (3 medium or 2 large) Idaho or Russet potatoes, scrubbed

One 4-pound whole chicken

1. In a bowl, combine the garlic cloves, 2 tablespoons of the oil, the lemon zest, thyme, 3 teaspoons of the salt, the paprika, and ½ teaspoon of the pepper and use a fork to mash them into a paste. Using your hands, loosen the skin of the breasts, thighs, and legs of the chicken, leaving it attached to the bird. Scoop a tablespoon of the garlic paste onto your fingers and rub it inside the cavity of the chicken. Flip the chicken and rub about half of the remaining paste under the chicken skin. Then rub the remaining paste all over the outside of the chicken, including the wings, so it's evenly coated. Chill for 4 hours and up to 24 hours, if desired.

2. Preheat the oven to 375°F. Use a mandoline or a sharp knife to slice the potatoes as thinly as possible (I aim for ⅛ inch thick, or 8 stacked slices per inch). Pat the sliced potatoes dry with a clean kitchen towel, then toss them in a large bowl with

RECIPE CONTINUES

the remaining 4 tablespoons oil, 1 teaspoon salt, and ½ teaspoon pepper.

3. Layer the potatoes in an overlapping concentric pattern all over the bottom of a large round or rectangular baking dish or small roasting pan (anywhere between 10 × 14 and 12 × 16 inches is good; a little bigger is better!), then arrange the chicken on top, breast side down (this keeps the chicken juicy). Roast until the potatoes surrounding the chicken are crisped, the chicken skin is golden, and a thermometer inserted into the thigh registers 165°F, 1 hour 15 minutes. Cool slightly, then carve the chicken and serve with the potatoes and any juices.

*If you're using fresh garlic instead of the confit, mince 7 garlic cloves on a cutting board and sprinkle 1 tablespoon kosher salt on top of the garlic. Place the heel of your hand on the upper portion of a large chef's knife and apply pressure, moving the garlic and salt around to form a paste; this will take about 30 seconds.

GARLIC CONFIT

Makes 1 cup each roasted garlic cloves and roasted garlic oil (recipe can be halved)
Active Time: 1 minute
Total Time: 50 minutes

2 cups (35 to 40) peeled garlic cloves

1 fresh thyme sprig

1½ cups extra-virgin olive oil

Preheat the oven to 250°F. Place the garlic cloves and the thyme in a small (½ to 1 quart) ceramic or metal ovenproof dish. Pour the olive oil over the garlic; it should just cover the cloves. Cover the dish tightly with foil and bake until the cloves are lightly golden and totally soft but not caramelized or dark brown, 50 to 55 minutes; cool completely. Refrigerated in an airtight container, confit and oil will keep for up to 2 weeks.

CIDER-BRAISED APPLE & JERUSALEM ARTICHOKE CHICKEN

While I was visiting Chen Koren's house for Shabbat preparations (see page 270), she made a delicious chicken with deep-fried sunchokes, also known as Jerusalem artichokes. I've adapted the recipe here by adding three apple elements—apple cider, cider vinegar, and apples themselves—for a sweet-tangy autumn-friendly Shabbat delicacy. Many people think Jerusalem artichokes have some sort of connection to the holy city, but surprisingly they don't. In fact, they're not artichokes at all. They're a member of the sunflower family, and in Italian the word for "sunflower" is *girasole*, which someone at some point mistook for *Jerusalem*. Thus a culinary misunderstanding—albeit a delicious one—was born. Instead of frying the artichokes as Chen did, I microwave the earthy, nutty, mildly sweet chokes first so they cook at the same pace as the apples. The sauce reduces as the dish finishes in the oven, thickening to perfection—and ideal for mopping up with slices of challah.

Serves 4

Active Time:
35 minutes

Total Time:
1 hour 25 minutes

---

1 pound Jerusalem artichokes, peeled and cut into ¼-inch pieces, or fingerling potatoes, halved lengthwise (or quartered if large)

1 tablespoon cornstarch

1½ cups low-sodium chicken broth

¾ cup apple juice or cider

3 tablespoons apple cider vinegar

1 tablespoon honey

1½ tablespoons Dijon mustard

2 teaspoons kosher salt

One 3½-pound chicken, skin on, cut into 8 pieces, patted dry

2 tablespoons olive oil

2 medium onions (¾ pound), each cut into 12 wedges

3 tablespoons very thinly sliced fresh sage, plus more for garnish

4 garlic cloves, thinly sliced

1 tablespoon finely minced fresh hot chili pepper

2 small apples, cored and cut into 8 wedges each

RECIPE CONTINUES

Preheat the oven to 400°F. In a microwave-safe bowl with a tight-fitting lid, place the Jerusalem artichokes and add 1 inch of water. Seal it tightly with the lid and microwave until the artichokes are cooked but still firm, 7 minutes. Remove, uncover, and drain the artichokes. In a medium bowl, whisk the cornstarch with a few tablespoons of the broth to dissolve, then whisk in the rest of the broth with the apple juice, vinegar, honey, mustard, and 1 teaspoon of the salt. Season the chicken on both sides with the remaining 1 teaspoon salt. In the largest heavy skillet you have (ideally 12 inches, but 10 will do too), heat the oil over medium heat. Add the chicken, skin side down, and cook until the fat is rendered and the skin is golden and crisp, 4 to 5 minutes. Flip and cook until the underside is lightly golden, 3 to 4 minutes. Remove to a plate, leaving any rendered fat and juices in the pan. Add the onions and Jerusalem artichokes and cook, stirring, until the onions are lightly golden and the artichokes take on a little color, 6 to 7 minutes. Add the sage, garlic, and chili and cook, stirring, 1 to 2 more minutes. Whisk the reserved broth mixture to reblend, add it to the skillet with the artichokes, and bring to a boil over medium-high heat, then reduce the heat to medium-low and simmer until the liquid thickens, 5 to 8 minutes. Nestle the chicken, skin side up, and apples into the pan. Carefully transfer the skillet to the oven and roast until the apples and Jerusalem artichokes are softened, the chicken skin is crisped and deep golden, and the sauce has reduced by about half, 35 to 40 minutes. Garnish with more sage, then divide the chicken and sauce among plates.

SCHUG-A-CHURRI PARGIYOT
with Persimmon Avocado Salsa

I love a recipe twist, and this one allowed me to take two classics—Yemenite schug and mango-avocado salsa—and put my own spin on them. Schug is hot and intense, but by loosening it up and introducing elements of chimichurri—more herbs, some shallots, and a splash of vinegar—it transforms into a marinade or condiment with a multitude of uses. We keep a jar on hand at all times to spread on sandwiches, dollop on grilled meats, or stir into a dressing. This salsa channels all of the persimmon's most admirable qualities—its naturally warm-spiced flavor profile, juicy but firm texture, and gorgeous color—and allows them to make a more expected chicken topping shine brightly. The chicken is, of course, fabulous right off the grill but also wonderful at room temperature with jewel-like salsa and sauce served alongside.

Serves 4 to 6

Active Time:
20 minutes

**Total Time
(including marinating time):**
1 hour 20 minutes

FOR THE CHICKEN:

2 pounds skinless, boneless chicken thighs (about 6)

1⅓ cups Schug-a-churri (recipe follows)

Kosher salt, for seasoning

Freshly ground black pepper, for seasoning

FOR THE SALSA:

1 large avocado, peeled and cut into small dice (about 2 cups)

4 small or 2 large persimmons, cut into small dice (about 2 cups)*

1 cup cilantro leaves and tender stems, finely chopped

½ cup finely diced red onion

1 small red jalapeño, cut into thin rings

3 tablespoons fresh lime juice (from 2 small or 1 large lime), plus more to taste

1 tablespoon olive oil

¼ teaspoon kosher salt

1. Marinate the chicken: In a bowl or plastic zip-top bag, combine the chicken and ⅔ cup of the schug-a-churri and stir or smush to make sure the marinade covers all parts of the chicken. Marinate on the counter for at least 1 hour and up to 2, or in the fridge for up to 24 hours.

2. Make the salsa: In a bowl, combine the avocado, persimmons, cilantro, onions, jalapeño, lime juice, olive oil, and salt and gently toss; refrigerate until ready to use.

3. Grill the chicken: Heat a grill or grill pan over medium-high heat. Scrape as much of the marinade off the chicken as you can and grill the chicken until it is done but still juicy and deep

RECIPE CONTINUES

grill marks form, 4 to 5 minutes per side. Season the chicken with salt and pepper, arrange on a platter, and serve with the salsa and remaining ⅔ cup schug-a-churri.

*Pitted and diced firm mango is a great substitute for the persimmons.

SCHUG-A-CHURRI

Makes a scant 2 cups

Active Time: 15 minutes

Total Time: 15 minutes

Make the schug-a-churri in advance and store it in the refrigerator for up to 2 weeks.

6 garlic cloves

4 medium jalapeños, preferably red, coarsely chopped (seeded, if desired, for a milder result)

2 small or 1 medium shallot, halved if small, quartered if large

½ cup tightly packed fresh parsley, leaves and tender stems

½ cup tightly packed fresh cilantro, leaves and tender stems

1½ teaspoons fresh oregano or za'atar leaves, or ½ teaspoon dried

½ cup olive oil

1½ tablespoons red wine vinegar

Finely grated zest and juice from ½ small lemon (1 teaspoon zest and 1 tablespoon juice)

1 teaspoon ground cumin

1 teaspoon freshly ground black pepper

1 teaspoon kosher salt

In the bowl of a food processor, process the garlic until very finely minced, stopping the processor and scraping down the sides once if necessary, 15 to 20 seconds. Add the jalapeños and shallots and pulse until everything is minced, 30 pulses. Empty into a bowl, then place the parsley, cilantro, and oregano in the processor and pulse until finely chopped but not wet, 20 to 25 pulses. Add to the bowl along with the olive oil, vinegar, lemon zest and juice, cumin, black pepper, and salt and stir to combine.

ONE-SKILLET CHICKEN & HERBY RICE

Some people stash their clothing purchases or other guilty pleasures away, pulling them out of closets when no one else is looking. But when the object of my hoarding is fresh herbs, hiding them is less of an option—I've got to use them. What could be a better vehicle for all my leafy green friends than an oversized skillet filled with lemony, herby chicken and rice that you can bring right to the table? This herb puree is the elegant solution to flavoring all the elements here. By quartering the chicken and letting the rice cook around it, you have the ultimate one-skillet dinner that remains juicy and flavorful to the last bite.

Serves 4

Active Time:
30 minutes

Total Time:
1 hour 35 minutes

One 3½-pound chicken, patted dry, cut into quarters

1½ tablespoons kosher salt, plus more for seasoning

1½ teaspoons freshly ground black pepper, plus more for seasoning

6 cups packed mixed fresh green herb leaves, such as parsley, cilantro, basil, and oregano, rinsed and dried

Zest and juice of 2 lemons

15 garlic cloves

1 medium jalapeño, seeded if desired

⅔ cup plus 3 tablespoons olive oil

3¼ cups chicken broth, plus more as needed

2 cups basmati rice

1. Preheat the oven to 400°F. Season the chicken generously with salt and pepper.

2. In a 12-inch skillet, heat the 3 tablespoons oil over medium-high heat. Place the chicken, skin side down, in the skillet and cook, without moving it, until golden and crisp, 5 to 6 minutes. Carefully flip the chicken and sear for an additional 4 to 5 minutes.

3. In a blender or the bowl of a food processor, blend the herbs, lemon zest and juice, garlic, jalapeño, salt, and black pepper until almost smooth, 15 seconds. With the blender running, drizzle in the remaining ⅔ cup oil until creamy, another 15 seconds.

4. Remove and reserve ½ cup of the herb mixture from the blender. To the rest of the mixture in the blender or processor, add the broth and swirl to collect any bits of green mixture. Place the rice in a bowl and pour in the broth mixture. Give it a stir and pour it into the skillet around the chicken, swirling the rice with a spatula to distribute it evenly and adding an extra ¼ cup broth if needed. Transfer the skillet to the oven. Bake until the chicken is cooked through and the rice is crisped on top and the edges are golden, 40 minutes, cooking an additional 2 to 3 minutes if the rice needs it. Season with more salt and black pepper to taste, cut the chicken into pieces, and serve with the remaining herb mixture.

MY MOTHER'S SHABBAT CHICKEN

This is simplicity, memory, and taste combined in a baking dish. It was our Friday-night staple, the one my mother made almost weekly, but we never tired of. My father remembers it as having carrots along with the onions, and my sister remembers celery, but I remember just onions, and lots of them, which became schmaltzy as the chicken pieces roasted and released their juices right into the roasting pan. The drift of dried spices she sprinkled on top rarely varied: onion powder, garlic powder, paprika, salt, pepper. Together they create a delicious coating that is deceptively simple and incredibly hard to resist. Mix and match the seasonings to your liking, but this classic blend is the original winner, winner, chicken dinner.

Serves 4

Active Time:
10 minutes

Total Time:
1 hour

1 large onion, very thinly sliced (about 2 cups)

1 tablespoon olive oil

1¼ teaspoons kosher salt

½ teaspoon freshly ground black pepper

1 3½- to 4-pound chicken, cut into 8 pieces, patted dry

1 teaspoon onion powder, plus more to taste

1 teaspoon garlic powder, plus more to taste

¼ teaspoon cayenne pepper

1½ teaspoons paprika

Preheat the oven to 350°F. In a 9 × 13-inch baking dish, toss the onions with the oil and ¼ teaspoon each of the salt and black pepper and evenly spread out the onions on the bottom. Place the onions in the oven and bake until they begin to soften, 10 minutes. Remove the onions from the oven, place the chicken pieces, skin side up, on top of the onions, and sprinkle with the remaining 1 teaspoon salt and ¼ teaspoon black pepper. Sprinkle the onion powder, garlic powder, cayenne, and paprika on top (do the paprika last for a beautiful color). Bake until the chicken is cooked through and juicy and the onions are soft and golden, 45 to 50 minutes. When the chicken is cooked, raise the oven temperature to broil and broil just until the top darkens in color and the onions sizzle a bit, 2 to 3 minutes. Serve the chicken with the schmaltzy onions.

BREADED PEACH CHICKEN

This recipe was inspired by one I learned from my college roommate Aviva Karzen's wonderful mother, Judith, who used lemon pepper and canned cling peaches to the most delicious effect. I remember standing in Judith's kitchen in Chicago, picking at leftover bits in the pan as Judith cooed over us in her strong Chicago accent. I've updated the recipe with fresh stone fruit, bread crumbs, and a homemade marinade, but if canned is what you've got, use it; Judith Karzen would definitely approve, and so would her daughter (don't worry, I checked with her).

Serves 4 to 6

Active Time:
20 minutes

**Total Time
(including marinating time):**
1 hour 40 minutes

½ cup plus 2 teaspoons olive oil

2 tablespoons apple cider vinegar

1 teaspoon Dijon mustard

1 teaspoon sweet paprika

1 teaspoon dried parsley

1 teaspoon onion powder

1 teaspoon kosher salt, plus more for seasoning

1 teaspoon sugar

½ teaspoon dried oregano

⅛ teaspoon cayenne pepper

One 3½- to 4-pound chicken, cut into 8 pieces

1 egg

1 cup all-purpose flour

2½ cups panko bread crumbs

2 medium, ripe peaches, pitted and each cut into 8 or 10 wedges

⅓ cup peach nectar

Fresh basil leaves, for garnish

1. Grease a 9 × 13-inch (or slightly larger) baking dish or a rimmed baking sheet with the 2 teaspoons oil. In a bowl, whisk together the remaining ½ cup oil, the vinegar, mustard, paprika, parsley, onion powder, salt, sugar, oregano, and cayenne. Put the chicken in a large bowl, add 3 tablespoons of the marinade, toss to coat, and let rest on the counter for at least 30 minutes and up to 2 hours.

2. Meanwhile, in a wide, shallow bowl, whisk the egg with two generous pinches of salt. Place the flour in another shallow bowl with three generous pinches of salt. In a third wide, shallow bowl, combine the panko with 3 tablespoons of the dressing and mix, using clean hands to blend, until the crumbs darken in color. Preheat the oven to 400°F. Working one piece at a time, remove the chicken from the marinade and into the flour, shaking off the excess, then into the egg, shaking off the excess. Press both sides into the seasoned panko, applying pressure so it adheres.

3. Arrange the chicken pieces in the prepared baking dish, then scatter any leftover crumbs among the pieces of chicken. In a medium bowl, toss the peaches in the remaining dressing and pour the peaches and any liquid all over the chicken, distributing the peaches evenly. Using a tablespoon, drizzle the peach nectar onto the crumbs nestled between the chicken pieces to moisten them. Bake until the crumbs are crisp and the chicken is cooked through, 45 to 50 minutes. Serve the chicken pieces with the peaches and any extra crumbs from the bottom of the pan. Garnish with basil.

SHABBAT, JERUSALEM-STYLE

"I can't wait for Shabbat to begin," Chen Koren told me, tightening the decorative kerchief covering her head as we began to cook in her airy kitchen. "It's the only time I get to sleep, talk to my husband, and really relax." We had just come back from Jerusalem's Machane Yehuda market, where Koren serves as a sort of unofficial mayor, giving tours and shipping boxes filled with the best products from her culinary playground to every corner of the earth. Koren's husband, Alon, a social worker, soon came in with their four young children, who went to play while he stepped in to peel potatoes,

crush garlic, and generally help shepherd the meal preparation forward. Alon is not religious; Chen is. He is mellow; she is infused with crackling, extroverted energy.

"My parents were the same way," she told me of her upbringing on a kibbutz in southern Israel. "It works for us." Soon she was unwrapping fish steaks she had purchased at the shuk, whipping up a spicy, paprika-heavy sauce for chraimeh, a traditional red-sauced Friday-night fish dish she learned to make from her Libyan mother. As the fish cooked, we fried almonds to top hummus she'd bought at the shuk, along with a few other salatim, challah, and desserts. "Luckily, when you have the best nearby, you don't have to make everything from scratch," she told me. Within two hours we'd completed a chicken and fish dish, multiple salads, and several sides and moved on to setting the table for later. As she arranged the candles and things became quieter in the house, we could hear the city outside winding down as well. "Shabbat shalom," she told me as I headed back to Tel Aviv. "Next time you're staying for dinner."

MEATBALLS in Dried Fruit Sauce

Never have I ever loved a meatball recipe more. The sweet, savory, spicy sauce, the herb-forward meatballs, and the soft dried fruit bring this dish together. Meatballs are a Shabbat no-brainer, in part because they're such a crowd-pleaser and also because they reheat so incredibly well. Feel free to swap in the dried fruit of your choice and also to double the recipe and freeze half for another week; it's the gift that keeps on giving.

Serves 4 to 6

Active Time:
30 minutes

Total Time:
1 hour 30 minutes

FOR THE SAUCE:

¾ cup dried apricots, chopped

¼ cup dried cherries

¼ cup dried currants or raisins

2 cups very hot water

¼ cup plus
2 tablespoons olive oil, plus more for greasing your hands

1 jumbo onion, finely diced

4 garlic cloves, minced

3 tablespoons tomato paste

Two 14-ounce cans crushed tomatoes

2 teaspoons kosher salt

½ teaspoon ground cumin

½ teaspoon dried red pepper flakes

2 tablespoons freshly squeezed lemon juice

FOR THE MEATBALLS:

1 slice white bread, torn into small pieces

1 pound 80/20 ground beef

1 egg yolk

¼ cup finely minced fresh parsley

2 teaspoons kosher salt

½ teaspoon ground cumin

2 tablespoons olive oil

Cooked rice, for serving

1. Make the sauce: In a bowl, cover apricots, cherries, and currants with hot water; soak until fruit is soft, 20 minutes; drain, reserving liquid (you should have about 1 cup). While fruit is soaking, heat oil in a 4- or 5-quart Dutch oven over medium heat. Cook onions, stirring, until lightly golden, 8 to 9 minutes. Remove half the onions and garlic to a large bowl and reserve. To the other half of the Dutch oven, add tomato paste and cook, stirring frequently, until caramelized and darkened in color, 2 minutes. Add crushed tomatoes, dried fruit, 1 cup reserved soaking water, salt, cumin, and red pepper flakes. Bring to a boil over medium-high heat, reduce heat to medium-low, and simmer, stirring occasionally, until sauce thickens slightly, 14 to 15 minutes (if needed, add water to loosen sauce to your desired consistency). Reduce heat to lowest setting, stir in 1 tablespoon lemon juice, and cover to keep warm.

2. Make the meatballs: In a small bowl, moisten bread with 2 tablespoons water. Let sit for 5 minutes, then squeeze out excess water. Add bread to the bowl with the reserved onion and garlic mixture along with meat, egg, parsley, salt, and cumin. Gently mix until incorporated.

3. Grease clean hands with a bit of olive oil (or water). Use 1½ to 2 tablespoons meat mixture at a time to form 20 walnut-sized meatballs.

4. Gently lower meatballs into the sauce, raise heat to medium-high, bring to a boil, then reduce heat to medium-low and simmer until meatballs are cooked through, 20 to 25 minutes. Stir in remaining 1 tablespoon lemon juice and season with salt and pepper to taste. Divide among bowls and serve with rice.

CAROL'S MEAT-STUFFED SICILIAN ARTICHOKES

As a kid in Palo Alto, I was a frequent visitor at the home of my friend Jessica Saal, a bright, funny classmate who tragically died from juvenile rheumatoid arthritis at the age of thirty-four. Jessica was great in her own right, but she had the added benefit of cool parents: Harry, a physicist-turned-start-up-guy, and Carol, who was sharp, witty, and a great cook who always felt more like a friend than someone's mom. Carol converted to Judaism before marrying Harry in 1968 and excelled in her adopted culinary canon of kugels, matzo ball soup, and bagel brunches. But she always remained fiercely proud of her Italian-American heritage, especially the recipes passed down by generations of Neapolitan women to her mother, Edith D'Esopo, who cooked them all throughout Carol's childhood in Hartford, Connecticut.

"My mother made things that, to this day, I still have not seen anywhere else," Carol told me. That included Christmas cookies fragrant with cloves, coffee, and chocolate; home-cured, fennel-laced sausages cut up and suspended in olive oil; and these delicious artichokes, which I once tasted at the Saals' home and never forgot. "I find many artichoke dishes aren't cooked enough, so give them a generous amount of time," Carol advised. The highly seasoned beef mixture adheres to the already meaty flesh on the artichoke leaves, making this a doubly indulgent delicacy. I love eating them cold from the fridge as well, squeezed with a little extra lemon juice.

Serves 4

Active Time:
40 minutes

Total Time:
2 hours

---

6 medium or 4 large artichokes

3 tablespoons freshly squeezed lemon juice

2 slices white bread

½ cup plus 1 tablespoon water

1 large egg plus 1 large egg yolk

¼ cup chopped fresh parsley, plus more for garnish

1 tablespoon finely chopped fresh za'atar leaves, 1½ teaspoons za'atar spice blend, or 1 tablespoon finely chopped fresh oregano

4 garlic cloves, finely minced

1 tablespoon plus ¼ teaspoon kosher salt

½ teaspoon freshly ground black pepper, plus more to taste

2½ tablespoons olive oil

2 teaspoons ground fennel

1 teaspoon dried red pepper flakes

1¼ pounds 80/20 ground beef

1 medium onion, cut into 8 wedges

1 medium potato, cut into chunks

¾ cup chicken broth

¾ cup white wine

½ cup water

1 bay leaf

RECIPE CONTINUES

1. Peel off any dry or dead-looking leaves from the artichokes, then use kitchen shears to trim off about ¼ inch of the thorny tips from the leaves. If there is a small, uneven stem jutting out of the bottom, trim it off and discard it; the artichokes should be able to sit upright in the pot. Spread the leaves as far as you can without breaking them, place the artichokes in a large bowl, cover with cold water, then add the lemon juice and let them soak while you prepare the meat.

2. Pulse the bread in the bowl of a food processor until crumbs form (you should have about 1 cup). In a large bowl, place ½ cup of the crumbs and moisten them with 1 tablespoon of the water, then add the egg, egg yolk, parsley, za'atar, garlic, 1 tablespoon of the salt, the black pepper, 1 tablespoon of the olive oil, the fennel, and red pepper flakes and mix to combine. Gently fold in the ground beef until incorporated.

3. Drain the artichokes and dry them well (a salad spinner works great for this). Using your fingers and 2 teaspoons of the meat mixture at a time, stuff the meat between the artichoke leaves, pressing it into the leaves. (Don't worry if you don't get every leaf, if some of the meat spills out of the artichokes, or if it doesn't look perfectly uniform.)

4. Place the artichokes in a pot that fits all of the artichokes in a neat single layer and fit the onions and potato chunks in between the artichokes to stabilize them.

5. Add the broth, wine, water, ½ tablespoon olive oil, and the bay leaf to the pot. Bring to a boil, cover, reduce the heat to medium-low, and cook until a leaf pulls easily off the artichokes, 45 to 55 minutes. Remove from the oven and preheat the broiler.

6. Toss the remaining ½ cup bread crumbs with the remaining 1 tablespoon olive oil and ¼ teaspoon salt and black pepper to taste. Uncover the artichokes, sprinkle the bread crumbs on top, and broil until the crumbs are golden, 3 to 4 minutes. Garnish with chopped parsley.

7. Serve one artichoke per person along with some potatoes and onions. To eat, pluck off the petals along with some stuffing, and scrape through your teeth to remove the soft flesh at the base of each. Discard the remaining leaf. Once all the petals are removed, you'll expose the fuzzy choke at the center, which should be discarded. Enjoy the remaining heart of the artichoke dipped in some of the braising liquid left at the bottom of the pot.

FIG & POMEGRANATE BRISKET

Considered one of the crown jewels of Shabbat and holiday cooking, brisket has decidedly humble beginnings. Inexpensive due to its toughness and originally considered a throwaway cut, brisket became a staple of cold-weather Eastern European Jewish cooking when farmers realized it was less expensive to butcher a cow than to feed it all winter long. Home cooks became experts at slow-cooking brisket to tender perfection, adding onions and often a tomato-based liquid to coax out the meat's flavor and ideal texture. Aside from my mother's recipe (see page 283), this is the version I find myself making the most. Tons of garlic and onions, white wine, and two types each of figs (fresh and dried) and pomegranate (molasses and fresh seeds) come together for a finished brisket that is simultaneously homey and elegant. Brisket is always better served the next day; if you have time, cool the whole cut in its braising liquid, then slice it against the grain and rewarm gently in the sauce.

Serves 8 to 10

Active Time:
1 hour

**Total Time
(including chilling time):**
13 hours

One 5-pound brisket with a good amount of fat

1 tablespoon plus 1 teaspoon kosher salt, plus more for seasoning

1½ teaspoons freshly ground black pepper, plus more for seasoning

¼ cup vegetable oil

3 large onions, thinly sliced (6 cups)

2 tablespoons all-purpose or gluten-free flour

10 garlic cloves, peeled and left whole

2 tablespoons tomato paste

2 cups dry white wine

1½ cups beef or chicken broth

⅓ cup pomegranate molasses

4 dried figs, chopped

¼ cup honey

1½ teaspoons red wine vinegar

1 tablespoon ground cumin

1 teaspoon dried red pepper flakes

6 fresh figs,* quartered

½ cup pomegranate seeds

Mint leaves, for garnish

1. Preheat the oven to 300°F.

2. Arrange the brisket on a large plate and season it generously on all sides with 1 tablespoon of the salt and 1 teaspoon of the black pepper. In a large, heavy Dutch oven, heat the oil over medium-high heat until very hot but not smoking. Add the brisket (fattier side down, if there is one) and sear until deeply browned and crisped in parts, 6 to 7 minutes. Carefully flip the brisket and sear another 6 minutes, then, if they're thick enough, sear each of the narrow sides, standing up the brisket, if possible, 3 minutes per side. Remove to a plate, leaving any fat and juices in the pan.

RECIPE CONTINUES

3. Add the onions and flour and cook, stirring occasionally, until the flour is absorbed, 1 minute, then add the garlic and tomato paste and cook, stirring occasionally, until the onions begin to soften, 5 minutes. Add the wine, raise the heat to high, bring to a boil, then turn down the heat and simmer until the wine reduces by half, 4 to 5 minutes. Add the broth, pomegranate molasses, dried figs, honey, vinegar, cumin, red pepper flakes, and the remaining 1 teaspoon salt and ½ teaspoon black pepper.

4. Bring to a boil over high heat, then reduce the heat to a simmer and gently lower the brisket back into the roasting pan, spooning some of the sauce and onions over the brisket. Cover the brisket with a piece of parchment paper (this will prevent the acid in the sauce from interacting with the foil), seal the roasting pan tightly with foil, and cook in the oven until the brisket is tender, 4 hours to 4 hours 30 minutes. Remove from the oven, unseal slightly, then let the brisket come to room temperature, about 1 hour.

5. If you have time, refrigerate the brisket overnight, then uncover it and remove and discard the congealed fat. Remove the brisket from the sauce and slice it against the grain into ¼-inch-thick slices. Heat the sauce in the roasting pan or another pot over medium-high heat, until boiling. Lower the heat and simmer until the sauce thickens to your liking, 10 to 15 minutes. Nestle the sliced brisket back in the sauce, cover with foil, and warm gently in a 200°F oven until everything is heated through, 45 minutes to 1 hour.

6. To serve, transfer the brisket and sauce to a platter, season with salt and black pepper, and garnish with the fresh figs, pomegranate seeds, and mint leaves.

*If you can't find fresh figs, garnish with more pomegranate seeds.

ALGERIAN MEATBALLS

During their childhood in Bucks County, Pennsylvania, Alex and Rebecca Mandel's French-Algerian mother, Roxane, pulled out all the stops for their Shabbat dinners. "The silver, the tablecloth, the beautiful glasses, they were all laid out in a room we only used for Shabbat," said Alex, a friend and neighbor of mine in Tel Aviv. Alex and Rebecca's father, Don, passed away suddenly in 2018, and the pain of loss is still palpable among the Mandel women. Don was Ashkenazi, but he loved Roxane's Algerian-Jewish dishes, letting them take center stage.

"Those are some of the best memories we have, just the four of us, eating that food," said Alex. Last summer, when Rebecca was visiting Tel Aviv from the Bay Area, we arranged a Zoom cooking session with Roxane so she could take us through her famously tender, juicy Shabbat boulettes (meatballs) and I could hear some of her stories. "Ma, how many eggs?" asked Alex, as Rebecca minced onions and I adjusted the camera so Roxane could supervise our every move.

Over the next few hours I learned about Roxane's enchanted childhood in Algiers, living close to the Mediterranean Sea and drying off with monogrammed towels brought home from her father's textile factory. The Jewish community remained relatively protected from discrimination until Algerian independence from the French in 1962, but when the situation worsened in the late 1960s, Roxane's parents, Simon and Marthe Bedjai, helped many people move to Israel or Paris. Simon died in Algiers in 1970, and Marthe, whom everyone now calls Grandmie, sold the family business, agreeing to pay a government official a 60 percent "commission" to leave with some of their assets.

Today, Grandmie is ninety-nine and lives in Paris. When she visited the Mandels in Bucks County, she'd hand-roll couscous and delicate meat-filled bestel pastries, her voice and laughter infusing the house with warmth. These meatballs are incredibly light and juicy, thanks to the addition of mashed potatoes, and are simmered in a tomatoey, generously spiced sauce that the family holds sacred.

Serves 6 to 8

Active Time:
1 hour 15 minutes

**Total Time
(including chilling time):**
2 hours 45 minutes

RECIPE AND INGREDIENTS CONTINUE

FOR THE MEATBALLS:

1 medium russet potato
(8 ounces), peeled and
quartered

1 pound ground turkey,
preferably a mix of light
and dark meat

1 small onion,
finely minced (1½ cups)

1 cup finely chopped
fresh parsley

2 teaspoons ground
cumin

2 teaspoons paprika

2 teaspoons garlic
powder

2 teaspoons ground
caraway

2 teaspoons ground
coriander

1 teaspoon ground
fennel

2 teaspoons kosher salt

½ teaspoon freshly
ground black pepper

FOR THE SAUCE:

¼ cup olive oil

2 jumbo onions,
finely diced (5½ cups)

2 tablespoons tomato
paste

3 pounds tomatoes,
peeled and cut into
½-inch cubes
(5½ cups cubed), or
three 14-ounce cans
diced tomatoes in juice

½ cup chopped fresh
cilantro

1½ teaspoons kosher salt

2 teaspoons ground
cinnamon

1 teaspoon sugar

2 bay leaves

2 chicken bouillon
cubes, crumbled

1¼ cups water, plus more
as needed

One 14-ounce can
chickpeas, drained and
rinsed

One 14-ounce can
artichoke bottoms or
hearts, drained and
quartered

**FOR FRYING AND
FINISHING:**

⅓ cup olive oil

Cooked rice, for serving

Chopped fresh mint,
for garnish

1. Make the meatballs: In a small saucepan, cover the chopped potato with 2 inches of cold water, bring to a boil, reduce the heat to medium, and simmer until tender, 16 to 17 minutes. Drain, cool slightly, transfer to a large bowl, and mash. Add the turkey, onion, parsley, cumin, paprika, garlic powder, caraway, coriander, fennel, salt, and pepper. Using your hands, gently combine everything, cover, and refrigerate at least 1 hour 30 minutes and up to 24 hours.

2. Make the sauce: In a very large, high-sided saucepan or soup pot, heat the oil over medium heat. Add the onions and cook, stirring occasionally, until lightly golden, 8 to 9 minutes. Add the tomato paste and cook 1 more minute, then add the tomatoes, cilantro, salt, cinnamon, sugar, bay leaves, and bouillon, bring to a boil, reduce the heat to a simmer, and cook, stirring occasionally, until the sauce thickens and reduces, 15 to 20 minutes. Add the water, chickpeas, and artichokes, bring the mixture back to a simmer, and continue to simmer over low heat while you fry the meatballs.

3. Fry the meatballs and finish the dish: Using lightly moistened hands, form the meat mixture into 27 or 28 walnut-sized balls and arrange them on a baking sheet. In a large skillet, heat the oil over medium-low heat. Working in batches if necessary to avoid overcrowding the pan, brown the meatballs, turning them often, until golden brown on all sides, 5 to 6 minutes total. Add the meatballs to the sauce, move them around gently to cover with the sauce, and simmer until the sauce thickens further, 15 to 20 minutes. Serve with cooked rice and garnish with mint.

STEFFI'S BRISKET

When she met my father on a blind date in 1961, my mother knew extremely little about kosher cooking—or cooking at all. Her mother, my grandmother Anne, was a child of the Great Depression who had been yanked out of school at age twelve to cook and clean for older siblings, assorted spouses, and other relatives all crammed into one house to save money. So by the time she got married, my grandmother approached cooking like an odious chore, an outlook she passed along to her children. Add to that the fact that my mother grew up with little connection to kosher or Jewish cooking; her annual birthday treat was a lobster dinner at a Queens restaurant called Perry Winkle's. So when she married my father at age twenty, she was starting from square one. She mastered brisket early and made it often, sticking closely to the classic Jewish formula of a tomatoey base, a little sweetness, and ample cooking time to tenderize the meat. When we had special Shabbat guests, this was the dish of choice, and it still is for me. I can make it virtually from muscle memory, and I have added a few touches of my own: red wine and red wine vinegar for acidity to cut through the richness.

Serves 8 to 10

Active Time:
30 minutes

**Total Time
(if serving immediately):**
5 hours 30 minutes

**Total Time
(if cooling and reheating):**
11 hours

One 5-pound brisket*
with a good amount of
fat

2 tablespoons kosher
salt, plus more to taste

1½ teaspoons freshly
ground black pepper,
plus more to taste

2 tablespoons neutral oil

6 medium carrots
(1¼ to 1½ pounds),
peeled and halved
crosswise

1¼ pounds onions
(3 medium), sliced

5 large garlic cloves,
smashed

3 tablespoons tomato
paste

2 tablespoons
all-purpose flour

1 cup dry red wine

2 cups beef broth

Two 14-ounce cans
crushed tomatoes

3 tablespoons dark
brown sugar

2 tablespoons red wine
vinegar

5 fresh herb sprigs of
your choice

2 bay leaves

6 small red or Yukon
Gold potatoes
(1¼ pounds)

1. Arrange the brisket on a large plate and season it generously on all sides with 1 tablespoon of the salt and 1 teaspoon of the pepper. In a large, heavy Dutch oven, heat the oil over medium-high heat until very hot but not smoking. Add the brisket (fattier side down, if there is one) and sear until deeply browned and crisped in parts, 6 to 7 minutes. Carefully flip the brisket and sear another 6 minutes, then, if they're thick enough, sear each of the narrow sides, standing up the brisket if possible, 3 minutes per side.

2. Arrange a rack somewhere between the center and lower third of the oven (you're making sure your covered pot will fit). Preheat the oven to 300°F. Remove the brisket to a rimmed baking sheet. Reduce the heat to medium-low, then add

RECIPE CONTINUES

the carrots to the oil in the pot and sear, turning, until they begin to brown, 5 to 6 minutes total. Transfer them to the baking sheet with the brisket. Add the onions and garlic to the pot and cook, stirring occasionally, until the onions soften but don't caramelize, 6 to 7 minutes. Add the tomato paste and cook, stirring, until absorbed, 2 minutes. Add the flour and cook, stirring, until absorbed, 1 more minute. Add the wine, bring to a boil over medium-high heat, and cook until most of the wine has evaporated, 2 to 3 minutes. Add the beef broth, tomatoes, brown sugar, vinegar, the remaining tablespoon salt and ½ teaspoon pepper, the herbs, and bay leaves. Bring to a boil over high heat, reduce the heat to low, and simmer until the sauce thickens a bit, 15 minutes.

3. Return the brisket and any accumulated juices to the pot, nestle the carrots and potatoes alongside the brisket, then spoon some of the sauce over the top, cover with a layer of parchment (this will prevent the acid in the sauce from interacting with the foil), seal with a layer of foil, and cook until the brisket is very tender, 5 to 5½ hours. Remove from the oven, uncover, cool at room temperature at least 1 hour, then re-cover and refrigerate for at least 5 hours and up to 24, if possible.

4. To serve, remove the brisket from the sauce to a cutting board, then remove and discard any hardened fat from the sauce and scrape any off the brisket. Warm the sauce slightly over medium-low heat, adding a few tablespoons of water to loosen it if the sauce is too thick. Remove and discard the bay leaves and any other stray herbs. Slice the brisket against the grain to your desired thickness, then nestle it back in the sauce in the pot, cover, and gently warm it in a 300°F oven for 15 to 20 minutes or on the stovetop over medium-low heat for 10 to 15 minutes. Season with salt and pepper to taste.

*Brisket is often sold as first-cut, which indicates a more premium, less fatty cut of meat, and second-cut or deckel, which contains more fat. I used a first-cut brisket here because I wanted to be able to get clean slices from the finished meat. But there is no denying the deliciousness of a second cut of brisket, meltingly rich and falling apart in the sauce. Both will work beautifully here.

NONNA'S WARM-SPICED LAMB & RICE

I arrived at Nelly Blanga's home in Herlizya, a stone's throw from Tel Aviv, just as three of her granddaughters—sisters Melissa, Sabrina, and Alessia Zeloof—descended from all directions, parking, hopping out of their cars, and hugging one another. "We've been trying to get her to cook with us for ages," Melissa told me. "Now we'll have the recipe for Nonna's lamb and rice." I had met Melissa a few months earlier at the cheese shop we both frequent in the Carmel Market, and within minutes we were talking about food, recipes, and her nonna Nelly. "She is an incredible cook," Melissa told me. Here I was, ready to meet her myself.

Nelly greeted us at the door, turquoise earrings dangling, hair elegantly coiffed, eyebrows etched to a level of precision I could only dream of. To the left of a spacious living room decorated with art and figurines sat the kitchen, with wraparound countertops looking out through picture windows at Nelly's well-tended garden. Almost all of Nelly's family lives within a mile radius of her home, where they gather for Shabbat and holiday meals to revel in her cooking and simply celebrate being together.

Nelly was born in the coastal Lebanese city of Sidon in 1941, and her family escaped to Beirut in 1948, after the founding of the state of Israel (today there are perhaps thirty Jews left in Lebanon). After marrying her husband, David, in 1962, they moved to Israel, then Milan, where David had a successful leather goods business. The Blangas followed their married daughters to London, eventually moving once more to Israel when their children settled there. Many memories—some edible—reflect her youth in the Levant (the countries bordering northern Israel, including Lebanon and Syria), and when the family gathers, she often makes this fall-off-the-bone lamb and its accompanying rice using a decidedly Levantine baharat-adjacent spice blend she grinds herself. The tender meat, combined with the rice rendered slightly sweet from the onions and spices, makes for an incredibly satisfying meal.

Serves 6 to 8

Active Time:
45 minutes

**Total Time
(including minimum
marinating time):**
12 hours

RECIPE AND INGREDIENTS CONTINUE

One 5- to 6-pound bone-in lamb shoulder, or 3½ to 4 pounds boneless lamb shoulder

¾ cup olive oil

9 garlic cloves, minced (3 tablespoons), plus 3 whole cloves, halved

4 tablespoons Nonna's Warm-Spice Blend (recipe follows) or Baharat Spice Blend (page 14 or store-bought)

3 tablespoons kosher salt, plus more to taste

3 tablespoons finely chopped fresh rosemary, plus 4 sprigs

½ cup whole almonds, roughly chopped

2 large onions, diced

2½ cups jasmine or basmati rice

3¾ cups water

½ teaspoon freshly ground black pepper, plus more as needed

½ cup finely chopped fresh parsley, plus more for garnish

1. Arrange the lamb in a large 9 × 13-inch roasting pan. In a bowl, combine ¼ cup of the olive oil with the minced garlic, 2 tablespoons each of the spice blend and the salt, and the chopped rosemary. Rub it all over the lamb. Nestle the rosemary sprigs in the roasting pan, cover with a layer of parchment, then seal tightly with aluminum foil and refrigerate at least 6 hours and up to 24 hours.

2. Arrange a rack in the center of the oven and another beneath it. Preheat the oven to 400°F. Still covered with foil, roast the lamb for 1 hour, then reduce the oven temperature to 300°F and continue to roast until the lamb is fork-tender, another 4 hours for boneless and 5 hours for bone-in.

3. During the last 15 minutes of cooking, arrange the almonds on a small rimmed baking sheet, place it on the oven rack below the lamb, and bake until the almonds are golden and fragrant, 15 minutes. Remove the almonds and lamb from the oven. Cool the almonds completely and let the lamb cool, covered, for 10 minutes before transferring it to a cutting board. Keep the lamb covered.

4. In a large (at least 4-quart) saucepan, heat the remaining ½ cup olive oil over medium-high heat. Add the onions, halved garlic cloves, and ½ teaspoon of the salt to the oil and cook, stirring occasionally, until golden and slightly caramelized, 20 minutes.

5. While the onions are cooking, place the rice in a colander and rinse it under cold water until the water runs clear, 2 minutes. Let the rice drain well. Once the onions are caramelized, add the rice to the pot along with the remaining 2 tablespoons spice blend and 2½ teaspoons salt, and stir to coat. Lower the heat to very low, and cook the rice without water, stirring every minute or two, for 10 minutes. Add the water, bring to a boil, reduce the heat to a simmer, cover, and cook until the rice is tender, 15 to 16 minutes. Let the rice rest, covered, for 10 minutes, then stir in the pepper and parsley and season with more salt to taste.

6. Uncover the meat, discard the rosemary, transfer as much liquid as possible into a degreasing cup or measuring cup, and skim off as much fat as you can (you can also freeze the liquid for 2 hours, then skim and remove the fat and reheat the pan juices).

7. Using your hands or two forks, pull the meat into large (1- to 2-inch) chunks. Return the meat to the pan with the juices and season with salt and pepper. Mound the rice onto a platter and top with the meat and the almonds. Garnish with more chopped parsley.

NONNA'S WARM-SPICE BLEND

Makes about 1 cup (save extra for other uses)
Active Time: 5 minutes
Total Time: 5 minutes

¼ cup ground allspice

¼ cup freshly ground black pepper

3 tablespoons ground cumin

2 tablespoons ground cinnamon

1½ teaspoons ground cardamom

1½ teaspoons ground cloves

In a small bowl, combine the allspice, pepper, cumin, cinnamon, cardamom, and cloves. Store in an airtight container for up to 3 months.

SABBATH STEWS

Sabbath Stews: Shabbat in a Pot

There may be no better expression of Shabbat cooking than a vessel filled with meat, grains, beans, and potatoes, covered and placed on the stove before Shabbat begins in order to sidestep the prohibition of cooking. It is known by many names, the most common are hamin, from the Arabic word for "hot"; dafina, Arabic for "buried"; and cholent, the Ashkenazi version, which some believe comes from the French word *chaud* ("hot"). Joel Haber, a Jerusalem-based food researcher, told me that the first evidence of a Sabbath stew can be traced to the city of Babel, where a dish called harisa—not to be confused with the spicy North African condiment—was prepared by combining wheat and meat and cooking it overnight for consumption on Shabbat morning. Jews who accompanied Muslims in the Arab conquest of Spain brought the dish with them, and it took on two names—dafina and hamin, essentially the same dish but from two different regions of Spain. Over the next several centuries the dish developed, and people customized their stews with what Haber calls "bonus foods" like kishka (stuffed derma), ta'amer (see Hamin Ta'amer on page 298), and kuklot (semolina dumplings; see Tbecha Belsalk, page 307). Eventually, these Spanish dishes migrated to Ashkenazi (Eastern European) territories, where they were called schalet, another word for "hot." In her masterwork *The Book of Jewish Food*, Claudia Roden writes that after their expulsion from Spain, Moroccan Jews took advantage of the residual heat from communal ovens that had been used to bake bread for Shabbat. Once the breads were done, women (or their domestic workers) would bring sealed pots of hamin to be deposited on numbered shelves, then return the following morning after prayers to collect the cooked hamin. In Egypt, the hamin was often cooked on embers used to heat the water for communal baths.

In my childhood home, my mother made cholent only in Palo Alto's relatively short California winter. In Israel, where winter is even less pronounced (especially in Tel Aviv), it's rain that is the defining weather event of Sabbath stew season. Once the weather report is confirmed, butchers are inundated with customers looking for cuts of meat suited to long cooking. Social media is filled with images of hamin being made. It's true, hamin can be purchased—and it can be good—but making hamin at home is the way to go. There's no substitute for the initial reveal of the contents of a pot of hamin, the divvying up, the customizing of plates with more or less barley, eggs, meat, or potatoes—and the singularly satisfying, nearly unavoidable nap that ensues after eating a bowl.

TBECHA BELSALK PAGE 307

CAULIFLOWER HAMIN
with Schug-a-churri Sauce

After many experiments dedicated to creating a truly delicious vegan Shabbat stew, I landed on using cauliflower as the centerpiece. Thanks to chefs like Eyal Shani and Michael Solomonov, whole roasted cauliflower has become a part of the Israeli cooking canon, and here I surround it with some of the elements of a traditional hamin—beans and grains—and some more unexpected ones in the form of whole tomatoes and sweet potatoes. Since there's no meat here, I really amp up the spice and tomato elements for a powerful flavor of vegetable-based umami. When the hamin is done, you should be able to slice through the cauliflower easily and portion it out with the rest of the ingredients; a shallow bowl is the perfect vessel here, and you can pile some cool, crunchy salad right into the bowl and top it with a bit of tahini.

Serves 12

Active Time:
1 hour

Total Time
(including soaking time):
8 hours 30 minutes

1½ cups dried cranberry beans or pinto beans

¼ cup olive oil

4½ teaspoons kosher salt

4 medium onions (1¼ pounds), cut into ½-inch-thick rounds

1½ cups uncooked wheat berries or farro

1 medium head cauliflower (1½ to 1¾ pounds)

3 medium sweet potatoes (1¾ to 2 pounds), halved lengthwise

6 medium Roma or vine-ripened tomatoes (or more if you have room!), stemmed and cored

10 garlic cloves

4 cups vegetable broth

4 cups water

¼ cup tomato paste

1½ tablespoons ground cumin

1½ tablespoons sweet paprika

½ teaspoon smoked paprika

1 teaspoon cayenne pepper

Schug-a-churri (page 262), Chopped Salad (recipe follows), and Tahini Sauce (page 14), for serving

1. In a medium bowl, cover the beans with at least 4 cups cold water. Cover with a kitchen towel and soak on the counter for 8 hours or refrigerate for 12 hours.* (You can also use the quick-soak method; see page 296.**)

2. Preheat the oven to 200°F. Pour the oil in a large (at least 8-quart) heavy pot with a lid, sprinkle ½ teaspoon of the salt over the oil, and arrange the onion slices to cover the bottom of the pot, in a few layers if needed, to fit. Flip the onion slices so that both sides are coated in the salted oil. Scatter the wheat berries and soaked beans on top of the onions. Trim the cauliflower so that most of the stem is removed and you can stand the cauliflower upright without it tipping over, then arrange the cauliflower on top of the beans and wheat berries. Nestle the sweet potato halves

RECIPE CONTINUES

and whole tomatoes around the cauliflower. Scatter the garlic cloves around the pot.

3. In a large bowl, whisk together the broth, water, tomato paste, cumin, sweet and smoked paprikas, cayenne, and the remaining 4 teaspoons salt.

4. Pour the liquid into the pot; it should come up to the top of the sweet potatoes, and the cauliflower head should stick out the top. Bring the pot to a boil, then cover it tightly (if your pot doesn't have a tight seal, seal it with foil first). Transfer the pot to the oven and cook until the beans and wheat berries are tender, the cauliflower is scoopable with a spoon, and the tomatoes are shriveled, 8 to 10 hours. Uncover, season with salt to taste and serve with Schug-a-churri, chopped salad, and tahini.

*Soaked beans can be drained, rinsed, and frozen, then used from their frozen state in recipes calling for soaked beans. Just make sure you mark freezer bags with the original amount of beans, pre-soaking, to avoid confusion when you're ready to use them.

**QUICK-SOAKED BEANS
This shortcut allows you to skip the soaking step and achieve beans almost as perfect as the ones that soak in the fridge overnight. Place the beans in a medium saucepan, cover with 4 inches of cold water, bring to a boil, and boil for 5 minutes. Remove the pan from the heat and let the beans cool in their water for 1 hour. Drain the beans and proceed with the recipe.

CHOPPED SALAD

Serves 6 to 8
Active Time: 15 minutes
Total Time: 15 minutes

¾ pound Persian cucumbers, trimmed and cut into ¼-inch dice (2½ cups)

1 pound ripe red tomatoes, cored and cut into ¼-inch dice (2½ cups)

¼ cup freshly squeezed lemon juice

¼ cup olive oil

½ teaspoon kosher salt, plus more to taste

Freshly ground black pepper to taste

Combine the cucumbers and tomatoes in a large bowl, making sure to use as much of the tomato juices as possible. Toss with the lemon juice, olive oil, salt, and pepper. If you are not eating the salad immediately after preparing it, strain the liquid from the salad and reserve it. When you are ready to serve, pour the juice over the salad and toss.

HAMIN TA'AMER

"In my childhood, it wasn't Shabbat if we didn't have hamin," Vered Tsabari said as we stood in her kitchen with her son, Avichai, a long-time friend of mine and the owner of a culinary travel company. Vered's Moroccan mother, Rosa, would tuck one of two extras into her hamin before setting it on the hot plate. "Sometimes there were marrow bones," Vered told me as we peeled potatoes. "And there was ta'amer. That was the real treat." A sort of meatloaf shot through with warm spices and a prodigious amount of nuts, the ta'amer (or ta'amara, roughly translated from the Arabic word for "stuffed") was suspended in the hamin, where it would cook overnight with the other components. "All my mother's pots were huge, and her hamin would feed sixteen people, twenty people, or whoever showed up," Vered told me as we mixed eggs with ground beef, nuts, and spices before enveloping them in cheesecloth and adding it to a giant pot filled with meat, beans, and barley. Before sealing Vered's decorative earthenware pot for cooking, we stirred in some of her tkilia, a condiment made of nothing more than hot chilies fried, ground, and suspended in oil. Just as Rosa passed down her traditional recipes to Vered, Vered is in the process of passing them along to Avichai, an accomplished cook in his own right. Vered sent me on my way with an extra ta'amer and a jar of tkilia to use when I went home to re-create the hamin for myself. "How many people are you having?" she asked me on my way out. "I'm sure there will be enough."

Serves 12

Active Time:
30 minutes

Total Time (including soaking and cooking time):
20 hours

FOR THE TA'AMER:

6 ounces shelled nuts, such as pecans, walnuts, or a combination (about 1½ cups)

¾ pound 80/20 ground beef

1 large egg plus 1 large egg yolk

½ teaspoon ground cinnamon

Pinch of ground cloves

Pinch of ground ginger

¾ teaspoon kosher salt

¼ teaspoon freshly ground black pepper

Pinch of ground white pepper

FOR THE HAMIN:

1¾ cups (¾ pound) dry white beans, soaked for 8 to 12 hours (see method, page 294, or use the quick-soak method on page 296)

2 tablespoons olive oil

2 large onions, chopped (4 cups)

1½ cups pearl barley (¾ pound), rinsed

5 medium potatoes (about 2 pounds), scrubbed, peeled, and quartered

2 small sweet potatoes (about 1 pound), scrubbed and left whole

2½ pounds short-rib meat, cut into large chunks on the bone

1½ tablespoons kosher salt, plus more for seasoning

2 to 3 tablespoons Tkilia (recipe follows)

3 tablespoons silan (date syrup)

6 large uncooked eggs, shells on

2 whole garlic heads, top ½ inch removed

RECIPE CONTINUES

1. Make the ta'amer: Place the nuts in the bowl of a food processor and process until the nuts resemble fine crumbs, 10 to 15 seconds, making sure to not overprocess them into a paste. Transfer to a bowl and, using your hands, gently mix with the beef, egg, egg yolk, cinnamon, cloves, ginger, salt, and black and white peppers until incorporated. Form the mixture into a 3 × 9-inch log and wrap it in cheesecloth, tying the ends in knots to secure it.

2. Make the hamin: Arrange a rack in your oven to leave space for a very large (10-to 12-quart) lidded pot, then preheat the oven to 200°F. Drain the soaked beans and reserve. In the pot, heat the oil over medium heat. Add the onions and cook, stirring, until they begin to soften, 5 to 6 minutes. Remove from the heat, then layer in the barley, beans, potatoes, sweet potatoes, and meat. Fill the pot with water until all of the ingredients are entirely covered by 1½ inches. Add the salt, tkilia, and silan, then nestle the ta'amer, the uncooked, shell-on eggs, and the garlic heads on top. Bring to a boil, then cover and transfer the pot to the oven.

Cook for at least 12 hours and up to 16, depending on how much you want to reduce the liquid in your hamin (you can also uncover it during the last hour or two of cooking to further reduce the liquid). Uncover, then remove and unwrap the ta'amer and shell the eggs. Taste the hamin and season with more salt if desired. Serve the hamin in bowls with pieces of the ta'amer and the eggs.

TKILIA

Makes ½ cup
Active time: 10 minutes
Total time: 15 minutes

½ cup vegetable oil

20 small dried hot chilies, such chilies de arbol, stems removed

In a medium skillet, heat ¼ cup of the oil over medium heat. Add the chilies and cook, stirring, until fragrant and crisp, 45 seconds to 1 minute. Cool, then transfer chilies and oil to a mini food processor or bowl of a standard food processor and process until smooth, 10 to 15 seconds. Scrape into a jar and cover with the remaining ¼ cup oil. Refrigerated in an airtight container, tkilia will keep for up to 1 year.

Instead of using the oven, many observant Jews cook their Sabbath stews in a Crock-Pot, a device invented in 1936 by a Jewish man named Irving Naxon, who was inspired by his own mother's Shabbat cooking rituals. Depending on your Crock-Pot, you may need to reduce recipes by one-third or one-half. Brown meat and any other elements first in the Crock-Pot if you like, and experiment a bit with heat levels to accommodate different models. Many also cook their stews overnight on a plata, or hotplate. To do so, follow regular instructions up to bringing your stew to its initial boil, then place on the preheated hotplate at a relatively low setting, where it will settle into a low simmer similar to cooking over a tiny flame on the stovetop (you will need to play with the heat levels and exact timing over a few weeks to perfect). In both cases, additional liquid may be necessary, and cooking times may vary slightly.

HAMIN MACARONI

For something as simple as noodles, chicken, onions, potatoes, and spices, hamin macaroni is outrageously delicious. "Using noodles for long-cooked dishes is a very Jerusalem thing," said Sherry Ansky, one of the high priestesses of Israeli cooking and an authority on hamin who wrote an entire book on the subject. (Lukshen, or noodles, appear in sweet, peppery Jerusalem kugel; see my previous cookbook, *Sababa*, for a recipe.) Ansky surmises that in ancient times, home cooks were always looking for ways to vary their Shabbat routines. "You have to imagine a very ancient and competitive world where every woman bringing a pot of hamin to the communal oven was competing with her mother-in-law, sisters-in-law, even her own grandma, for best in show," said Ansky. "The more carbohydrates you add, the more unique your hamin becomes." In this case, the spaghetti is cooked and well drained, then the onions, chicken, and potatoes are browned before they are layered in a heavy, lidded pot. Something magical happens to the ingredients as they cook in their microclimate, and they become caramelized and downright luxurious.

Serves 8 to 10

Active Time:
1 hour

**Total Time
(including baking time):**
10 hours

---

1 pound uncooked spaghetti

6 tablespoons vegetable oil

4 large skin-on, bone-in chicken thighs (about 1¾ pounds)

4 chicken drumsticks (1 pound)

4½ teaspoons kosher salt, plus more as needed

1½ teaspoons freshly ground black pepper

3 large or 4 medium potatoes (about 1¾ pounds), peeled and cut into ½-inch rounds

3 large onions, coarsely chopped (6 cups)

5 garlic cloves, minced

2 tablespoons sweet paprika

1 teaspoon cayenne pepper, plus more to taste

1. Bring a wide, heavy pot (at least 6 quarts, as you will use it later to layer and cook the hamin) of generously salted water to a boil over high heat. (It may sound like a lot, but I like to add 1½ teaspoons kosher salt per quart of water. So if you fill a 6-quart pot halfway, add 4½ teaspoons kosher salt.) Following the package directions, cook the spaghetti 1 minute less than al dente, then drain well, transfer to a large bowl, and toss with 1 tablespoon of the oil.

2. Preheat the oven to 350°F. Pat the chicken thighs and legs dry, then season both sides with 1 teaspoon of the salt and ½ teaspoon of the black pepper. Season the potatoes on both sides with 1 teaspoon of the salt.

RECIPE CONTINUES

3. Heat 2 tablespoons of the oil in the large pot over medium heat, then add the chicken (in batches if your pot is not wide enough), skin side down, and cook until the skin is browned and crisp, 4 to 5 minutes. Flip and cook for 2 additional minutes. Remove the chicken to a plate, then add the potatoes to the pot and fry until lightly golden, 3 to 4 minutes per side. Remove to another plate, add another tablespoon of the oil to the pot, then add the onions and ½ teaspoon of the salt and cook, stirring, until lightly golden, 8 to 9 minutes. Add the garlic and cook for 1 additional minute. Add half of the onion mixture to the spaghetti with the remaining 2 tablespoons oil, 1 tablespoon of the paprika, 1 teaspoon of the salt, and ½ teaspoon each of the black pepper and cayenne.

4. In another bowl, gently combine the chicken with the other half of the onions and season with the remaining 1 tablespoon paprika, 1 teaspoon salt, and ½ teaspoon each black pepper and cayenne.

5. Line the bottom and sides of the large pot with parchment, then add the browned potatoes, packing them tightly into the bottom of the pot. Layer half the spaghetti mixture on top of the potatoes, then layer in the chicken and onion mixture, then the rest of the spaghetti mixture. Fold in the sides of the parchment to cover, filling in the center with another piece if the top is exposed.

6. Cover with the lid and bake for 1 hour. Reduce the oven temperature to 200°F and bake until everything is deeply golden and the chicken is falling off the bone, 9 to 10 hours. Uncover, remove the parchment from the top, and tear the parchment from around the sides of the pasta so it's at the same level as the hamin. Place a plate, slightly larger than the circumference of the pot, over the top and, using oven mitts to hold it, carefully invert the pot. Peel away the parchment and bring the hamin to the table.

ASHKIE (ASHKENAZI) CHOLENT

In my eyes, religious Jewish women are the ultimate hostesses, making what many of us call "dinner parties" week in and week out, every Shabbat, for most of their adult lives. By my accounting, since she married at age twenty-one, my sister, Sharon, who is now fifty-five, has prepared about 3,500 Shabbat meals. Sharon and I were not tight as children. Four years younger than she is, I was annoyingly precocious, wanting in on every aspect of her life. Although she tolerated my encroachments, the poor girl understandably needed some space. It was only after she left for college that we began to come toward each other, and today we are as close as can be in spite of vast differences in lifestyle and culture.

She married young, deeply believing and Orthodox, and is a mother of three. I married at forty-five, childless, having left much of the ritual behind to focus instead on Jewish culture and food. And still, she is my touchstone, the safest space and the most loving heart in existence (not to mention, she laughs at my jokes). In my years living in New York, my sister and brother-in-law Ari's Shabbat table was my softest landing place, and crossing the George Washington Bridge into New Jersey meant I was coming home to their warm embrace—and to Sharon's delicious food.

When she makes her cholent—in the Eastern European style, without hard-boiled eggs or a lot of spice—I feel enveloped by the two most important women in my life—her and our late mother, who also made a killer cholent in her oversized, black-handled Farberware pot. This is a fusion of their two recipes, with a few twists of my own in the form of short-rib meat, whole garlic cloves, and pastrami. I purposely don't sear the meat to keep it simple, but if you want to, by all means do so. The secret sauce in my mother's cholent was ketchup, so I approximate those flavors with a combination of tomato paste, vinegar, and sugar. The smoky notes from the pastrami, the rich, falling-off-the-bone meat, and the whole cloves of sweet, long-cooked garlic are the ultimate Shabbat comfort food.

Serves a lot of people

Active Time:
30 minutes

Total Time:
16 hours 30 minutes

RECIPE AND INGREDIENTS CONTINUE

1¼ cups (8 ounces) dried white beans, such as navy, cannellini, or lima, soaked for 8 to 12 hours (see method, page 294, or use the quick-soak method on page 296)

2 large onions, chopped (4 cups)

6 garlic cloves

2½ pounds red potatoes, peeled and halved

2½ pounds English-style short ribs (meat on top of the bones), cut between the bones into large chunks

¾ cup pearl barley or rice

7 cups water, plus more as needed

2 cups beef broth

2 tablespoons tomato paste

1½ tablespoons kosher salt, plus more as needed

1 tablespoon sugar

2 teaspoons paprika

2 teaspoons apple cider vinegar

One 8-ounce chunk pastrami or 8 ounces sliced

1. In a medium saucepan, cover the beans with 4 inches of cold water. Bring to a boil, boil for 5 minutes, remove from the heat, and let the beans cool in their water for 1 hour. Drain and rinse the beans. Layer the onions and garlic on the bottom of a large (8- to 10-quart) slow cooker or lidded heavy pot, then top with the potatoes. Layer the short ribs on top of the potatoes, then scatter the drained beans and barley over the top.

2. In a large bowl, whisk together the water, broth, tomato paste, salt, sugar, paprika, and vinegar. Pour the liquid into the pot, making sure all the ingredients are just covered; add a little water if needed. Arrange the pastrami across the top of the pot. Cover the slow cooker and cook on low for 15 to 16 hours, or place the pot in a 200°F oven for at least 12 hours and up to 16 hours, until the short ribs are very tender and falling off the bone. Check during the last 4 hours to make sure there is enough liquid but not too much liquid; if there's too much, crack the top of the slow cooker or pot for a couple of hours; if there's not enough, add a bit of liquid and keep the pot sealed until cooking is finished. Season with salt to taste and serve the cholent in shallow bowls.

TBECHA BELSALK
(Swiss Chard, Bean, Meat & Dumpling Stew)

In 2008, I stumbled into Casserole, a tiny Tel Aviv restaurant in the Neve Zedek neighborhood. I had a soulful meal of Libyan-Jewish dishes including tbecha belsalk, a stew of meat, beans, Swiss chard, and semolina dumplings that was new to me. Casserole closed soon after, and only when Benny Briga and I collaborated on a book that was released in 2021 did I learn that Casserole had been his, with his mother, Leah, in the kitchen. Leah invited me to her home in Or Yehuda, not far from Tel Aviv, to learn how to make the dish.

In 1972, Leah, who was born in Israel to Turkish parents, was newly married to Benny's Libyan-born father, Avraham. Soon she was standing next to her mother-in-law, Miriam, learning how to make the essential components of the recipe.

The stew was put on the stove before Shabbat and eaten in the morning, either at home or at synagogue after services to mark a special occasion like a circumcision or an upcoming wedding. "Whoever got up first in the morning would open the pot to 'check' on it," said Benny. "A check obviously included a taste."

Adding onion, parsley, turmeric, and black pepper at the end adds an element of freshness that elevates the dish even further.

Serves 8 to 10

Active Time:
1 hour

**Total Time
(including bean soaking time):**
14 hours

FOR THE BEANS:

1¼ cups dried white beans (8 ounces), such as navy or cannellini

FOR THE DUMPLINGS:

2½ cups semolina

¼ cup vegetable oil

¼ cup (1¾ ounces) ground lamb fat (ask your butcher) or additional vegetable oil

2 teaspoons sweet paprika

2 teaspoons kosher salt

1 teaspoon ground caraway

2 large eggs, beaten

¾ cup water

**FOR THE BELSALK
& STEW:**

1 large bunch Swiss chard (about 1 pound)

½ cup vegetable oil

9 cups hot water, plus more as needed

2 beef marrow bones (¾ pound)

1½ pounds beef stew meat, cut into 2-inch cubes

2 chicken leg quarters (1 pound) or more stew meat

2 pounds small potatoes, peeled

2 teaspoons kosher salt, plus more for seasoning

FOR FINISHING:

1 large onion, finely minced (2 cups)

1 bunch fresh parsley (leaves and tender stems), finely chopped

1 heaping teaspoon ground turmeric

1 teaspoon finely ground black pepper

Lemon wedges, for serving

RECIPE CONTINUES

1. Soak the beans: Place the beans in a medium bowl and cover with at least 4 cups of cold water. Cover with a kitchen towel and soak on the counter for 8 hours or refrigerate for 12 hours. (Alternatively, you can also use the method for Quick-Soaked Beans on page 296.) Drain and rinse the beans after soaking.

2. Make the dumplings: In a medium bowl, combine the semolina, oil, lamb fat, paprika, salt, and caraway and use a fork to mix until the semolina resembles wet sand. Using your hands, mix in the eggs and the water until well incorporated; the dough will be wet and loose. Press plastic wrap onto the surface of the mixture and refrigerate for at least 3 hours and up to 12 hours to tenderize the semolina.

3. Make the belsalk: While the dumpling dough rests, separate the leaves from the stems on the chard; discard the stems or reserve them for another purpose.

4. In a large, heavy (10- to 12-quart) Dutch oven, heat the oil over medium-high heat. Add the chard in batches, letting it wilt before adding more, then continue to cook the chard, stirring occasionally, until it gets really dark in color and almost crispy but not burnt, 25 to 30 minutes.

5. When the chard is ready, to the pot add 2 cups of the water, the drained beans, bones, stew meat, chicken quarters, potatoes, and salt. Add the remaining 7 cups water so the contents are covered by about ½ inch of water; add more water if needed, but leave 2 inches headroom at the top of the pot. Bring everything to a low boil over medium heat, skimming off any scum during the first 5 minutes. Remove the semolina mixture from the fridge; use your hands to form golf ball–sized pieces of dough into torpedo-shaped dumplings. As you shape them, nestle the dumplings into the soup, gently shaking the pot to submerge them into the stew.

6. Cook, uncovered, making sure the liquid is only lightly bubbling and not boiling, until the water level is reduced by an inch and the meat is tender, 3 hours. (You can also cook this overnight, covered, in a 200°F oven or on a low-heat hot plate, for 10 to 12 hours or more.) Thirty minutes before serving, scatter the onion, most of the parsley, the turmeric, and black pepper on top of the stew and very gently stir them in. Cook over very low heat for 30 minutes until everything is absorbed, then spoon the dumplings and stew into bowls and garnish with more parsley. Season with salt to taste and serve with lemon wedges.

SPRING BEEF STEW

This rich, classic stew welcomes some of spring's best ingredients into the fold with the addition of fresh tarragon and mint, and I think it has what it takes to win over even the most stewed-out among us. Be sure to add the peas and asparagus just before serving so that they retain their springtime green color and are crisp-tender.

Serves 8

Active Time:
30 minutes

Total Time:
3 hours 30 minutes

3 pounds beef stew meat, cut into 2-inch cubes

5 teaspoons kosher salt

1½ teaspoons freshly ground black pepper, plus more to taste

4 tablespoons olive oil

1 jumbo onion, chopped (3 cups)

6 garlic cloves, chopped

2 tablespoons tomato paste

3 tablespoons all-purpose or gluten-free flour

2 cups dry red wine

4 cups beef broth

1 bay leaf

2 fresh thyme sprigs

1½ teaspoons silan (date syrup), honey, or sugar

1 cup water, as needed

4 medium carrots (1 pound), peeled and cut into ½-inch chunks

1 pound fingerling or baby white potatoes, scrubbed

8 ounces asparagus, cut into 2-inch pieces

1 cup frozen peas

Chopped fresh mint and tarragon, for serving

1. Arrange a rack in the lower third of the oven and preheat the oven to 325°F. Pat the meat dry and season with 2 teaspoons of the salt and ½ teaspoon of the pepper. In a large (at least 6-quart) Dutch oven or heavy pot with a lid, heat 2 tablespoons of the olive oil over medium-high heat. Working in two batches, brown the meat on all sides, turning once midway, about 6 minutes per batch. Transfer the meat to a plate but leave the juices and fat in the pot.

2. Reduce the heat to medium, and add the remaining 2 tablespoons olive oil to the pot followed by the onions and garlic. Cook, stirring often, until the onions are tender and lightly golden, 8 to 9 minutes. Add the tomato paste and cook, stirring occasionally, 1 more minute. Add the flour and cook, stirring, until absorbed, 1 minute. Add the wine, raise the heat to high, bring to a boil, and continue to boil until the wine is reduced by three-quarters, 4 to 5 minutes. Return the beef and any juices to the pot, then add the broth, bay leaf, thyme sprigs, silan, 2 teaspoons of the salt, the remaining 1 teaspoon pepper, and up to 1 cup of water as needed so that the meat is just covered. Raise the heat to medium-high, bring to a boil, cover the pot tightly, transfer to the oven, and bake, not opening the oven until the meat is almost tender, 2 hours.

3. Uncover the pot, stir in the carrots and potatoes, cover again, and return the pot to the oven until the meat is totally tender and the potatoes and carrots are cooked through, 1 more hour. Remove and discard the bay leaf and thyme, season with the remaining 1 teaspoon salt and pepper to taste, add the asparagus and peas, cover, and let them "cook" until the asparagus is crisp-tender, 5 to 6 minutes. Divide among bowls and garnish with mint and tarragon.

DRINKS & COCKTAILS

PINK LEMONADE
(Vodka Optional)

The blueberry flavor is subtle here, but I love the way the berries tint lemonade the absolutely perfect shade of pink. Here I'm using an old trick I learned on Food52 about a decade ago: maximize lemon peel's impact by finely zesting it, allowing the lemon oil to carry its powerful citrus essence directly into the drink. This is just as refreshing in its zero-proof version, so feel free to keep it alcohol-free.

Makes 5½ cups

Active Time:
15 minutes

Total Time:
15 minutes

8 large lemons,
plus more lemon slices
for garnish

1 cup fresh or frozen
blueberries (defrosted
if frozen), plus more for
garnish

¾ cup sugar

4 cups water

3 drops orange flower
water or rose water,
plus more to taste
(optional)

Chilled vodka (optional)

Ice cubes for serving

Finely zest 6 of the lemons, reserve the zest, then juice all of the lemons. You should have about 1½ cups lemon juice and 6 tablespoons zest. In a medium bowl, mash the blueberries with ½ cup of the lemon juice, ¼ cup of the sugar, and 4 tablespoons of the zest until the blueberries are pulverized and as mashed as possible. Press the liquid through a fine-mesh sieve into a large pitcher, discarding the solids; you should have about ½ cup blueberry liquid. Combine the remaining ½ cup sugar with the remaining 2 tablespoons lemon zest in a small bowl and rub it with your fingers until the sugar is moistened. Add it to the pitcher with the remaining 1 cup lemon juice, the water, and the orange flower water. Stir until the sugar is dissolved, about 1 minute. Chill, add a splash of vodka (if desired), add a drop more orange flower water (if desired), then serve the lemonade in glasses over ice, garnished with whole blueberries and lemon slices.

SHAKEN ICED TAHINI COFFEE

This deceptively simple "milky" iced coffee comes together lickety-split, yielding something very different and very indulgent, very fast. Tahini enriches the drink with its signature goodness, lightening the coffee so it looks positively creamy. Make sure to follow the order I recommend for mixing the ingredients; that way, the tahini won't freeze and stick to the ice cubes. If you like stronger coffee, feel free to add an extra shot of espresso!

Makes 1 drink

Active Time:
5 minutes

Total Time:
5 minutes

---

3 tablespoons pure tahini paste

1 tablespoon maple syrup*

½ teaspoon pure vanilla extract

Dash of kosher salt

¾ cup cold coffee of your choice

1 cup ice**

1. In a large (16-ounce) jar with a tight-fitting lid or in a cocktail shaker, place the tahini, maple syrup, vanilla, and salt. Add the coffee, seal, and shake for 5 seconds to combine.

2. Open the jar or shaker, add the ice, reseal, and shake vigorously until the drink is lightened in color and frothy, 10 to 15 seconds.

3. Pour, along with the ice, into a tall glass.

*You can make a large batch of the tahini and maple syrup using the proportions in the recipe, then add ¼ cup of the tahini-maple syrup to each drink you make.

**If you prefer, you can blast everything in a blender for a more Frappuccino-esque experience.

SESAME OLD-FASHIONED COCKTAIL

To give the classic old-fashioned cocktail a new-fashioned twist, I infused bourbon with sesame seeds, then shook the toasty, nutty spirit with maple syrup and sesame oil.

Makes 1 cocktail

Active Time:
5 minutes

**Total Time
(including cooling time):**
4 hours 15 minutes

**FOR THE SESAME-INFUSED BOURBON
(makes 2 cups):**

½ cup white sesame seeds

2 cups bourbon

FOR THE COCKTAIL:

2 teaspoons maple syrup

⅛ teaspoon (5 drops) toasted sesame oil

1 tablespoon water

Orange twist and Luxardo or maraschino cherries, for garnish

1. Make the sesame-infused bourbon: Preheat the oven to 350°F. Spread the sesame seeds on a rimmed baking sheet and roast, stirring once or twice, until deeply golden and fragrant, 16 to 18 minutes. Transfer the sesame seeds to a bowl or a resealable container and, while still warm, add the bourbon. Cool to room temperature, then refrigerate for at least 4 hours and up to 24. Strain well, reserving the sesame seeds if you plan to dry and reuse them.*

2. Combine 2 ounces of the sesame-infused bourbon with the maple syrup, sesame oil, and water in an 8-ounce jar (at minimum) with a tight-fitting lid and shake vigorously. Completely fill a short rocks glass with ice, pour in the cocktail mixture, and garnish with an orange twist and a cherry.

*To dry out the seeds for future use, preheat the oven to 350°F, spread the sesame seeds on a rimmed baking sheet, and roast, stirring every few minutes, until they dry out and become fragrant and lightly golden, 13 to 14 minutes. They'll retain a surprising amount of bourbon flavor, making them perfect for desserts (like the cookies on the following page) or for sprinkling over ice cream for a surreptitiously boozy garnish.

SESAME SEED WAFER COOKIES

I use the bourbon-infused sesame seeds from the cocktail on page 318 to make these tasty little cookies; serve them with the drink if you like. They're the perfect after-dinner cookie or little treat to go with a cup of tea or a digestif.

Makes 19 to 20 cookies

Active Time:
10 minutes

Total Time:
25 minutes

Roasted bourbon-soaked sesame seeds (see page 318), or ½ cup (70 grams) white sesame seeds

4 tablespoons (½ stick/57 grams) unsalted butter, softened

½ cup (106 grams) lightly packed light brown sugar

¼ teaspoon (1 gram) fine sea salt

⅛ teaspoon baking soda

1 large egg yolk

½ cup (65 grams) all-purpose flour

Vegetable oil, for oiling your hands

1. Arrange two racks in the top and bottom thirds of the oven. Preheat the oven to 350°F and line two rimmed baking sheets with parchment paper. If you're using the repurposed sesame seeds from the cocktail recipe, you're ready to go. If you're using plain sesame seeds, spread the sesame seeds on a third rimmed baking sheet and roast until fragrant, 5 to 6 minutes. Cool completely.

2. In a medium bowl, vigorously beat the butter, brown sugar, salt, baking soda, and egg yolk with a wooden spoon until fluffy, 30 seconds. Stir in the flour and then the sesame seeds until just incorporated. Press plastic wrap onto the surface, chill for 15 minutes, then use lightly oiled hands to divide the dough into 19 or 20 equal-sized balls (about 1 inch in diameter). Arrange the cookies on the prepared baking sheets, leaving about 3 inches between them. Bake, rotating and switching the sheets once midway through, until the cookies spread and are golden brown, 9 to 10 minutes. Remove from the oven and cool on the baking sheets. Store in an airtight container for up to 1 week or freeze for up to 3 months.

POMEGRANATE SUMAC MARGARITAS

We make this tart-and-sweet drink in the fall, when pomegranates are at their peak but the weather still begs for margaritas—by far summer's best cooling agent in my eyes. For an extra layer of tartness with minimal effort, I make a sumac simple syrup, then reinforce the concept with a salty-sugary rim that adds even more tang with every sip.

Makes 4 drinks

Active Time:
20 minutes

**Total Time
(including steeping time):**
1 hour 20 minutes

---

6 small limes, plus lime wheels for garnish

½ cup plus
2 tablespoons sugar

½ cup water

4 tablespoons ground sumac

1 tablespoon plus a pinch of kosher salt

8 ounces tequila

8 ounces pomegranate juice

Ice cubes

1. Finely zest 2 of the limes (you should have 2 teaspoons zest). Use a Y-peeler to peel wide strips of zest from a third lime. Juice all 6 limes (you should have about ¾ cup [6 ounces] juice).

2. Bring ½ cup of the sugar, the water, and the wide lime zest strips to a simmer over medium-low heat in a small saucepan, stirring to dissolve the sugar. Simmer for 2 minutes, remove from the heat, then stir in 3 tablespoons of the sumac and a pinch of the salt; let steep 1 hour. Press the syrup through a fine-mesh sieve; discard the solids (you should have ½ cup syrup).

3. To make 2 drinks, combine 4 ounces each of the tequila and pomegranate juice, 3 ounces of the lime juice, and 2 tablespoons of the sumac syrup in a large cocktail shaker.

4. Before you shake the cocktails, combine the remaining 2 tablespoons sugar and 1 tablespoon each kosher salt and sumac with the finely grated lime zest on a small plate.

5. Place 1 tablespoon of the syrup on another small plate and dip the rim of 2 rocks glasses in the syrup, then in the sumac-salt mixture. Add ½ cup ice cubes to the shaker and shake vigorously until a little frothy, 5 to 10 seconds. Carefully fill the rimmed glasses with ice, then divide the cocktail among the 2 glasses. Repeat with the remaining ingredients to make the 2 additional cocktails. Garnish the glasses with lime wheels, if desired.

PITCHER COCKTAILS

To make a pitcher of margaritas, combine ½ cup of the syrup with 16 ounces each of tequila, lime juice, and pomegranate juice in a pitcher. Stir, then pour into ice-filled glasses rimmed with the sumac-salt mixture using the method above.

CUCUMBER-GIN COOLERS

I like to think of this cocktail as summer on steroids. The drink's gorgeous jade-green hue is its visual calling card, one that lives up to its promise from the first sip. The vegetal nature of cucumber is sweetened with a minty ginger syrup, and a spike of gin finishes the proceedings in style. This one was born to be batched and chilled, then served whenever you need something simultaneously light and lifting.

Makes 6 to 8 drinks

Active Time:
20 minutes

**Total Time
(including cooling time):**
2 hours 20 minutes

---

2 large or 3 medium lemons

1 cup sugar

1½ cups water

2-inch piece fresh ginger, cut into thin matchsticks

½ cup packed fresh mint leaves, plus sprigs for garnish

2¼ pounds Persian cucumbers, washed (about 9 cucumbers)

12 ounces gin

Ice cubes, for serving

1. Use a Y-peeler to peel wide strips of zest from one of the lemons. In a small saucepan, combine the sugar, ½ cup of the water, the ginger, and lemon zest strips and bring to a simmer over medium-low heat. Simmer until the sugar dissolves, 2 minutes. Remove from the heat and add the mint. Let cool to room temperature or ideally for at least 2 hours to infuse the flavors into the syrup. Juice the lemons (you should have about ½ cup juice).

2. Reserve 1 of the cucumbers to garnish the drinks. Trim the remaining cucumbers, peel half (4) of them, and discard the peels. Cut all of the cucumbers into large pieces, place in a blender or bowl of a food processor with the remaining 1 cup water, and blend until smooth, 15 to 20 seconds. Strain the mixture through a fine-mesh strainer, pressing the solids to release all the juice; discard the solids. It takes a bit of time, but it's worth it (you should have about 2½ cups juice).

3. Combine the cucumber mixture, gin, lemon juice, and the syrup in a pitcher and divide it among ice-filled glasses. Cut the remaining cucumber into spears and garnish the glasses with the spears and some mint sprigs.

DIRTY FETA & OLIVE MARTINI

A more surprising martini you will not find. This one's for fans of the classic cocktail's dirtiest version, containing not one, not two, but three salty pickling brines to make you pucker up. The idea came to me one day when trying to figure out what to do with the brine feta bathes in, and then I saw a bottle of gin out of the corner of my eye. The combination is surprising, and the skewered, feta-stuffed olive on top makes this a drink *and* a snack at the same time.

Makes 1 cocktail

Active Time:
10 minutes

Total Time:
10 minutes

¼ ounce firm feta, plus ¾ ounce (1½ tablespoons) strained feta brine

2 large pitted green olives, such as Castelvetrano

1 small pickled cocktail onion, plus a dash (optional) of its pickling liquid

2½ ounces (5 tablespoons) vodka or dry gin

½ ounce (1 tablespoon) dry white vermouth

¼ ounce (1½ teaspoons) olive brine

Place a martini glass in the freezer. Cut the feta into small batons about the circumference of the empty area where the olives have been pitted, and stuff them inside the olives. Thread one or both of the olives onto a skewer with the cocktail onion. Combine the vodka, feta brine, vermouth, olive brine, and onion brine (if using) in an ice-filled cocktail shaker or large glass, stir for 15 seconds, and strain into the chilled glass. Garnish with the olive skewer.

DESSERTS

FUDGY MEDJOOL DATE BROWNIES

For a family that made virtually all of its desserts from scratch—kosher desserts were highly impossible to find store-bought—a pan of crinkly-on-the-outside, fudgy-on-the-inside Duncan Hines brownies was an easy treat we whipped together in minutes that gave us enjoyment all Shabbat long, often as the chocolatey supporting player to a platter of fresh fruit or apple cake. This is my update using dates; their texture works brilliantly in the brownie batter, upping the moisture quotient and adding an extra caramelly note.

Makes 16 brownies

Active Time:
10 minutes

Total Time:
40 minutes

---

12 large (7.5 ounces/ 210 grams) plump Medjool dates, pitted and split (or ¾ cup pure date paste* and 4 large pitted dates, split)

3 large eggs

½ cup (100 grams) granulated sugar

½ cup (1 stick/4 ounces/ 114 grams) unsalted butter, coconut oil, or vegetable oil, melted and cooled

1½ teaspoons (8 grams/ ml) pure vanilla extract

¼ cup (30 grams) confectioners' sugar

⅓ cup (43 grams) all-purpose flour

⅓ cup (28 grams) cocoa powder

1 teaspoon (3 grams) espresso powder

½ teaspoon (3 grams) fine sea salt

½ cup (65 grams) walnut halves

½ cup (90 grams) bittersweet mini chocolate chips

1. Preheat the oven to 325°F. Line the bottom and sides of an 8 × 8-inch metal baking pan with parchment paper.

2. Arrange 8 of the dates in a small bowl, cover with boiling water by 1 inch, and soak until the dates soften, 10 minutes. Drain and discard the liquid, cool slightly, then transfer the dates (or ¾ cup date paste) to a food processor, add the eggs and granulated sugar, and blend until the dates are pulverized and only small bits are visible, 1½ minutes. Add the butter, vanilla, and confectioners' sugar and blend until just combined, 5 seconds.

3. Add the flour, cocoa, espresso, and salt and blend until just combined, scraping down the sides of the processor if necessary, 5 to 10 seconds.

4. Add the walnuts and pulse until coarsely chopped, 4 seconds. Add the chocolate chips and pulse three times to incorporate. Spread the batter into the prepared pan and arrange the 8 date halves on top of the batter.

5. Bake until the top is set but the center is still soft, 23 to 25 minutes. Cool completely, then cut into 16 squares.

*Pure date paste can be found in many Middle Eastern and Indian markets and online from DateLady.com.

CARDAMOM BERRY CRISP

Desserts like these typically indicate a summery climate, but a dish brimming with sweet, ripe fruit might be even more important in the winter, when unearthing a frozen stash of juicy berries, then baking them underneath a shattering, melt-in-your mouth shell, can truly feel like a ray of sunshine.

   Pouring the butter over the top of the sandy crisp mixture may be a new technique to you, but have faith—justice will prevail, and the topping will transform into a layer begging to be cracked open. It's heaven warm out of the oven, and possibly even better the next day, eaten with a spoon right out of the dish.

Serves 8

Active Time:
15 minutes

Total Time:
1 hour

¾ cup (1½ sticks/ 6 ounces/170 grams) unsalted butter or coconut oil, melted, or neutral oil, plus more for greasing the pan

1 pound (450 grams) fresh cherries, preferably sour, stemmed and pitted (about 3 cups), or frozen (not thawed)

1 pound (450 grams) assorted fresh berries, such as blueberries, raspberries, and blackberries (about 3 cups), or frozen (not thawed)

1 cup (130 grams) plus 2 tablespoons (16 grams) all-purpose flour

1 tablespoon (2 grams) finely grated lemon zest

1 tablespoon (15 grams/ml) freshly squeezed lemon juice

1½ teaspoons (7.5 grams) ground cardamom

½ teaspoon (3 grams) fine sea salt

1 cup (200 grams) sugar

1¼ teaspoons (5 grams) baking powder

1 large egg white, beaten

½ cup (45 grams) sliced almonds

Vanilla ice cream, for serving (optional)

1. Preheat the oven to 350°F. Grease a 9-inch round baking dish generously with butter. In a large bowl, toss the cherries and berries with 2 tablespoons of the flour, the lemon zest and juice, ½ teaspoon of the cardamom, and ¼ teaspoon of the salt. Transfer to the prepared dish.

2. In a large bowl, whisk together the remaining 1 cup (130 grams) flour with the sugar, the remaining 1 teaspoon cardamom and ¼ teaspoon salt, the baking powder, and the egg white until a sandy mixture forms, then stir in the almonds. Sprinkle the topping over the fruit, then drizzle the melted butter evenly all over the surface.

3. Bake until golden and bubbling around the edges, 35 to 45 minutes. Let cool slightly before serving. Serve with ice cream, if desired.

LEMON BLACK-SESAME BUNDT CAKE

I replaced the poppy seeds in this Bundt-pan classic with black sesame, grounding this dessert in the place I live, with flavors that I love. I added sesame oil to both the batter and the icing and was delighted by the way it intensifies the sesame flavor of the cake, using an ingredient more commonly associated with Asian cuisine. You may be surprised by the number of lemons required here, but after living in Israel for the better part of the past decade, six lemons feels like child's play. After much fiddling around, I found that in order for the cake to really, really have that zesty lemon magic, prodigious juicing must ensue. This one's a showstopper, so serve it to a crowd for dessert, then enjoy any leftover slices with a cup of tea or coffee.

Serves 10 to 12

Active Time:
45 minutes

**Total Time
(including cooling time):** 3 hours

⅓ cup (46 grams) black sesame seeds

1 cup (2 sticks/ 8 ounces/226 grams) plus 2 tablespoons (¼ stick/1 ounce/ 28 grams) unsalted butter or solid, scoopable coconut oil or vegan butter, softened

8 large lemons, plus more if needed

3 cups (390 grams) all-purpose flour, sifted

1½ teaspoons (6 grams) baking powder

1 teaspoon (6 grams) fine sea salt, plus a pinch

½ teaspoon (3 grams) baking soda

1½ cups (300 grams) plus ⅔ cup (133 grams) granulated sugar

1 tablespoon (14 grams/ ml) pure vanilla extract

4 large eggs

1 teaspoon (6 grams) toasted sesame oil

1 cup (227 grams) full-fat yogurt (dairy or nondairy)

1½ cups (180 grams) confectioners' sugar

1. Preheat the oven to 350°F and arrange a rack in the center of the oven. Place the sesame seeds on a rimmed baking sheet and toast the seeds until fragrant, 5 to 6 minutes; remove from the oven and cool.

2. Use the 2 tablespoons butter to grease a 10-inch Bundt pan (using your fingers works great, allowing you to get into every crevice of the pan and reduce sticking post-baking). Finely zest 7 of the lemons (try to only zest the yellow part, leaving the more bitter white pith on the lemon) to end up with ⅓ cup tightly packed zest. Peel the zest off the remaining lemon in strips, then halve and juice all the lemons to yield 1½ cups juice (juice an extra lemon if you need to). In a bowl, whisk together the flour, sesame seeds, baking powder, 1 teaspoon of the salt, and the baking soda.

RECIPE CONTINUES

3. In the bowl of a stand mixer fitted with the paddle attachment, beat 1½ cups (300 grams) of the granulated sugar with the remaining 1 cup butter on medium-high speed until light and fluffy, 2 to 3 minutes, scraping down the sides of the bowl if necessary. Add the vanilla and the eggs, one at a time, beating 15 seconds after each addition and scraping down the sides of the bowl if necessary, until creamy, 2 to 3 minutes. Add ⅔ cup of the lemon juice, the finely grated zest, and ½ teaspoon of the sesame oil and beat until creamy, 1 minute. In two batches each, add the dry ingredients and yogurt, mixing after each addition until just incorporated. Spoon the batter into the prepared Bundt pan, smooth the top, and bake until a toothpick or tester inserted into the center comes out clean, 50 minutes to 1 hour.

4. Meanwhile, in a small saucepan, bring the remaining ⅔ cup (133 grams) granulated sugar, ⅔ cup of the lemon juice, the lemon zest strips, and a pinch of salt to a simmer over medium heat. Stir to dissolve the sugar, then remove from the heat and let cool with the lemon strips in the syrup.

5. When the cake has finished baking, remove it from the oven, let cool for 10 minutes, then invert it onto a rack set over a large rimmed baking sheet. Use a toothpick or skewer to poke a LOT of holes in the cake, trying to get around the outside and the inner circle of the cake as well (make 60 to 75 holes—it's a great stress reliever).

6. Remove the zest strips from the syrup (this is the most delicious treat for a kid of any age) and, a few tablespoons at a time, pour the syrup all over the cake to soak in. Some will pool on the sheet below; if you like, carefully tip it back into the saucepan and pour it over the cake again; repeat until most of the syrup is used, and let the cake cool completely. This takes a little longer than you think—like a good 1 hour 15 minutes—otherwise the glaze will melt off.

7. In a small bowl, whisk together the confectioners' sugar and the remaining lemon juice (about 3 tablespoons) and ½ teaspoon sesame oil. Drizzle half the glaze over the cake, let it set for 15 minutes, then drizzle the other half over the cake and let it set for another 15 minutes. Transfer to a serving plate. Leftover cake can be stored, covered, on the counter for up to 3 days.

LIME-COCONUT CUSTARD PIE
with Press-In Crust

Since I wrote *Sababa* a few years back, limes have become more widely available in Israel, powered by the popularity of both craft cocktails and Asian food. But they're still highly seasonal, so when limes are around and not prohibitively expensive (no five-for-a-dollar deals here), I make this delicious pie, which happens to be 100 percent dairy-free in addition to being 100 percent insanely delicious. The crust comes together in a snap using Medjool dates, shredded coconut, and pecans (a recipe I learned from my friend Shari Leidich many years ago in Boulder, Colorado), forming a base for a lime-and-coconut filling that will illustrate in one bite how these two elements were born to live together in a dessert. The thickness of coconut milk (plus a little coconut oil) subs in for the butter that usually helps solidify custard-like fillings. This one can be made up to three days in advance (except for the whipped cream) and is best served cold, right out of the fridge, making it ideal for a hot summer day.

Serves 12

Active Time:
25 minutes

**Total Time
(with minimum cooling time):**
6 hours 45 minutes

FOR THE CRUST:

2 cups (260 grams) pecans

1 cup (75 grams) shredded, unsweetened coconut

2 large pitted Medjool dates (57 grams), torn into pieces

¼ teaspoon (1 gram) fine sea salt

Neutral oil, for greasing the pan and your hands

FOR THE FILLING:

3 large limes

3 large egg yolks

5 tablespoons (35 grams) cornstarch

Two 13.5-ounce (400 ml/380 grams) cans full-fat coconut milk (800 ml/760 grams total coconut milk)

⅔ cup (133 grams) granulated sugar

¼ teaspoon (1 gram) fine sea salt

3 tablespoons (43 grams) coconut oil

2 teaspoons (9 grams/ml) pure vanilla extract

FOR THE TOPPING:

One 13.5-ounce (400 ml) can full-fat coconut milk, chilled, or ½ cup (118 ml) cold heavy cream

3 tablespoons (23 grams) confectioners' sugar

RECIPE CONTINUES

1. Make the crust: Preheat the oven to 350°F. Arrange the pecans on a large rimmed baking sheet and the coconut on another baking sheet and roast until the coconut is golden and toasty, 7 to 8 minutes, and the pecans are fragrant and a deep brown color but not burnt, 10 to 12 minutes. Remove both from the oven and cool completely, then transfer both to the bowl of a food processor with the dates and salt. Pulse until the mixture is very finely chopped and holds together when pinched between your fingers, about 20 to 25 pulses. Lightly oil a 9-inch springform pan with neutral cooking spray, then spray your hands and press the crust into the bottom and up the sides of the pan.

2. Make the filling: Zest and juice 2 of the limes; you should have about 1½ tablespoons zest and 6 tablespoons juice. In a medium saucepan off the heat, whisk together the egg yolks, cornstarch, coconut milk, 3 tablespoons of the lime juice, the granulated sugar, and salt. Place over medium heat and cook, whisking constantly, until the pudding bubbles and thickens and the whisk leaves a slight impression in the custard, 7 to 8 minutes. Remove from the heat, whisk in the remaining 3 tablespoons lime juice and all the lime zest, the coconut oil, and vanilla. Cool slightly, then pour the filling into the crust. Cover tightly with plastic wrap, placing it directly on the surface to prevent a skin from forming, and chill until firm, at least 6 hours and up to 24 hours.

3. Make the topping: Chill the can of coconut milk in the refrigerator for at least 4 hours and up to 24, then open the can and scoop out the solidified "cream" that has risen to the top and place it in a medium bowl. (Alternatively, for whipped cream, pour the cold heavy cream in a medium bowl.) For either alternative, beat the cold cream with the confectioners' sugar either by hand or using an electric mixer on high speed until soft peaks form, 2 to 3 minutes.

4. To serve, top the pie with the whipped topping. Zest the remaining lime over the top of the pie, then cut the lime into thin segments (use the same method as for oranges in the Spinach Salad with Oranges & Pine Nuts, page 138). Scatter the segments over the pie. Pie can be refrigerated, covered, for up to 3 days.

VEGAN RICE PUDDING
with Quick Plum Preserves

My paternal grandfather, Jack Nadrich, who supplied restaurant equipment to mom-and-pop Greek diners in Queens, New York, was an avowed rice pudding fan, the result of decades of customer visits that inevitably ended with a cup of coffee and some dessert. He always asked for it when we dined out, and I started making it after he died. When I moved to Israel, I discovered other forms of rice pudding, including sutlache, a baked Turkish version, and the many vegan varieties available on restaurant menus (Israel has more vegans per capita than any country in the world). My version harnesses the starchiness of Arborio rice to create a rich, thick texture. There are a variety of nondairy milks available today, and any will work well here; I like to use the so-called barista blends, which are richer and have a slightly higher fat content.

Serves 6 to 8

Active Time:
45 minutes

Total Time:
55 minutes

FOR THE PUDDING:

4 cups barista-blend (higher-fat) oat milk or almond milk, plus more for loosening the chilled pudding

Two 13.5-ounce cans unsweetened coconut milk, or 3½ cups nondairy milk of your choice

1 cup Arborio rice

⅔ cup sugar

1 cinnamon stick, or ½ teaspoon ground

½ teaspoon freshly grated or ground nutmeg

¾ teaspoon kosher salt

2 tablespoons chopped shelled pistachios

FOR THE PLUM PRESERVES
(makes 2 cups):

5 medium-sized ripe plums, pitted and cut into 8 wedges

⅓ cup sugar

2 teaspoons freshly squeezed lemon juice

2 teaspoons brandy or pure vanilla extract (optional)

Pinch of kosher salt

1. Make the rice pudding: In a 3- or 4-quart saucepan, combine the oat milk, 1 can of the coconut milk (or an additional 1¾ cups oat milk), the rice, sugar, cinnamon stick, nutmeg, and ½ teaspoon of the salt. Bring to a boil, reduce the heat to medium-low, and cook, stirring often, until the rice releases most of its starch and the liquid thickens, 35 minutes. Stir in the remaining can of coconut milk (or the remaining 1¾ cups additional oat milk), return to a boil, then reduce the heat again to a simmer and cook, stirring, until the pudding thickens again and the rice appears even more swollen, 5 minutes. Remove from the heat, take out and discard the cinnamon stick, stir in the remaining ¼ teaspoon salt, and cool to room temperature. Serve at room temperature or refrigerate in a sealed container,

RECIPE CONTINUES

letting the pudding sit out for an hour before serving and loosening with more oat milk, if desired.

2. Make the preserves: In a medium saucepan, combine the fruit and sugar over medium heat and bring to a low boil. Reduce the heat to medium-low and cook, stirring occasionally, until the plums release their liquid but don't break down completely, 10 to 12 minutes. Remove from the heat, cool slightly, then stir in the lemon juice, brandy (if using), and salt. Transfer to a bowl, cover, and chill until ready to use.

3. Top the rice pudding with some of the preserves and chopped pistachios.

STRAWBERRY UPSIDE-DOWN CAKE

So that all of our desserts would be eligible for consumption after a meal that contained meat, my mother's baked goods were always made dairy-free. The "butter" of choice was a rectangular ingot of gold foil-wrapped Nucoa margarine (margarine has been a part of Jewish baking for a long time, and though some people have found replacements, it's still exceedingly popular in kosher kitchens. I'm not here as judge, only messenger).

This dairy-free status, called pareve, was an important one in our house, making everything, as we called it, "Switzerland," as in neutral, available to be eaten at all times with all other foods, thus maximizing their practicality. Pareve (pronounced PAR-eh-veh in Hebrew) is one of my favorite Jewish kitchen words, because it goes so far beyond its intended use. When I am searching for the perfect word to describe someone without a lot of personality, to me they're "pareve." Though this cake is dairy-free (butter-lovers, you have a swap-in option as well), it is anything but pareve. Ever since I had my first upside-down cake made with canned pineapple rings, I've been hooked. Here I use strawberries, and the result is marvelous. The finished product is a slightly messy affair: The juices of the berries release into the batter, creating a few custardy spots here and there, but that's the beauty of this cake. It's got a distinct look, a strong personality . . . anything but pareve.

Serves 8 to 10

Active Time:
40 minutes

Total Time:
1 hour 50 minutes

¾ cup (165 grams/ml) plus 3 tablespoons (42 grams/ml) vegetable oil, or 1 cup (2 sticks/ 8 ounces/226 grams) unsalted butter, melted and slightly cooled, plus more for greasing the sides of the pan

¼ cup (58 grams) lightly packed brown sugar

1½ cups (300 grams) granulated sugar

1½ pounds hulled strawberries (about 1 mounded quart), sliced into ¼-inch pieces (about 5 cups sliced)

2 tablespoons (15 grams) cornstarch

2 cups (260 grams) all-purpose flour

½ cup (78 grams) yellow cornmeal

1 tablespoon (12 grams) plus 1 teaspoon (4 grams) baking powder

½ teaspoon (3 grams) fine sea salt

One 13.5-ounce (400 ml/ 380 grams) can full-fat unsweetened coconut milk, shaken, or 1⅔ cups (385 ml) half-and-half

3 large eggs

Finely grated zest and juice of 1 small lemon (about 1 teaspoon zest and 2 tablespoons (30 grams/ml) lemon juice)

1 teaspoon (4 grams/ml) pure vanilla extract

Lightly sweetened whipped cream, for serving

RECIPE CONTINUES

1. Preheat the oven to 350°F and arrange a rack in the center position. Lightly grease the bottom and sides of a 10-inch springform pan with a bit of the oil and line the bottom with parchment paper. Drizzle 3 tablespoons (42 grams/ml) of the oil over the parchment, then tilt the pan to evenly distribute it across the bottom. Sprinkle the brown sugar and ¼ cup (50 grams) of the granulated sugar evenly over the oil. In a bowl, gently toss the strawberries with the cornstarch and scatter them evenly on top of the sugars. Place the prepared springform pan on a baking sheet.

2. In a large bowl, whisk together the flour, cornmeal, the remaining 1¼ cups (250 grams) granulated sugar, the baking powder, and salt.

In a separate bowl, whisk together the coconut milk, the remaining ¾ cup (165 grams/ml) oil, the eggs, lemon zest and juice, and vanilla. Add the wet ingredients to the dry and fold until just combined. Pour the batter over the strawberries and bake until the top is golden brown, the center feels set, and a cake tester or toothpick inserted into the center comes out clean, 1 hour 10 minutes to 1 hour 15 minutes. Remove from the oven and cool for 5 minutes, then run a knife around the edges to loosen the sides of the pan and invert the cake onto a serving platter. Release the sides of the pan, peel away the parchment, and cool completely before serving. The cake will be very moist on the top—as intended! Serve with whipped cream.

APRICOT TAHINI SHORTBREAD BARS

I took a classic Israeli recipe for crumbly, melt-in-your-mouth tahini cookies and turned it into a shortbread-like base for ripe, juicy apricots—the kind you would eat out of hand but that might make it into jam if they sat on the counter for another day or two. Ideally, the fruit should slump into the crust, baking to silky softness so that you can bite straight through on the way to the crunchy-nutty crust.

Makes 16 squares

Active Time:
15 minutes

**Total Time
(including chilling and cooling
time):** 2 hours

½ cup (1 stick/4 ounces/ 114 grams) unsalted butter, softened, or ½ cup (4 ounces/ 114 grams) coconut oil in solid form, at room temperature, plus more for greasing the pan

⅔ cup (133 grams) granulated sugar

¾ cup (188 grams) pure tahini paste, stirred

½ teaspoon (2 grams/ml) pure vanilla extract

2 cups (260 grams) all-purpose flour

2 teaspoons (8 grams) baking powder

½ teaspoon (3 grams) fine sea salt

10 ripe medium apricots, pitted and halved, or 8 very ripe small plums, pitted and quartered*

2 tablespoons (25 grams) demerara sugar, such as Sugar in the Raw

1. Grease a 9-inch square baking pan with butter. Line the pan with 2 crisscrossing strips of parchment paper, greasing between each layer and leaving a 2-inch overhang on all sides. In the bowl of a stand mixer fitted with the paddle attachment, combine the granulated sugar, tahini, butter, and vanilla and beat on medium speed, stopping to scrape down the sides of the bowl if necessary, until fully incorporated and slightly fluffy, about 2 minutes. In a small bowl, combine the flour, baking powder, and salt, add it to the butter mixture, and beat on medium-low speed just until fully incorporated and slightly crumbly, 30 seconds.

2. Press the dough into the pan and chill for 30 minutes. During the last 15 minutes of chilling, preheat the oven to 350°F. Arrange the apricots, cut side up, on top of the dough (they can overlap if necessary), sprinkle with the demerara sugar, and bake until the edges of the dough are golden and the apricots are slumped and softened, 45 to 50 minutes. Remove from the oven, cool completely, about 1 hour, and cut into 16 squares.

*If ripe fruit isn't in season, spread 1 cup apricot or plum preserves over the top and bake as directed.

GRANDMA MILDRED'S FRUIT COMPOTE

Compote—which has origins in seventeenth-century France—is so synonymous with Jewish grandma cooking that I assumed the dish hailed from Eastern Europe. Ever since I was a little girl, I looked forward to my grandma Mildred's version, lush with prunes and apricots swimming in a sweet, amber-colored syrup. My grandmother would fly out to California for the Jewish holidays every year, sending a shopping list in advance that called for the assorted dried fruit she used in what she humorously mispronounced as "compost." I was always amazed at how little time it took to make something I enjoyed so much, and she explained that you just add everything to the pot and let the gentle heat of the fire do most of the work. I've updated her recipe here, adding wine, ginger, and a bit of lemon, which reduces the sweetness a drop. You'll have some poaching liquid left; consider stirring it into seltzer with a squeeze of lemon or lime or mixing it with bourbon or rum for a Shabbat cocktail.

Serves 6

Active Time:
25 minutes

**Total Time
(including minimum
cooling time):** 3 hours

---

1 large lemon

2¾ cups water

1 cup dry white wine

⅔ cup sugar

1 cinnamon stick

¾ cup pitted,
dried apricots
(about 4 ounces)

¾ cup pitted prunes
(about 4½ ounces/
120 grams)

¼ cup golden raisins
(1½ ounces/40 grams)

1 tablespoon finely
grated fresh ginger

2 tablespoons thinly
sliced crystallized ginger

1 teaspoon pure vanilla
extract

⅛ teaspoon kosher salt

Use a Y-peeler to peel thick strips of zest from the lemon; place them in a medium saucepan. Juice the lemon and reserve the juice (you should have 3 tablespoons). To the saucepan with the zest strips, add the water, wine, sugar, and cinnamon stick. Bring to a boil, stirring occasionally to help the sugar dissolve, then reduce the heat to medium-low and simmer until thickened slightly, 10 minutes. Add the apricots, prunes, raisins, and fresh and crystallized gingers, then return to a boil. Reduce the heat to low and simmer gently until the fruit plumps but doesn't fall apart, 25 to 30 minutes. Remove from the heat and stir in 1 tablespoon of the lemon juice (or more to taste), the vanilla, and salt. Chill the compote for at least 2 hours and up to 24 hours; as it chills, the liquid will thicken slightly and the flavor will deepen. Remove the cinnamon stick and divide the fruit and liquid among bowls (discard the lemon peels if you like, or enjoy eating them since they're semi-candied after cooking). Store in an airtight container in the fridge for up to 1 week.

PEAR & CHERRY PHYLLO STRUDEL

I was about to embark on a make-from-scratch strudel dough expedition, but I then reminded myself to relax and enjoy the benefits of phyllo, which—with the help of multiple dustings of confectioners' sugar between layers—bakes up flaky and crisp and cradles this gingery filling like a champ. I swapped in pears and dried cherries for the more expected apples and raisins, and amped up the lemon and ginger to give the finished product a slightly sharper edge. The trick is to get the fruit soft, but not so soft that it turns into jam. A dusting of confectioners' sugar fancies up the finished product.

Serves 8

Active Time:
35 minutes

Total Time:
1 hour 10 minutes

1¾ pounds (800 grams) firm, ripe pears (about 4 medium or 6 small), peeled, cored*, and cut into ½-inch pieces (3¾ cups)

⅓ cup dried cherries

3 tablespoons (38 grams) granulated sugar

3 tablespoons (44 grams) light brown sugar

1 tablespoon finely grated lemon zest (from 1 large lemon)

1 tablespoon freshly squeezed lemon juice

3 tablespoons finely grated fresh ginger** (from a peeled 3-inch piece)

1 teaspoon (3 grams) ground ginger

1 teaspoon (3 grams) ground cinnamon

¼ teaspoon fine sea salt

3 tablespoons panko bread crumbs

¼ cup (33 grams) all-purpose flour

⅔ cup (75 grams) confectioners' sugar

7 standard (10 × 14-inch) phyllo sheets, thawed

9 tablespoons (139 grams/4½ ounces) unsalted butter, melted

2 tablespoons sanding sugar or demerara sugar (such as Sugar in the Raw)

1. Place the cut pears into a large bowl and add the cherries, granulated and light brown sugars, lemon zest and juice, fresh and ground ginger, cinnamon, and salt and gently toss to coat. Gently fold in the panko, then add the flour and stir until uniformly absorbed into the mixture.

2. Preheat the oven to 375°F and line a rimmed baking sheet with parchment.

3. Fit a fine-mesh strainer over a bowl and spoon the confectioners' sugar into the strainer. Place a piece of parchment on the counter with the short side aligned with the counter. Place a phyllo sheet on the parchment, lightly brush it with about 1 tablespoon of butter, then use the strainer to lightly sprinkle about 1½ tablespoons confectioners' sugar on top. Repeat with the remaining phyllo sheets, butter, and confectioners' sugar, stacking sheets on top of another as you go and reserving about 2 tablespoons confectioners' sugar for the top.

RECIPE CONTINUES

4. Spoon the filling onto the prepared phyllo, leaving a 2½-inch border along the top and bottom and a 3-inch border along the long sides.

5. Use the parchment to fold one long side of the phyllo over the filling, then fold the bottom and top edges up over the folded pastry. Fold the strudel over to seal it. Use a fish spatula or grill spatula to transfer the strudel to the prepared baking sheet, seam side down. Lightly brush the top and sides of the strudel with the reserved 2 tablespoons butter, then sprinkle it with the sanding sugar. Use a paring knife to score six ½-inch slits along the top of the strudel, leaving about 1 inch between slits.

6. Bake until golden brown, rotating the sheet halfway through, 40 to 45 minutes. Using a long metal spatula, transfer the strudel to the cutting board. Cool for at least 15 minutes, dust the top with the remaining 2 tablespoons confectioners' sugar, and cut into slices.

*To easily core pears while saving the maximum amount of fruit, halve the fruit, then use a melon baller to extract the seeds and any tough pieces of the core.

**I grate my ginger on a Microplane, but you can also do it on the small holes of a box grater. Alternatively, very thinly slice the peeled ginger into planks, stack them up, cut them first into very thin julienne (batons), cut crosswise into very tiny dice, and then go over the ginger a bit more with a knife.

CINNAMON BABKA RING

For Shabbat breakfast or anytime, I present you with this gorgeous, comforting, incredibly delicious dessert. Cinnamon is my current favorite babka flavoring: less sweet than chocolate, a tad spicy even, and a gorgeous match for the tender, buttery dough I cribbed from my last book (why mess with perfection?). Here, I double the dough, then fit it into a springform pan, where it bakes up fluffy and deeply golden, the inner layers revealing a cinnamon-toast-worthy swirl that will stay with you long after the last bite has been taken.

Serves 10 to 12

Active Time:
40 minutes

**Total Time
(including resting and rising time):**
9 hours 30 minutes

FOR THE DOUGH:

4 cups (520 grams) all-purpose flour, plus more for flouring your hands and the work surface

¼ cup (50 grams) granulated sugar

2½ teaspoons (9 grams) instant (rapid-rise) yeast

1 teaspoon (6 grams) fine sea salt

⅔ cup (155 grams/ml) whole milk

2 large eggs, beaten

1 tablespoon (14 grams/ml) pure vanilla extract

½ cup (1 stick/4 ounces/ 114 grams) unsalted butter, slightly softened, cut in half, plus more for buttering the pan

FOR THE FILLING:

¾ cup (1½ sticks/ 6 ounces/170 grams) unsalted butter, softened

½ cup (115 grams) lightly packed dark brown sugar

½ cup (100 grams) granulated sugar

3 tablespoons (25 grams) ground cinnamon

3 tablespoons (24 grams) all-purpose flour

½ teaspoon (3 grams) fine sea salt

FOR THE SYRUP:

½ cup (100 grams) granulated sugar

½ cup (118 g/ml) water

1 cinnamon stick, broken into 3 pieces, or ½ teaspoon ground

1. Make the dough: In the bowl of a food processor fitted with the dough blade (the plastic one you never use!), pulse the flour, granulated sugar, yeast, and salt 5 times.* Warm the milk in the microwave just long enough to take off the chill, 15 seconds. Add the milk, eggs, and vanilla to the processor, pulse 5 times, then process until a soft, tacky dough is formed, 1 minute. Add the butter and pulse 5 times, then process again until a very soft, tacky, loose dough forms, another 30 to 45 seconds. Open the processor, press some plastic wrap right on top of the dough, and let it rest for 45 minutes.

2. Lay out a large piece of plastic wrap, scrape the dough into the center of the plastic wrap, flour your hands lightly, and form the dough into a 7-inch square. Wrap it in plastic and chill it for at least 6 hours and up to 24 hours; the longer you chill the dough, the more manageable it becomes, and the flavor of the dough deepens and develops.

RECIPE CONTINUES

3. Butter the bottom and sides of a 10-inch springform pan, then line the bottom and sides of the pan with parchment. Butter the bottom and sides of the parchment-lined pan.

4. Make the filling: Combine the butter, brown sugar, granulated sugar, cinnamon, flour, and salt in a medium bowl.

5. Clear and lightly flour a large work surface. Remove the dough from the fridge and roll it out into a 12 × 28-inch rectangle. Spread the butter-sugar mixture all over the dough, leaving a 1-inch border around the edges. Working from the long end, roll the dough into a tight log, then cut it in half to make two 14-inch logs. Slice each log up the middle lengthwise into 2 equal strips (4 total); you should see stripes of cinnamon and sugar facing up. Cross two of the strips to form an *X*, then twist the strips around each other from the center on each side, trying not to stretch out the length too much, until you have a lovely twist with the filling exposed. Repeat with the remaining 2 dough strips. Fit the twisted babkas into the parchment-lined pan in a ring shape, curving them against the walls of the pan (the babka ends will meet or almost meet as they rise, then fuse together as they bake). Cover with a clean kitchen towel and let the babka rise in a warm place until doubled in size, 1 hour 30 minutes to 2 hours.

6. Preheat the oven to 350°F. When the babka has doubled, place the pan on a baking sheet and bake it until deeply golden brown on top, 45 to 50 minutes.

7. While the babka is baking, make the syrup: Combine the granulated sugar, water, and cinnamon stick in a small saucepan over medium heat and bring to a low boil. Reduce the heat and simmer until the sugar dissolves, 2 to 3 minutes. Remove from the heat and cool.

8. When the babka is done, remove it from the oven and, while still warm, brush it with the syrup, letting the syrup soak into the babka between brushings. As the babka cools, the top will harden to a pleasing crunch.

*To knead the dough by hand: In a large wide-mouthed bowl, stir together the flour, granulated sugar, yeast, and salt. Warm the milk in the microwave just long enough to take off the chill, 15 seconds. Add the milk, eggs, and vanilla to the bowl and stir together with a wooden spoon or a spatula until a tacky dough forms; it'll take about 2 minutes. Cut the butter into 6 to 8 pieces, then start to knead the butter into the dough by folding the dough over and kneading the butter in with the heel of your hand. It'll be sticky—add a tablespoon of flour if the dough is too wet—and continue to knead until the butter is fully incorporated and the dough comes together in a supple, more evenly textured dough, 6 to 7 minutes. Lay some plastic wrap right on top of the dough, let it rest for 45 minutes, and proceed with the recipe as directed.

NO-MACHINE TURKISH COFFEE ICE CREAM

At Fahoum, a wonderful Arab coffee shop in the historic shuk in the coastal northern Israeli city of Akko, you can buy some of the best coffee on earth, roasted to perfection on a vintage machine and ground with whole cardamom pods to lend it an incredible aroma. That coffee is the inspiration for this ice cream, which requires no more than a stand mixer (or, if you're motivated, a whisk and bowl) and any receptacle that will fit in your freezer. Folding espresso-infused sweetened condensed milk into whipped cream is about as easy as making dessert gets. The only key is to very gently fold the two elements together to keep the texture as airy as possible.

Serves 8 to 10

Active Time:
15 minutes

**Total Time
(including freezing time):**
5 hours 15 minutes

---

1 tablespoon espresso powder or other strong instant coffee

1 teaspoon boiling water

One 14-ounce can sweetened condensed milk

¾ teaspoon ground cardamom

1 teaspoon pure vanilla extract

¼ teaspoon kosher salt

2 cups (475 ml) heavy cream, chilled

1. Clear a flat surface in a cold part of your freezer that is large enough to fit a 9 × 5 × 3-inch metal loaf pan. Place the loaf pan in the freezer to chill while you prepare the cream mixture.

2. In a small bowl, dissolve the espresso powder in the boiling water. In a large bowl, combine the sweetened condensed milk, dissolved espresso powder, cardamom, vanilla, and salt and mix thoroughly.

3. In a large bowl of a stand mixer fitted with the whisk attachment, whip the heavy cream on medium-high speed until stiff peaks appear, 1½ to 2 minutes. (Alternatively, pour the heavy cream in a large bowl and whisk by hand until stiff peaks appear.)

4. Gently fold ½ cup of the whipped cream into the condensed milk mixture to combine, then slowly fold the condensed milk mixture into the whipped cream until combined. Remove the chilled pan from the freezer and gently spoon the mixture in, gently smooth the top, cover with plastic wrap, and freeze until solid, at least 5 hours. The ice cream will keep in the freezer, stored in an airtight container, for up to 1 month.

FROZEN MANGO & POMEGRANATE POPS

Just as pomegranates come into season in Israel, mangoes are on their way out of the shuk after nearly six months of pleasing millions of satisfied customers. That's when I make these beautiful pops, marveling at how the tart crimson-hued pomegranate seeds contrast in flavor and color with the luxuriously sweet, velvety mango pulp. Frozen mangoes work wonderfully in this recipe, and in fact, if the choice is between subpar ripe and frozen, choose the latter, since fruit is usually frozen at its peak.

Makes 6 ice pops

Active Time:
10 minutes

**Total Time
(including freezing time):**
4 hours 10 minutes

3 cups fresh or frozen very ripe mango chunks, defrosted if frozen

¼ cup sugar

½ cup pomegranate seeds

Zest of 1 lime

2 tablespoons fresh lime juice

Pinch of kosher salt

6 wooden sticks

1. Make space in the freezer for 6 ice-pop molds. Place the mango and sugar in a blender and blend until smooth, 15 to 20 seconds. Transfer the mixture to a bowl and stir in the pomegranate seeds, lime zest, lime juice, and salt.

2. Transfer the mixture to the ice-pop molds, center a wooden stick in each mold, and freeze until solid, 4 hours. Remove from the freezer and let the pops defrost for 2 to 3 minutes (or run the molds under warm water for 10 to 15 seconds) before sliding them out of their molds. The pops will keep in the freezer for 6 months.

JEWEL-TOPPED CHOCOLATE BARKS

The idea of enjoying Shabbat can be sourced to the book of Isaiah, which compels us to make Shabbat as delightful as possible. One of the ways Jewish people fulfill this admittedly easy commandment is at a Friday night post-Shabbat dinner gathering called an oneg shabbat. Friends are invited, songs are sung, alcoholic beverages are served, and the idea is to relax into the sanctity of the time and to revel in every moment of Shabbat's beauty. Sweets are often served, and I can think of nothing more oneg-worthy than these barks, which pair wonderfully with a glass of whiskey and are far more impressive to present than they are difficult to execute. Start with good chocolate, be generous with your toppings, don't skimp on the flaky salt and sumac—and let the festivities begin.

Serves 10 to 12

Active Time:
15 minutes

**Total Time
(including chilling time):**
45 minutes

½ cup pomegranate seeds

½ cup coarsely chopped roasted pistachios

¾ pound (340 grams) good-quality white chocolate, finely chopped

½ teaspoon ground sumac

½ teaspoon flaky sea salt, such as Maldon

¾ pound (340 grams) good-quality dark chocolate, finely chopped

1. Line the bottom and sides of two 9 × 13-inch quarter-sheet pans (or any 9 × 13-inch baking dishes will also work) with parchment. Make room in your fridge for the pans; you'll need the space to chill them. Spread the pomegranate seeds out on a paper towel–lined plate or baking sheet to absorb any moisture. If the pistachios are still in their papery skins, rub them between two clean kitchen towels to remove as much as possible (this is an optional step, more for beauty than for function).

2. Place the white chocolate in a microwave-safe bowl and microwave on high, stopping and stirring every 45 seconds, until the chocolate is smooth, 1½ to 2 minutes. Pour the melted white chocolate into one of the prepared pans, spreading the chocolate with an offset spatula to within 1 inch of the edge of the parchment; top with the pistachios and sprinkle with the sumac and ¼ teaspoon of the flaky salt. Repeat with the dark chocolate, pouring it into the second pan and topping it with the pomegranate seeds and the remaining ¼ teaspoon flaky salt.

3. Chill until hardened, 30 minutes (you can also pop them into the freezer if you're in a hurry to eat them). Break into smaller pieces to serve. The pomegranate bark lasts, stored covered in the fridge, for up to 4 days; the white chocolate bark will last indefinitely.

PISTACHIO FRANGIPANE & BLOOD ORANGE GALETTE

Rich, nutty frangipane is traditionally made with almonds, but I couldn't resist the opportunity to get just one last pistachio recipe into this book. Blending them with eggs, sugar, and citrus zest creates a dreamy spread that I envelop in a flaky pie crust to make a galette. Baking blood orange slices right on top concentrates their flavor yet leaves the citrus whole and sliceable. It can be hard to find shelled pistachios, so if your only option is the salted and roasted ones you often find in large bags at big-box stores, by all means use them and omit half the salt in the frangipane.

Serves 8

Active Time:
30 minutes

**Total Time
(including chilling and cooling
time):** 1 hour 30 minutes

**FOR THE CRUST
(makes 2 crusts*):**

2½ cups (325 grams) all-purpose flour, plus more for the work surface and rolling pin

2 teaspoons (10 grams) granulated sugar

1 teaspoon (6 grams) fine sea salt

1 cup (2 sticks/8 ounces/ 226 grams) unsalted butter, cut into ½-inch cubes, chilled in the freezer for 20 minutes

8 tablespoons (118 grams/ml) ice water, plus more as needed

1 large egg, beaten, for the egg wash

1 tablespoon (12.5 grams) demerara sugar, for sprinkling

FOR THE FILLING:

1½ cups (195 grams) shelled pistachios

⅔ cup (133 grams) granulated sugar

6 tablespoons (¾ stick/ 3 ounces/85 grams) unsalted butter, softened

2 large eggs

1 teaspoon (4 grams/ml) pure vanilla extract

¼ teaspoon (1 gram) fine sea salt

2 tablespoons (16 grams) all-purpose flour

2 small blood oranges (or regular), rind removed, cut into ¼-inch rounds

**FOR THE
WHIPPED CREAM
(optional):**

½ cup (117 ml) heavy cream

1½ tablespoons (19 grams) granulated sugar

RECIPE CONTINUES

1. Make the crust: In the bowl of a food processor, pulse the flour, granulated sugar, and salt until incorporated. Add the butter and pulse until the mixture is mealy and pea-sized lumps of butter remain, 20 to 25 pulses. Add 4 tablespoons of the ice water and pulse the dough, then add the remaining 4 tablespoons ice water, 1 tablespoon at a time and pulsing in between, and pulse until the dough just comes together and small pieces of butter are still visible (be careful not to overwork the dough). Divide the dough in half and form two 5-inch disks about 1 inch thick. Wrap each disk in plastic and chill for at least 30 minutes. (Refrigerate the second crust for up to 48 hours for another use or freeze, tightly sealed, for 3 months.)

2. While the dough is chilling, make the frangipane: Place the shelled pistachios in the bowl of a food processor or mini chopper and process until very fine crumbs form, 20 to 25 seconds. In the bowl of a stand mixer fitted with the whisk attachment, beat the granulated sugar, butter, and pistachios until well creamed, 1 to 2 minutes (you can also do this with an electric hand mixer). Beat in the eggs, vanilla, and salt until fluffy and combined, 1 to 2 minutes, then reduce the speed and fold in the flour until just incorporated into a creamy, thick paste, 15 seconds.

3. Preheat the oven to 375°F. On a lightly floured surface and using a lightly floured rolling pin, roll out the dough, rotating and carefully flipping the dough occasionally and sprinkling flour lightly on the dough as needed, until you have a 12-inch round (the dough should be smooth and not sticky). Center the dough on a parchment-lined baking sheet. Spread the frangipane on the dough, leaving a 1-inch border around the edge. Arrange the orange slices over the top in a free-form pattern. Fold the dough over the filling, forming a 1-inch folded edge. Brush the beaten egg over the crust and sprinkle with the demerara sugar. Chill for 20 minutes (this helps the crust hold its shape while baking), then bake until the filling is puffed and the crust is flaky and golden, 18 to 20 minutes.

4. Remove from the oven and cool completely. Use a sharp knife to cut the tart into slices. If serving with whipped cream, beat the cream and sugar with a whisk in a medium bowl until soft peaks form, 2 minutes. Serve with the tart.

*You can halve the pie crust recipe and make it in the small bowl of a food processor.

RINA'S NUT CRESCENT COOKIES

One morning at Caffe Tamati in Tel Aviv, Avishai Ben Arosh offered me an almond-crusted, crescent-shaped cookie that was chewy and nutty, with a hint of lemon—a cross between amaretti and marzipan. Once I found out that the cookie maker was Avishai's mother, Rina, we set a date for a baking lesson at his childhood home in Kiryat Ata, a suburb north of Haifa. Rina welcomed us at the door and immediately plied us with coffee and homemade tahini-filled truffles.

"I've been on my feet since age thirteen," said Rina, one of nine children of parents who had immigrated to Israel in 1950 from the Tunisian island of Djerba, where there was once a thriving Jewish community. Rina grew up in Israel, but after marrying and living in Paris with her husband, Yonatan, for several years, she fell in love with patisserie. A trip to Morocco cemented her love of homemade cookies and pastries, and she now bakes dozens of varieties, always keeping several kinds in the freezer for Shabbat and holiday meals, not to mention the epic, gluten-filled dessert-centric Mimouna celebration she throws every year to celebrate the end of Passover and the beginning of springtime. The secret to these cookies is gently dissolving the egg whites and sugar over a double boiler, then giving the dough time to chill before baking.

Makes 18 to 20 cookies

Active Time:
30 minutes

**Total Time
(including dough chilling time):**
8 hours 25 minutes

½ cup (100 grams) granulated sugar

2 large egg whites

1 cup (130 grams) whole walnuts, hazelnuts, or a mix

¾ cup (106 grams) whole almonds

1 tablespoon (2 grams) finely grated lemon zest (from 2 large lemons)

½ teaspoon ground cinnamon

1 teaspoon (4 grams/ml) pure vanilla extract

1 cup (90 grams) sliced almonds

Confectioners' sugar, for dusting

1. Bring 3 inches of water to a simmer in a pot, then set a metal bowl over the pot to create a double boiler (the bottom of the bowl shouldn't touch the water below). Add the granulated sugar and egg whites to the upper bowl and whisk, stirring, until the sugar is just dissolved, about 2 minutes. Remove from the heat and cool slightly.

RECIPE CONTINUES

2. In the bowl of a food processor, process the walnuts and almonds until a fine flour forms, 20 to 25 seconds, making sure not to overprocess them into a nut butter. Add the lemon zest, cinnamon, vanilla, and the egg-sugar mixture and process until a wet, sticky dough forms, 10 to 15 seconds. Transfer the mixture to an airtight container and refrigerate for at least 8 hours or overnight.

3. Arrange racks in the upper and lower thirds of the oven and preheat the oven to 350°F. Line two baking sheets with parchment and clear a clean work surface. Place the sliced almonds on a plate. Pull off a tablespoon of the chilled dough from the bowl and roll it in the almonds, pressing so the nuts adhere on all sides. Roll it into a ball in your hands, sprinkle a few more nuts into your hand, and roll the ball into a ¾-inch-thick, 4-inch-long rope, tapering the ends slightly. Place the rope on the prepared baking sheet and bend the ends downward to form a crescent shape. Repeat with the remaining dough and nuts, arranging the cookies 2 inches apart on the sheets; you should have 18 to 20 cookies. Bake, rotating and switching the baking sheets halfway through, until fragrant and the almond coating is very lightly golden, about 15 minutes. Cool completely on the baking sheet. Dust with confectioners' sugar before serving. Store on the counter in an airtight container for up to 1 week, or in the freezer for up to 6 months.

HAVDALAH

As Shabbat comes to a close, a set of special rituals known as Havdalah mark its end, allowing for one last opportunity to linger in the otherness of the day. For Hedai Offaim, an Israeli farmer, restaurateur, and entrepreneur, the lead-up to Havdalah is yet another opportunity to distinguish between the holy and the mundane.

Born to nonreligious socialist immigrant parents in Israel, Offaim—who is not Sabbath observant in the traditional sense of the word—became inter-

ested in Hasidism, a spiritual sect of Judaism more commonly known for its rigorously Orthodox adherents, as a way to further explore his own Jewish identity. He uses the hours leading up to Havdalah to host friends and family and soften the blow of Shabbat's departure with food, drink, and song. Everyone gathers at his home for se'udah shlishit (the "third meal," known in Yiddish as Shaleshudes), rounding out the three meals the Talmud indicates Jews are meant to eat on Shabbat.

When I walked into the house on a late spring Shabbat afternoon, an AC/DC soundtrack selected by his nine-year-old son played on the stereo and fog hung low over his 125 acres visible through the expansive back windows, all framed by the Jerusalem hills.

In the spacious, wood-accented kitchen, a skillet sizzled with onions

CONTINUES

HAVDALAH *(continued)*

cooking in goose fat, and yapchik (see recipe, page 154), a potato kugel enriched with tender chunks of meat, was completing its time in the oven (most people eat a dairy se'udah shlishit, but Offaim does it his own way). After he put the finishing touches on a meal that included chopped liver, herring, challah, and three kinds of kreplach (filled dumplings)—chopped liver, pulled meat, and potato, each shaped according to its filling—we sat down to eat.

The stereo was turned off, and soon Hedai began singing a Hasidic ni-gun (melody), "Kol Dodi Dofek" ("The Voice of My Love Is Knocking"), that he had long ago committed to memory. As darkness descended, he lit the

Havdalah candle and began the service. A cup of wine was filled to over-flowing, meant to symbolize life's abundance of blessings, and as a small bunch of sage was passed around and we all inhaled from its earthy scent, spiritual smelling salts helped calm our journey back to normal.

We held our fingers up to the flame, letting the light illuminate the whites of our nails, another traditional ritual part of the ceremony. Then he spilled wine onto a plate, extinguished the candle, and just like that, Shabbat was over and the week began. As we filed out and said our goodbyes, thoughts dissolved into anticipation of the week ahead. Thankfully, Shabbat was less than six days away.

ACKNOWLEDGMENTS

Dan Perez: How lucky am I that *you* chose to work with *me* in 2017. Your incredible photography reflects the person you are: filled with natural, Israeli light.

Nurit Kariv: My talented, fun, inspiring, visionary creative partner. Thank you for never stopping until it's perfect. THE COVER!

Lucia Watson: Powerfully gracious, and wonderful in every way. You are equal parts sharp editor, scheduling coach, cheerleader, and friend. I'm the luckiest to have you in my corner.

Anne Kosmoski, Farin Schlussel, Lindsay Gordon, Suzy Swartz, Ashley Tucker: A dream team of the most supportive, passionate, and smart people who comprise my publishing family. All the gratitude!

Janis Donnaud: You are irreplaceable. I feel incredibly fortunate for your constant presence, tenacity, support, loyalty, and all of the laughs. If only it were easier to schedule dinner together!

Leora Mietkewicz: Heaven-sent as a colleague and friend. Working with you elevates my day in every way. It is my great privilege to see how you move through the world; I learn from you daily. Oh, and thank you, Azura!

Jazzie Morgan, you bring my work to life with energy and talent (but absolutely no gluten). Thank you for helping me share my world while remaining totally myself.

Galia Schipper: A ray of spicy sunshine in my life! Love you! xoxo

Talia Trup—British class and sass all in one. Thank you for sliding into my DMs!

Maddie Pine: We met for a reason! So grateful we did, and for all that you are.

My Caffe Tamati family, Mickey, Merav, Tamati, Avishai, and Saar. My second home around the corner. Caffeine, community, and so much more.

Michael Solomonov, my brother, confidant, and fearless leader in many things. The coolest mensch. Always there for me! Asima, David, and Lucas, Jay and I love you.

Avichai Tsabari and Via Sabra, you are family. Thank you for believing in me.

Melissa Roberts Matar, Mary Frances Heck, Ian Knauer, Karl Wagner, and Shelley Wiseman, thanks for what you do!

To the wonderful group of volunteer testers, thank you! Aliza Sokolow, Cecily McAndrews, Emily Teel, Jeffrey Yoskowitz, Leslie Jonath, Mari Levine, Amy Sowder, Amy Treadwell, Danielle Rehfeld, Gabriella Gershenson, Helen Baldus, Jamie Forester, Julia Bainbridge, Julie Tanous, Jyl Benson, Kyra Werbin, Linnea Covington, Maia Baff, Maren King, Miriam Rubin, Pamela Lewy Murphy, Sheila Jarnes, Stephanie Banyas, Alyssa Langer, Danielle Centoni, Danielle DeSiato Kuhn, Ingrid Goldfein, Jessica Fox, Katherine Martinelli, Nicole Putzel, Rebeccah Marsters, Tina Ujlaki, Wendy Paler, Fran Pine, Gayle Squires, Jodie Chase, Meghan Glass, Kirsten Schofield, Marisa Robertson-Textor, Jackie Alpers, Meredith Kellman, Nicole Fisher, Mandy Morris, Shira Koschitzky, Rebecca Pliner, Miri Polachek, Michal Levine, and Adina Jaffe Lipson.

Barak Nadav, Boris Kabakov, David Zarbiv, and Itai Talbi—thank you all.

Gil Hovav, thank you for always leading me to the best people and places. SH SH!!!

Joan Nathan, Sherry Ansky, Gil Marks, Claudia Roden, and Merav Sarig—your work inspires and leads me.

To Naama Shefi—for preserving our work and celebrating our world.

Gady Levy, Erika Resnick, Gabriella Gershenson: Thanks for making Streicker my home away from home.

My dad and stepmom, Stan and Bette Sussman—what a wonder to spend to Shabbat with you whenever I desire. An hour drive sure beats a fifteen-hour flight. Thank you for the open home and the open heart. Dad, so much of what I love about Shabbat, I learned through watching you. How fortunate am I to have grown up at your (and Mom's) table.

Sharon and Ari Wieder, Tova and Ezra Elyashmerni, Akiva Wieder, and Jack Wieder: I fill your home with packages to secure my permanent place on Winthrop Road. Happy to hold all of your packages until you all make aliya!

Jessica Steinberg, Dina Kraft, Elianna Bar-On, Anat Abramov Shimoni, Karen Lerman, Tova Dorfman, and Marni Mandel: Better friends a girl couldn't ask for!

Chrissy Teigen, cooking with you infuses my kitchen with love and inspiration.

Libby Goldberg, Lisa Hostein, and *Hadassah Magazine*—to another twenty years together!

Yaffees, Ollechs, and Katzes—so lucky to have such kind, generous mishpocha. Much love!

Nadav, Shani, Or, Yuval, and Shir: The best family I could ask for.

Jay, for being relentlessly optimistic about this book, and so supportive and fun. You are my forever Shabbat (and everything else) partner. Together, in our little corner of Tel Aviv, we create the Kitchen Table of our (and Shirley's) dreams.

INDEX

Note: Page numbers in *italics* indicate photographs.